D1270930

The
Supernatural in Modern
English Fiction

By

Dorothy Scarborough

1967

OCTAGON BOOKS, INC.

New York

To

GEORGE AND ANNE SCARBOROUGH

Reprinted 1967
by special arrangement with G. P. Putnam's Sons

OCTAGON BOOKS, INC.
175 FIFTH AVENUE
NEW YORK, N. Y. 10010

LIBRARY OF CONGRESS CATALOG CARD NUMBER: 67-18784

Printed in U.S.A. by
NOBLE OFFSET PRINTERS, INC.
NEW YORK 3, N. Y.

PREFACE

THE subject of the supernatural in modern English fiction has been found difficult to deal with because of its wealth of material. While there has been no previous book on the topic, and none related to it, save Mr. C. E. Whitmore's work on *The Supernatural in Tragedy*, the mass of fiction itself introducing ghostly or psychic motifs is simply enormous. It is manifestly impossible to discuss, or even to mention, all of it. Even in my bibliography which numbers over three thousand titles, I have made no effort to list all the available examples of the type. The bibliography, which I at first intended to publish in connection with this volume, is far too voluminous to be included here, so will probably be brought out later by itself.

It would have been impossible for me to prosecute the research work or to write the book save for the assistance generously given by many persons. I am indebted to the various officials of the libraries of Columbia University and of New York City, particularly to Miss Isadore Mudge, Reference Librarian of Columbia, and to the authorities of the New York Society Library for permission to use their priceless out-of-print novels in the Kennedy Collection. My interest in English fiction was increased during my attendance on some courses in the history of the English novel, given by Dr. A. J. Carlyle, in Oxford University, England, several years ago. I have received helpful bibliographical suggestions from Professor Blanche Colton Williams, Dr. Dorothy Brewster, Professor Nelson Glenn McCrea, Professor John Cunliffe, and Dean Talcott

v

45900

Williams, of Columbia, and Professor G. L. Kittredge, of Harvard. Professors William P. Trent, George Philip Krapp, and Ernest Hunter Wright very kindly read the book in manuscript and gave valuable advice concerning it, Professor Wright going over the material with me in detail. But my chief debt of gratitude is to Professor Ashley H. Thorndike, Head of the Department of English and Comparative Literature in Columbia, whose stimulating criticism and kindly encouragement have made the book possible. To all of these—and others—who have aided me, I am deeply grateful, and I only wish that the published volume were more worthy of their assistance.

D. S.

COLUMBIA UNIVERSITY,
April, 1917.

CONTENTS

                                                                PAGE

      INTRODUCTION   I

CHAPTER

   I.—THE GOTHIC ROMANCE   6

  II.—LATER INFLUENCES   54

 III.—MODERN GHOSTS   81

 IV.—THE DEVIL AND HIS ALLIES   .   .   .   130

  V.—SUPERNATURAL LIFE   174

 VI.—THE SUPERNATURAL IN FOLK-TALES   .   .   242

VII.—SUPERNATURAL SCIENCE   251

VIII.—CONCLUSION.   281

The Supernatural in Modern English Fiction

INTRODUCTION

THE supernatural is an ever-present force in literature. It colors our poetry, shapes our epics and dramas, and fashions our prose till we are so wonted to it that we lose sense of its wonder and magic. If all the elements of the unearthly were removed from our books, how shrunken in value would seem the residue, how forlorn our feelings! Lafcadio Hearn in the recently published volume, *Interpretations of Literature*, says:

There is scarcely any great author in European literature, old or new, who has not distinguished himself in his treatment of the supernatural. In English literature I believe there is no exception from the time of the Anglo-Saxon poets to Shakespeare, and from Shakespeare to our own day. And this introduces us to the consideration of a general and remarkable fact, a fact that I do not remember to have seen in any books, but which is of very great philosophical importance: there is something ghostly in all great art, whether of literature, music, sculpture, or architecture. It touches something within us that relates to infinity.[1]

[1] The word *ghostly* is used here in its earlier sense signifying spiritual.

This continuing presence of the weird in literature shows the popular demand for it and must have some basis in human psychosis. The night side of the soul attracts us all. The spirit feeds on mystery. It lives not by fact alone but by the unknowable, and there is no highest mystery without the supernatural. Man loves the frozen touch of fear, and realizes pure terror only when touched by the unmortal. The hint of spectral sounds or presences quickens the imagination as no other suggestion can do, and no human shapes of fear can awe the soul as those from beyond the grave. Man's varying moods create heaven, hell, and faery wonder-lands for him, and people them with strange beings.

Man loves the supernatural elements in literature perhaps because they dignify him by giving his existence a feeling of infinity otherwise denied. They grant him a sense of being the center of powers more than earthly, of conflicts supermortal. His own material life may be however circumscribed and trivial yet he can loose his fancy and escape the petty tragedies of his days by flight beyond the stars. He can widen the tents of his mortal life, create a universe for his companionship, and marshal the forces of demons and unknown gods for his commands. To his narrow rut he can join the unspaced firmament; to his trivial hours add eternity; to his finite, infinity. He is so greedy of power, and has so piteously little that he must look for his larger life in dreams and in the literature of the supernatural.

But, whatever be the reasons, there has been a continuity of the ghostly in literature, with certain rise and fall of interest. There is in modern English fiction, as likewise in poetry and the drama, a great extent of the supernatural, with wide diversity of elements. Beginning with the Gothic romance, that curious architectural excrescence that yet has had enormous influence on our

novel, the supernatural is found in every period and in
every form of fiction. The unearthly beings meet us in
all guises, and answer our every mood, whether it be
serious or awed, satiric or humoresque.

Literature, always a little ahead of life, has formed our
beliefs for us, made us free with spirits, and given us
entrance to immortal countries. The sense of the unearthly is ever with us, even in the most commonplace
situations,—and there is nothing so natural to us as the
supernatural. Our imagination, colored by our reading,
reveals and transforms the world we live in. We are
aware of unbodied emotions about us, of discarnate
moods that mock or invite us. We go a-ghosting now in
public places, and a specter may glide up to give us an
apologia pro vita sua any day in Grand Central or on Main
Street of Our-Town. We chat with fetches across the
garden fence and pass the time of day with demons by
way of the dumb-waiter. That gray-furred creature that
glooms suddenly before us in the winter street is not a
chauffeur, but a were-wolf questing for his prey. Yon
whirring thing in the far blue is not an aeroplane but
a hippogriff that will presently alight on the pavement
beside us with thundering golden hoofs to bear us away
to distant lovely lands where we shall be untroubled by
the price of butter or the articles lost in last week's wash.
That sedate middle-aged ferry that transports us from
Staten Island is a magic Sending Boat if only we knew
its potent runes! The old woman with the too-pink
cheeks and glittering eye, that presses August bargains
upon us with the argument that they will be in style
for early fall wear, is a witch wishful to lure away our
souls. We may pass at will by the guardian of the narrow
gate and traverse the regions of the Under-world. True,
the materialist may argue that the actual is more marvelous than the imagined, that the aeroplane is more a

thing of wonder than was the hippogriff, that the ferry is really the enchanted boat, after all, and that Dante would write a new *Inferno* if he could see the subway at the rush hour, but that is another issue.

We might have more psychal experiences than we do if we would only keep our eyes open, but most of us do have more than we admit to the neighbors. We have an early-Victorian reticence concerning ghostly things as if it were scandalous to be associated with them. But that is all wrong. We should be proud of being singled out for spectral confidences and should report our ghost-guests to the society columns of the newspaper. It is hoped that this discussion of comparative ghost-lore may help to establish a better sense of values.

In this book I deal with ghosts and devils by and large, in an impressionistic way. I don't know much about them; I have no learned theories of causation. I only love them. I only marvel at their infinite variety and am touched by their humanity, their likeness to mortals. I am fond of them all, even the dejected, dog-eared ghosts that look as if they were wraiths of poor relations left out in the rain all night, or devils whose own mothers wouldn't care for them. It gives me no holier-than-thou feeling of horror to sit beside a vampire in the subway, no panic to hear a banshee shut up in a hurdy-gurdy box. I give a cordial how-do-you-do when a dragon glides up and puts his paw in mine, and in every stray dog I recognize a Gladsome Beast. Like us mortals, they all need sympathy, none more so than the poor wizards and bogles that are on their own, as the Scotch say.

While discussing the nineteenth century as a whole, I have devoted more attention to the fiction of the supernatural in the last thirty years or so, because there has been much more of it in that time than before. There is now more interest in the occult, more literature produced dealing with psychal powers than ever before in our history. It is apparent in poetry, in the drama, the novel, and the short story. I have not attempted, even in my bibliography, to include all the fiction of the type, since that would be manifestly impossible. I have, however, mentioned specimens of the various forms, and have listed the more important examples. The treatment here is meant to be suggestive rather than exhaustive and seeks to show that there is a genuine revival of wonder in our time, with certain changes in the characterization of supernatural beings. It includes not only the themes that are strictly supernatural, but also those which, formerly considered unearthly, carry on the traditions of the magical. Much of our material of the weird has been rationalized, yet without losing its effect of wonder for us in fact or in fiction. If now we study a science where once men believed blindly in a Black Art, is the result really less mysterious?

CHAPTER I

The Gothic Romance

THE real precursor of supernaturalism in modern English literature was the Gothic novel. That odd form might be called a brief in behalf of banished romance, since it voiced a protest against the excess of rationalism and realism in the early eighteenth century. Too great correctness and restraint must always result in proportionate liberty. As the eternal swing of the pendulum of literary history, the ebb and flow of fiction inevitably bring a reaction against any extreme, so it was with the fiction of the period. The mysterious twilights of medievalism invited eyes tired of the noonday glare of Augustan formalism. The natural had become familiar to monotony, hence men craved the supernatural. And so the Gothic novel came into being. *Gothic* is here used to designate the eighteenth-century novel of terror dealing with medieval materials.

There had been some use of the weird in English fiction before Horace Walpole, but the terror novel proper is generally conceded to begin with his Romantic curiosity, *The Castle of Otranto*. The Gothic novel marks a distinct change in the form of literature in which supernaturalism manifests itself. Heretofore the supernatural elements have appeared in the drama, in the epic, in ballads and other poetry, and in folk-tales, but not noticeably in the novel. Now, however, for a considerable time the ghostly

6

themes are most prominent in lengthy fiction, contrasted with the short story which later is to supersede it as a vehicle for the weird. This vacillation of form is a distinct and interesting aspect of the development of supernaturalism in literature and will be discussed later.

With this change in form comes a corresponding change in the materials of ghostly narration. Poetry in general in all times has freely used the various elements of supernaturalism. The epic has certain distinct themes, such as visits to the lower world, visions of heaven, and conflict between mortal and divine powers, and brings in mythological characters, gods, goddesses, demigods, and the like. Fate is a moving figure in the older dramas, while the liturgical plays introduced devils, angels, and even the Deity as characters in the action. In the classical and Elizabethan drama we see ghosts, witches, magicians, as *dramatis personæ*. Medieval romances, prose as well as metrical and alliterative, *chansons de geste*, *lais*, and so forth, drew considerably on the supernatural for complicating material in various forms, and undoubtedly much of our present element comes from medievalism. Tales of the Celtic Otherworld, of fairy-lore, of magic, so popular in early romance, show a strong revival to-day.

The Gothic novel is more closely related to the drama than to the epic or to such poetry as *The Faerie Queene* or *Comus*. On the other hand, the later novels and stories, while less influenced by the dramatic tradition, show more of the epic trace than does the Gothic romance. The epic tours through heaven and hell, the lavish use of angels, devils, and even of Deity, the introduction of mythological characters and figures which are not seen in Gothic fiction, appear to a considerable extent in the stories of recent times. In Gothicism we find that the Deity disappears though the devil remains. There are no vampires, so far as I have been able to find, though the were-wolf and the lycanthrope appear, which were absent from the drama (save in *The Duchess of Malfi*). Other elements are seen, such as the beginnings of the scientific supernaturalism which is to become so prominent in later times. The Wandering Jew comes in and the elixir of life and the philosopher's stone achieve importance. Mechanical supernaturalism and the uncanny power given to inanimate objects seem to have their origins here, to be greatly developed further on. Supernaturalism associated with animals, related both to the mythological stories of the past and to the more horrific aspects of later fiction, are noted in the terror romance.

Allegory and symbolism are present in a slight degree, as in *Melmoth* and Vathek's Hall of Eblis, though not emphasized as in more modern literature. Humor is largely lacking in the Gothic romance, save as the writers furnish it unintentionally. In Gothicism itself we have practically no satire, though Jane Austen and Barrett satirize the terror novel itself in delicious burlesques that laugh it out of court.

Elements of Gothicism. In the terror tale the relationship between supernatural effect and Gothic architecture, scenery, and weather is strongly stressed. Everything is ordered to fit the Gothic plan, and the conformity becomes in time conventionally monotonous. Horace Walpole, the father of the terror novel, had a fad for medievalism, and he expressed his enthusiasm in that extraordinary building at Strawberry Hill, courteously called a Gothic castle. From a study of Gothic architecture was but a step to the writing of romance that should reproduce the mysteries of feudal times, for the shadows of ancient, gloomy castles and cloisters suggested the shades of ghost-haunted fiction, of morbid terrors. *The Castle of Otranto* was the outcome of a dream suggested by the author's thinking about medieval structures.

The Gothic castle itself is represented as possessing all the antique glooms that increase the effect of mystery and awe, and its secret passage-ways, its underground vaults and dungeons, its trap-doors, its mouldy, spectral chapel, form a fit setting for the unearthly visitants that haunt it. A feudal hall is the suitable domicile for ghosts and other supernatural revenants, and the horrific romance throughout shows a close kinship with its architecture. The novels of the class invariably lay their scenes in medieval buildings, a castle, a convent, a monastery, a château or abbey, or an inquisitional prison. The harassed heroine is forever wandering through midnight corridors of Gothic structure. And indeed, the opportunity for unearthly phenomena is much more spacious in the vast piles of antiquity than in our bungalows or apartment-houses.

Mrs. Radcliffe erected many ruinous structures in fiction. Her *Mysteries of Udolpho* shows a castle, a convent, a château, all Gothic in terror and gloomy secrets, with rooms hung with rotting tapestry, or wainscoted with black larch-wood, with furniture dust-covered and dropping to pieces from age, with palls of black velvet waving in the ghostly winds. In other romances she depicts decaying castles with treacherous stairways leading to mysterious rooms, halls of black marble, and vaults whose great rusty keys groan in the locks. One heroine says:[1] "When I entered the portals of this Gothic structure a chill—surely prophetic—chilled my veins, pressed upon my heart, and scarcely allowed me to breathe."

The Ancient Records of the Abbey of St. Oswyth[2] says of its setting: "The damp, cold, awe-inspiring hall seemed to conjure up ten thousand superstitious horrors and terrific imaginary apparitions." In Maturin's *Al-*

---

[1] In *The Romance of the Castle.*   [2] By T. J. Horsley-Curties.

bigenses the knights assemble round the great fire in the baronial hall and tell ghost tales while the storm rages outside. In *Melmoth, the Wanderer* the scene changes often, yet it is always Gothic and terrible,—the monastery with its diabolical punishments, the ancient castle, the ruined abbey by which the wanderer celebrates his marriage at midnight with a dead priest for the celebrant, the madhouse, the inquisition cells, which add gloom and horror to the supernatural incidents and characters. In *Zofloya*,[1] the maiden is imprisoned in an underground cave similar to that boasted by other castles. This novel is significant because of the freedom with which Shelley appropriated its material for his *Zastrozzi*, which likewise has the true Gothic setting. In Shelley's other romance he erects the same structure and has the devil meet his victim by the desolate, dear old Gothic abbey

Regina Maria Roche wrote a number of novels built up with crumbling castles, awesome abbeys, and donjon-keeps whose titles show the architectural fiction that dominates them. A list of the names of the Gothic novels will serve to show the general importance laid on antique setting. In fact, the castle, abbey, monastery, château, convent, or inquisition prison occupied such an important place in the story that it seemed the leading character. It dominated the events and was a malignant personality, that laid its spell upon those within its bounds. It shows something of the character that Hawthorne finally gives to his house of seven gables, or the brooding, relentless power of the sea in Synge's drama.[2] The ancient castle becomes not merely haunted itself but is the haunter as well.

Not only is architecture made subservient to the needs of Gothic fiction, but the scenery likewise is adapted to

[1] By Mrs. Dacre, better known as "Rosa Matilda."
[2] *Riders to the Sea.*

fit it. Before Mrs. Radcliffe wrote her stories interlarded with nature descriptions, scant notice had been paid to scenery in the novel. But she set the style for morose landscapes as Walpole had for glooming castles, and the succeeding romances of the *genre* combined both features. Mrs. Radcliffe was not at all hampered by the fact that she had never laid eyes on the scenes she so vividly pictures. She painted the dread scenery of awesome mountains and forests, beetling crags and dizzy abysses with fluent and fervent adjectives, and her successors imitated her in sketching nature with dark impressionism.

The scenery in general in the Gothic novel is always subjectively represented. Nature in itself and of itself is not the important thing. What the writer seeks to do is by descriptions of the outer world to emphasize the mental states of man, to reflect the moods of the characters, and to show a fitting background for their crimes and unearthly experiences. There is little of the light of day, of the cheerfulness of ordinary nature, but only the scenes and phenomena that are in harmony with the glooms of crimes and sufferings.

Like the scenery, the weather in the Gothic novel is always subjectively treated. There is ever an artistic harmony between man's moods and the atmospheric conditions. The play of lightning, supernatural thunders, roaring tempests announce the approach and operations of the devil, and ghosts walk to the accompaniment of presaging tempests. In *The Albigenses* the winds are diabolically possessed and laugh fiendishly instead of moaning as they do as seneschals in most romances of terror. The storms usually take place at midnight, and there is rarely a peaceful night in Gothic fiction. The stroke of twelve generally witnesses some uproar of nature as some appearance of restless spirit. Whenever the heroines in Mrs. Radcliffe's tales start on their midnight ramble through subterranean passages and halls of horror, the barometer becomes agitated. And another[1] says: "The storm, that at that moment was tremendous, could not equal that tempest which passed in the thoughts of the unhappy captive."

In *Zofloya* Victoria's meetings in the forest with the Moor, who is really the devil in disguise, are accompanied by supernatural manifestations of nature. The weather is ordered to suit the dark, unholy plots they make, and they plan murders against a background of black clouds, hellish thunder, and lurid lightning. When at last the Moor announces himself as the devil and hurls Victoria from the mountain top, a sympathetic storm arises and a flood sweeps her body into the river. This scene is accusingly like the one in the last chapter of Lewis's *Monk*, where the devil throws Ambrosio from the cliff to the river's brink.

Instantly a violent storm arose; the winds in fury rent up rocks and forests; the sky was now black with clouds, now sheeted with fire; the rain fell in torrents; it swelled the stream, the waves over-flowed their banks; they reached the spot where Ambrosio lay, and, when they abated, carried with them into the river the corse of the despairing monk.

No Gothic writer shows more power of harmonizing the tempests of the soul with the outer storms than does Charles Robert Maturin.[2] As Melmoth, doomed to dreadful life till he can find some tortured soul willing to exchange destinies with him, traverses the earth in his search, the preternatural aspects of weather both reflect and mock his despair. As the young nephew alone at midnight after his uncle's death reads the fated manuscript, "cloud after cloud comes sweeping on like the dark banners of an approaching host whose march is for

[1] St. Oswyth.   [2] In *Melmoth, the Wanderer* and *The Albigenses*.

destruction." Other references may illustrate the motif. "Clouds go portentously off like ships of war . . . to return with added strength and fury." "The dark and heavy thunder-clouds that advance slowly seem like the shrouds of specters of departed greatness. Peals of thunder sounded, every peal like the exhausted murmurs of a spent heart."

In general, in the Gothic novel there is a decided and definite attempt to use the terrible forces of nature to reflect the dark passions of man, with added suggestive-ness where supernatural agencies are at work in the events. This becomes a distinct convention, used with varying effectiveness. Nowhere in the fiction of the period is there the power such as Shakespeare reveals, as where Lear wanders on the heath in the pitiless clutch of the storm, with a more tragic tempest in his soul. Yet, although the idea of the inter-relation of the passions of man and nature is not original with the Gothicists, and though they show little of the inevitability of genius, they add greatly to their supernatural effect by this method. Later fiction is less barometric as less architectural than the Gothic.

The Origin of Individual Gothic Tales. The psycholog-ical origin of the individual Gothic romances is interesting to note. Supernaturalism was probably more generally believed in then than now, and people were more given to the telling of ghost stories and all the folk-tales of terror than at the present time. One reason for this may be that they had more leisure; and their great open fires were more conducive to the retailing of romances of shudders than our unsocial steam radiators. The eighteenth century seemed frankly to enjoy the pleasures of fear, and the rise of the Gothic novel gave rein to this natural love for the uncanny and the gruesome.

Dreams played an important part in the inspiration of

the tales of terror. The initial romance was, as the author tells us, the result of an architectural nightmare. Walpole says in a letter:

Shall I even confess to you what was the origin of this romance? I waked one morning from a dream, of which all that I could recall was that I had thought myself in an ancient castle (a very natural dream for a head filled like mine with Gothic story) and that at the uppermost banister of a great staircase I saw a gigantic hand in armor. In the evening I sat down and began to write, without knowing in the least what I intended to say or relate. The work grew on my hands.

Mary Shelley's *Frankenstein* was likewise born of a dream. "Monk" Lewis had interested Byron, Polidori, and the Shelleys in supernatural tales so much so that after a fireside recital of German terror stories Byron proposed that each member of the group should write a ghostly romance to be compared with the compositions of the others. The results were negligible save *Franken-stein*, and it is said that Byron was much annoyed that a mere girl should excel him. At first Mrs. Shelley was unable to hit upon a plot, but one evening after hearing a discussion of Erasmus Darwin's attempts to create life by laboratory experiments, she had an idea in a half waking dream. She says:

I saw—with shut eyes but acute mental vision—I saw the pale student of unhallowed arts kneeling beside the thing he had put together. I saw the hideous phantasm of a man stretched out, and then, on the working of some powerful engine, show signs of life. . . . The artist sleeps but he is awakened; and behold, the horrid thing stands at his bedside, looking on him with watery, yellow yet speculative eyes!

And from this she wrote her story of the man-monster.
The relation of dreams to the uncanny tale is interesting.

Dreams and visions, revelatory of the past and prophetic of the future, played an important part in the drama (as they are now widely used in motion-picture scenarios) and the Gothic novel continues the tradition. It would be impossible to discover in how many instances the authors were subconsciously influenced in their choice of material by dreams. The presaging dreams and visions attributed to supernatural agency appear frequently in Gothic fiction. The close relation between dreams and second sight in the terror novel might form an interesting by-path for investigation. Dream-supernaturalism becomes even more prominent in later fiction and contributes passages of extraordinary power of which De Quincey's *Dream-Fugue* may be mentioned as an example.

The germinal idea for *Melmoth, the Wanderer* was contained in a paragraph from one of the author's own sermons, which suggested a theme for the story of a doomed, fate-pursued soul.

At this moment is there one of us present, however we may have departed from the Lord, disobeyed His will, and disregarded His word—is there one of us who would, at this moment, accept all that man could bestow or earth could afford, to resign the hope of his salvation? No, there is not one—not such a fool on earth were the enemy of mankind to traverse it with the offer!

True, the theme of such devil-pact had appeared in folk-tales and in the drama previously, notably in Marlowe's *Doctor Faustus*, but Maturin here gives the idea a dramatic twist and psychologic poignancy by making a human being the one to seek to buy another's soul to save his own. A mortal, cursed with physical immortality, ceaselessly harried across the world by the hounds of fate, forever forced by an irresistible urge to make his impitiable offer to tormented souls, and always meeting a tragic refusal, offers dramatic possibilities of a high order and Maturin's story has a dreadful power.

Clara Reeve's avowed purpose in writing *The Old English Baron* was to produce a ghost story that should be more probable and realistic than Walpole's. She stated that her book was the literary offspring of the earlier romance, though Walpole disclaimed the paternity. She deplored the violence of the supernatural machinery that tended to defeat its own impressiveness and wished to avoid that danger in her work, though she announced: "We can conceive and allow for the appearance of a ghost." Her prim recipe for Romantic fiction required, "a certain degree of the marvelous to excite the attention; enough of the manners of real life to give an air of probability to the work; and enough of the pathetic to engage the heart in its behalf." But her ingredients did not mix well and the result was rather indigestible though devoured by hungry readers of her time.

Mrs. Anne Radcliffe, that energetic manipulator of Gothic enginery, wrote because she had time that was wasting on her hands,—which may be an explanation for other and later literary attempts. Her journalist husband was away till late at night, so while sitting up for him she wrote frightful stories to keep herself from being scared. During that waiting loneliness she doubtless experienced all those nervous terrors that she describes as being undergone by her palpitating maidens, whose emotional anguish is suffered in midnight wanderings through subterranean passages and ghosted apartments. There is one report that she went mad from over-much brooding on mormo, but that is generally discredited.

Matthew Gregory Lewis was impelled to write *The Monk* by reading the romances of Walpole and Mrs. Radcliffe, together with Schiller's *Robbers*, which triple influence is discernible in his lurid tale. He defended the indecency of his book by asserting that he took the plot from a story in *The Guardian*,[1] ingeniously intimating that plagiarized immorality is less reprehensible than original material. Shelley, in his turn, was so strongly impressed by Lewis's *Monk*, and Mrs. Dacre's *Zofloya* in writing his *Zastrozzi*, and by William Godwin's *St. Leon* in his *St. Irvyne, or The Rosicrucian*, that the adaptation amounts to actual plagiarism. Even the titles show imitation. In writing to Godwin, Shelley said he was "in a state of intellectual sickness" when he wrote these stories, and no one who is familiar with the productions will contradict him in the matter.

The influence of the crude scientific thought and investigation of the eighteenth century is apparent in the Gothic novels. *Frankenstein*, as we have seen, was the outcome of a Romantic, Darwinian dream, and novels by Godwin, Shelley, and Maturin deal with the theme of the elixir of life. William Beckford's *Vathek* has to do with alchemy, sorcery, and other phases of supernatural science. Zofloya, Mrs. Dacre's diabolical Moor, performs experiments in hypnotism, telepathy, sorcery, and satanic chemistry. And so in a number of the imitative and less known novels of the *genre* science plays a part in furnishing the material. There is much interest in the study of the relation of science to the literature of supernaturalism in the various periods and the discoveries of modern times as furnishing plot material. The Gothic contribution to this form of ghostly fiction is significant, though slight in comparison with later developments.

The Gothic Ghosts. The Ghost is the real hero or heroine of the Gothic novel. The merely human characters become for the reader colorless and dull the moment a specter glides up and indicates a willingness to relate

[1] "The History of Santon Barsis," *The Guardian*, Number 148.

the story of his life. The continuing popularity of the shade in literature may be due to the fact that humanity finds fear one of the most pleasurable of emotions and truly enjoys vicarious horrors, or it may be due to a childish delight in the sensational. At all events, the ghost haunts the pages of terror fiction, and the trail of the supernatural is over them all. In addition to its association with ancient superstitions, survivals of animistic ideas in primitive culture, we may see the classical and Elizabethan influence in the Gothic specter. The prologue-ghost, naturally, is not needed in fiction, but the revenge-ghost is as prominent as ever. The ghost as a dramatic personage, his talkativeness, his share in the action, reflect the dramatic tradition, with a strong Senecan touch. The Gothic phantoms have not the power of Shakespeare's apparitions, nothing approaching the psychologic subtlety of *Hamlet* or *Julius Cæsar* or the horrific suggestiveness of *Macbeth*, yet they are related to them and are not altogether poor. Though imitative of the dramatic ghosts they have certain characteristics peculiar to themselves and are greatly worth consideration in a study of literary supernaturalism.

There are several clearly marked classes of ghosts in Gothicism. There is the real ghost that anybody can pin faith to; there is the imagined apparition that is only a figment of hysterical fear or of a guilty conscience; and there is the deliberate hoax specter. There are ghosts that come only when called,—sometimes the castle dungeons have to be paged for retiring shades; others appear of their own free will. Some have a local habitation and a name and haunt only their own proper premises, while others have the wanderlust. There are innocent spirits returning to reveal the circumstances of their violent demise and to ask Christian burial; we meet guilty souls sent back to do penance for their sins in the place of their commission; and there are revenge ghosts of multiple variety. There are specters that yield to prayers and strong-minded shades that resist exorcism. It is difficult to classify them, for the lines cross inextricably.

The genealogical founder of the family of Gothic ghosts is the giant apparition in *The Castle of Otranto*. He heralds his coming by an enormous helmet, a hundred times larger than life size, which crashes into the hall, and a sword which requires a hundred men to bear it in. The ghost himself appears in sections. We first see a Brobdignagian foot and leg, with no body, then a few chapters later an enormous hand to match. In the last scene he assembles his parts, after the fashion of an automobile demonstration, supplies the limbs that are lacking and stands forth as an imposing and portentous shade. After receiving Alfonso's specter—Alfonso will be remembered as the famous statue afflicted with the nose-bleed—he "is wrapt from mortal eyes in a blaze of glory." That seems singular, considering the weighty material of which he and his armor are made. There is another interesting specter in the castle, the monk who is seen kneeling in prayer in the gloomy chapel and who, "turning slowly round discovers to Frederick the fleshless jaws and empty sockets of a skeleton wrapped in a hermit's cowl."

Clara Reeve's young peasant in *The Old English Baron*, the unrecognized heir to the estate, who is spending a night in the haunted apartment, sees two apparitions, one a woman and the other a gentleman in armor though not of such appalling size as the revenant in *Otranto*. The two announce themselves as his long-lost parents and vanish after he is estated and suitably wed. Mrs. Radcliffe[1] introduces the shade of a murdered knight, a chatty personage who haunts a baronial hall full of men,

[1] In *Gaston de Blondeville*.

and at another time engages in a tournament, slaying his opponent.

Mrs. Bonhote[1] shows us a migratory ghost of whom the old servant complains in vexation:

Only think, Miss, of a ghost that should be at home minding its own business at the Baron's own castle, taking the trouble to follow him here on special business it has to communicate! However, travelling three or four hundred miles is nothing to a ghost that can, as I have heard, go at the rate of a thousand miles a minute on land or sea.

In this romance the baron goes to visit the vault and has curdling experiences.

"A deep groan issues from the coffin and a voice exclaims, 'You hurt me! Forbear or you will crush my bones to powder!'" He knocks the coffin in pieces, whereupon the vocal bones demand decent burial and his departure from the castle. Later the baron sees the ghost of his first wife, who objects to his making a third matrimonial venture, though she has apparently conceded the second. In the same story a young woman's spook pursues one Thomas, almost stamping on his heels, and finally vanishing like a sky-rocket, leaving an odor of brimstone behind. A specter rises from a well in *The History of Jack Smith, or the Castle of Saint Donats*,[2] and shakes its hoary head at a group of men who fire pistols at it.

The Castle of Caithness[3] shows a murdered father indicating his wounds to his son and demanding vengeance. An armored revenge ghost appears in *Count Roderick's Castle*, or *Gothic Times*, an anonymous Philadelphia novel, telling his son the manner of his murder, and scaring the king, who has killed him, to madness. The revenge ghosts in the Gothic do not cry "Vindicta!" as frequently as in

[1] In *Bungay Castle*.
[2] By Charles Lucas, Baltimore.   [3] By F. H. P.

the early drama, but they are as relentless in their hate. In *Ancient Records*, or *The Abbey of St. Oswyth*,[1] the spirit of a nun who has been wronged and buried alive by the wicked baron returns with silent, tormenting reproach. She stands beside him at midnight, with her dead infant on her breast.

Suddenly the eyes of the specter become animated. Oh!— then what flashes of appalling anger dart from their hollow orbits on the horror-stricken Vortimer! Three dreadful shrieks ring pealing through the chamber now filled with a blaze of sulphurous light. The specter suddenly becomes invisible and the baron falls senseless on his couch.

Scant wonder! In the same story Rosaline, the distressed heroine, is about to wed against her will, when a specter appears and forbids the bans. Again, Gondemar has a dagger at her throat with wicked intent, when a spook "lifts up his hollow, sunken countenance and beckons with angry gestures for his departure." Gondemar departs!

Another revenge ghost creates excitement in *The Accusing Spirit*. A murdered marquis appears repeatedly to interested parties and demands punishment on his brother who has slain him. Another inconsiderate specter in the same volume wakes a man from his sleep, and beckoning him to follow, leads him to a subterranean vault, stamps his foot on a certain stone, shows a ghastly wound in his throat and vanishes. On investigation, searchers find a corpse in a winding-sheet beneath the indicated spot. Another accusing spirit appears in the same story—that of Benedicta, a recreant nun, who glides as a headless and mutilated figure through the cloisters and hovers over the convent bed where she "breathed out her guilty soul." The young heroine who has taken

[1] By T. J. Horsley-Curties.

temporary refuge in the convent and has to share the
cell with this disturbing room-mate, is informed by an
old nun that, "Those damned spirits who for mysterious
purposes receive permission to wander over the earth can
possess no power to injure us but that which they may
derive from the weakness of our imagination." Never-
theless, the nervous girl insists on changing her room!
Another famous cloistered ghost, one of the pioneer
female apparitions of note, is the Bleeding Nun in Lewis's
The Monk, that hall of Gothic horrors. He provides an
understudy for her, who impersonates the nun in times
of emergency, providing complicating confusion for the
other characters and for the reader.

Ghosts begin to crowd upon each others' heels in later
Gothic novels. No romance is so poor as not to have a
retinue of specters, or at least, a ghost-of-all-work. Em-
boldened by their success as individuals, spooks appear in
groups and mobs. William Beckford in his *Vathek* presents
two thousand specters in one assembly. Beckford was no
niggard! In Maturin's *The Albigenses*, de Montfort, passing alone through a dark forest, meets the phantoms of
countless victims of his religious persecution. Men, women,
young maidens, babes at the breast, all move toward him
with unspeakable reproach, with "clattering bones, eye-
less sockets, bare and grinning jaws." Aside from Dante
the most impressive description of unhappy spirits in
a large number is given in *Vathek* in that immortal
picture of the Hall of Eblis. Beckford shows here a
concourse of doomed souls, each with his hand forever
pressed above his burning heart, each carrying his own
hell within him, having lost heaven's most precious boon,
the soul's hope! In the Hall of Eblis there are the still
living corpses, "the fleshless forms of the pre-adamite
kings, who still possess enough life to be conscious of their
deplorable condition; they regard one another with looks

of the deepest dejection, each holding his right hand motionless above his heart." The prophet Soliman is there, from whose livid lips come tragic words of his sin and punishment. Through his breast, transparent as glass, the beholder can see his heart enveloped in flames.

In James Hogg's *The Wool-Gatherer*, a man of very evil life is haunted by the wraiths of those he has wronged. As he lies on his death-bed, not only he, but those around him as well, hear the pleading voices of women, the pitiful cries of babes around his bed, though nothing is visible. We have here a suggestion of the invisible supernaturalism that becomes so frequent and effective a motif in later fiction. After the man is dead, the supernatural sounds become so dreadful that "the corpse sits up in the bed, pawls wi' its hands and stares round wi' its dead face!" When the watchers leave the room for a few moments, the body mysteriously disappears and is never found. A somewhat similar instance occurs in one of Ambrose Bierce's modern stories of dead bodies.

There is some attempt to exorcise restless spirits in a number of Gothic novels. On various occasions the priests come forth with bell, book, and candle to pronounce anathema against the troublesome visitants. In one story a monk crosses his legs to scare away the specter, but forgets and presently tumbles over. In another,[1] the priest peremptorily bids the ghosts depart and breaks the news firmly to them that they cannot return for a thousand years. But one bogle, whether of feeble understanding or strong will, comes in to break up the ceremonies of incantation, and scares the priest into hysterics.

The imagined ghost appears in many of the Gothic tales, whose writers lack the courage of their supernaturalism. Mrs. Radcliffe, for instance, loves to build up a tissue of ghostly horrors, yet explains them away on natural

[1] *The Spirit of Turrettville.*

grounds after the reader fancies he sees a spirit around every corner.

The ghosts that are deliberately got up for the purposes of deception form an interesting feature of Gothic methods. The reasons behind the spectral impersonations are various, to frighten criminals into restitution after confession, to further crime, or merely to enliven the otherwise lagging story. In *The Spirit of Turrettville* two youths follow the sounds of plaintive music till, in a deserted, spookish apartment, they see a woman playing at an old harp. As they draw near, they see only skeleton hands on the keys and the apparition turns toward them "a grinning, mouldering skull." She waves her hands with haughty rebuke for their intrusion and "stalks" out of the oratory. She gives further performances, however, singing a song composed for the occasion. But the reader, after such thrills, resents finding out later that she is the living wife, attempting to frighten the villain into confession.

In *The Accusing Spirit* a bogus spook is constructed by means of phosphorus, aided by a strong resemblance between two men, to accuse an innocent man of murder. The apparition dramatically makes his charge, but is unmasked just in time to save the victim's life. A tall, cadaverous young man makes up for a ghost in an anonymous novel,[1] while a mysterious woman in a black veil attends a midnight funeral in the castle, then unaccountably disappears.

In *Melmoth* the monks persecute a despised brother by impersonating spirits in his cell. They cover the walls with images of fiends, over which they smear phosphorus, and burn sulphur to assist the deception. They utter mocking cries as of demons, seeking to drive him mad. In Lewis's *Monk* there is a false Bleeding Nun as well as

---

[1] In *Ariel, or the Invisible Monitor.*

the *bona fide* specter. In other Gothic novels there are various spectral frauds cleverly planned, and then revealed, but their explanation does not altogether dispel the uncanny impression they make.

The ghost that stays at home in a definite place, haunting its own demesne, is a familiar figure in the fiction of the period. Every castle has its haunted tower or dungeon or apartment with its shade that walks by night. Several appear carrying candles or lamps to light them through the blackness of architectural labyrinths. Several evince a fondness for bells and herald their coming by rings. In one romance,[1] the ghost takes the form of a white cow. (Doubtless many ghosts in real life have had a similar origin.) In another,[2] a specter in armor appears to terrify his murderer, and supernatural lightning aids in his revenge.

It would be impossible to designate all the ghosts in Gothic fiction for there is wholesale haunting. They appear in the plot to warn, to comfort or command, and seem to have very human characteristics on the whole. Yet they are not so definitely personated, not so individual and realistic as the spirits in later fiction, though they do achieve some creepy effects. It is not their brute force that impresses us. We are less moved by the armored knight and the titanic adversary in Otranto than by the phantoms in the Hall of Eblis. The vindictive ghosts, mouldy from the vault, are less appalling than the bodiless voices of wronged women and children that haunt the death-bed and bring a corpse back to dreadful life. The specters with flamboyant personality, that oppress us with their egotistic clamor, may be soon forgotten, but the ghostly suggestiveness of other spirits has a haunting power that is inescapable. Some of the

[1] *The Spirit of the Castle.*
[2] *Ethelwina, or the House of Fitz-Auburne,* by T. J. Horsley-Curties.

Gothic ghosts have a strange vitality,—and, after all, where would be the phantoms of to-day but for their early services?

Witches and Warlocks. While not at all equal in importance to the ghosts, witches and warlocks add to the excitement in Gothic fiction. There is but little change from the witch of dramatic tradition, for we have both the real and the reputed witch in the terror novel, the genuine antique hag who has powers given her from the devil, and the beautiful young girl who is wrongly suspected of an unholy alliance with the dark spirits.

In *Melmoth*, there is an old woman doctor who has uncanny ability. She tells fortunes, gives spells against the evil eye and produces weird results "by spells and such dandy as is beyond our element." She turns the mystic yarn to be dropped into the pit, on the brink of which stands "the shivering inquirer into futurity, doubtful whether the answer to her question 'Who holds?' is to be uttered by the voice of a demon or lover." In *The Albigenses* three Weird Sisters appear that are not altogether poor imitations of Shakespeare's own. Matilda in *The Monk* possesses dæmonic power of enchantment and in the subterranean passages of the monastery she works her unhallowed arts. The hag Carathis, in *Vathek*, is a witch of rare skill, who concocts her magic potions and by supernatural means forces all things to her will. There are several witches and warlocks in James Hogg's *The Hunt of Eildon*, who work much mischief but at last are captured and convicted. They have the choice of being burned alive or being baptized, but with wild cries they struggle against the holy water and face the flames.

In Hogg's *Brownie of Bodbeck*, Marion Linton believes her own daughter is a witch and thinks she should be given the trial by fire or water. There is an innocent young reputed witch in *The Hunt of Eildon*, who is sentenced to death for her art.

The Devil. The devil incarnate is one of the familiar figures in the terror novel. Here, as in the case of the ghost, we see the influence of the dramatic rather than of the epic tradition. He is akin to Calderon's wonder-working magician and Marlowe's Dr. Faustus rather than to the satanic creations of Dante and Milton. He is not a dread, awe-inspiring figure either physically or as a personality, though he does assume terrifying, almost epic proportions in the closing scenes of *The Monk* and *Zofloya*. Neither is he as human, as appealing to our sympathies as the lonely, misjudged, misunderstood devils in later fiction. We neither love nor greatly fear the Gothic demon. Yet he does appear in interesting variants and deserves our study.

In Hogg's *Hunt of Eildon* the devil comes in as a strange old man who yet seems curiously familiar to the king and to everyone who sees him, though no one can remember just when he knew him. There is a clever psychologic suggestiveness here, which perhaps inspired a similar idea in a recent play, *The Eternal Magdalen*. Later he is recognized and holy water thrown on him.

The whole form and visage of the creature was changed in a moment to that of a furious fiend. He uttered a yell that made all the abbey shake to its foundations and forthwith darted away into the air, wrapt in flames. As he ascended, he waved his right hand and shook his fiery locks at his inquisitors.

There is nothing dubious about his personality here, certainly!

Satan appears dramatically in *The Monk* as well. His first visits are made in the form of attractive youth. Ambrosio, who has been led into sin by the dæmonic agent, Matilda, is awaiting death in the Inquisition cell, when she comes to see him to urge that he win release by selling his soul to the devil. But the repentant monk refuses her advice, so she departs in a temper of blue flame. Then he has a more dread visitant,—Lucifer himself, described as follows:

His blasted limbs still bore the marks of the Almighty's thunders; a swarthy darkness spread itself over his gigantic form; his hands and feet were armed with long talons. . . . Over his huge shoulders waved two enormous sable wings; and his hair was supplied by living snakes which twined themselves with frightful hissings. In one hand he held a roll of parchment, and in the other an iron pen. Still the lightnings flashed around him and the thunder bursts seemed to announce the dissolution of nature.

Ambrosio is overawed into selling his soul and signs the compact with his blood, as per convention.

The devil doesn't keep to his agreement to release him, however, for Lewis tells us that taking his victim to the top of a mountain and "darting his talons into the monk's shaven crown, he sprang with him from the rock. The caves and mountains rang with Ambrosio's shrieks. The demon continued to soar aloft till, reaching a dreadful height, he released the sufferer. Headlong fell the monk." He plunges to the river's brink, after which a storm is evoked by the devil and his body swept away in the flood.

A similar dæmonic manifestation occurs in *Zofloya*. Victoria has been induced to bind herself to the Evil One, who has appeared as a Moorish servant of impressive personality and special powers. He grants her wishes hostile to her enemies, holding many conferences with her in the dark forest where he is heralded by flute-like sounds. He appears sometimes like a flame, sometimes like a lightning flash. He comes with the swiftness of the wind and tells her that her thoughts summoned him. At last, he announces himself as Satan, and assumes his own hideous form of gigantism.

Behold me as I am, no longer that which I appeared to be, but the sworn enemy of all created nature, by men called Satan. Yes, it was I that under semblance of the Moor appeared to thee.

As he spoke, he grasped more firmly the neck of Victoria, with one push he whirled her headlong down the dreadful abyss!—as she fell his loud dæmonic laugh, his yells of triumph echoed in her ears; and a mangled corpse she fell, she was received into the foaming waters below.

The devil is seen in *Vathek* as a preternaturally ugly old man with strange powers. James Hogg has rather a penchant for the demon, for he uses him in *The Wool-Gatherer*, and in *Confessions of a Justified Sinner*, which is a story of religious superstition, of the use of diablerie and witchcraft, introducing a satanic tempter. On the whole, the appearances of the devil in Gothic fiction lack impressiveness, are weak in psychologic subtlety, and have not the force either of the epic or of the dramatic representations. Nor have they the human appeal that the incarnations of the devil in later fiction make to our sympathies.

In addition to the unholy powers possessed by the devil and given by him to his agents, the witches, warlocks and magicians, we see in Gothic fiction other aspects of dæmonology, such as that associated with animals and with inanimate objects. Supernaturalism in the horror novel is by no means confined to human beings, but extends to beasts as well. Animals are supposed to be peculiarly sensitive to ghostly impressions, more so than men, and the appearance of a specter is often first announced by the extreme terror of some house-

hold pet, or other animal. Gothic dogs have very keen
noses for ghosts and howl lugubriously when an apparition
approaches. Ravens are represented as showing the
presence of evil powers, somewhat as the Southern darkey
believes that the jay-bird is the ally of the devil and
spends every Friday in torment. And one does not
forget the snaky coiffure that writhed around the demon's
head in *The Monk*.

Maturin's *Albigenses* introduces the story of a gruesome
loup-garou, or werewolf, which figures extensively in
folk-tales. In this case the husband of a beautiful young
woman is a werewolf who during his savage metamor-
phosis tears her to pieces then disappears to return no
more. This is suggestive—with a less satisfactory ending
—of Marie de France's charming little *lai*, *Le Bisclaveret*.
Professor Kittridge has shown the frequency of the werewolf motif in medieval story, by the variants he brings
together in his *Arthur and Gorlogon*. In *The Albigenses*
a lycanthrope also is described, a hideous human being
that fancies himself a mad wolf.

There is much use of animal supernaturalism in James
Hogg's romances. In one,[1] Sandy is saved from going
over a precipice by the warning of a hare that immediately after vanishes, having left no tracks in the snow.
In another,[2] the two white beagles that the king uses in
hunting are in reality maidens bound by enchantment,
who are forced to slay human beings then transform them
into deer for the king and his company to eat. The other
dogs are aware of the unnatural state of affairs, while the
men are too stupid to realize it. The clownish Croudy is
changed into a hog, which brings amusing and almost
tragic complications into his life. His old dog knows him
and follows him pathetically, and a drove of cows go off
in a stampede at his approach, for they, too, sense the

[1] *The Wool-Gatherer.*   [2] *The Hunt of Eildon.*

supernatural spell. Croudy is put on the block to be killed for pork, when the fairy changes him back suddenly to the consternation of the butcher. But Croudy does not behave well after his transformation, so he is changed into a cat with endless life. He may resume mortal shape one night in the year and relate his feline experiences.

In the same story the king of Scotland is proposing a toast when his favorite dog dashes the cup from his hand. This is repeated several times, till the king learns that the drink is poisoned, and the dog has thus by supernatural knowledge saved his life. An innocent young girl, sentenced to death for witchcraft because a fairy has taken her form and worked enchantment, and her lover are transformed into white birds that fly out of the prison the night before the execution and live eternally on the shores of a far lake.

The ghostly power extends to inanimate objects as well as to human beings and animals. Armor and costumes seem to have a material immortality of their own, for it is quite common to recognize spectral visitants by their garments or accouterments. Armor clanks audibly in the terror scenes. In *The Castle of Otranto*, the giant ghost sends his immense helmet crashing into the hall to shatter the would-be-bridegroom and the hopes of his father. The head-gear has power of voluntary motion and moves around with agility, saves the heroine from danger by waving its plumes at the villain and generally adds excitement to the scenes. Later a titanic sword leaps into place of itself, after having been borne to the entrance by a hundred men fainting under the weight of it, while a statue of Alfonso sheds three drops of blood from its nose and a portrait turns round in its frame and strolls out into the open.

Pictures in general take a lively part in horrific fiction. The portrait of a murdered man in *The Spirit of the Castle* picks itself up from the lumber heap where it has been thrown, cleans itself and hangs itself back on the wall, while[1] a portrait in a deserted chamber wags its head at a servant who is making the bed. The portrait of Melmoth is endowed with supernatural power, for its eyes follow the beholder with awful meaning, and as the nephew in desperation tears it from its frame and burns it, the picture writhes in the flames, ironically, and mocks him. This might be compared with Oscar Wilde's *Picture of Dorian Grey* and with other later stories.

The statue of Alfonso in Walpole's *Castle* moves from its place with no visible means of support, and[2] a great effigy of black marble is said to "march all round and come back into its place again with a great groan." In *St. Oswyth* the soil of the abbey grounds obtained by gross injustice is haunted by the ghost of the wronged nun who inflicts a curse upon it, rendering it "spell-blighted, unprolific, and impossible to till." The key to the room in the old house in which Melmoth's diabolic portrait is kept, turns in its lock with a sound like the cry of the dead.

Gothic romance contains magic mirrors wherein one can see any person he wishes no matter how distant he may be, and watch his movements after the fashion of a private moving-picture show,-- such as that used by Ambrosio.[3] There are enchanted wands with power to transform men to beasts or *vice versa*, as in *The Hunt of Eildon*. There are crystal balls that reveal not only what is going on in distant parts, but show the future as well.[4] The same volume describes magic swords that bear changing hieroglyphics to be read only by enchantment and other uncanny objects. These will serve to illustrate the preternatural powers possessed by inanimate objects

[1] In *The Spirit of Turrettville*.
[2] In *Ariel*.
[3] In *The Monk*.
[4] As in *Vathek*.

in the terror literature. In some instances the motif
is used with effectiveness, definitely heightening the
impression of the weird in a way that human supernaturalism could not accomplish. We do not see here the mechanistic supernaturalism, which is to become important in
later tales, and the effects here are crude, yet of interest
in themselves and as suggesting later uses of the idea.

Dæmonology manifests itself in the supernatural science
in the Gothic novels as well as in the characterization of
the devil and his confreres. We have diabolical chemistry
besides alchemy, astrology, hypnotism, ventriloquism,
search for the philosopher's stone, infernal biology, and
the other scientific twists of supernaturalism. In *Vathek*,
where we have a regular array of ghostliness, we see a
magic potion that instantly cures any disease however
deadly,—the progenitor of the modern patent medicine.
There is an Indian magician who writes his messages on
the high heavens themselves. Vathek's mother is an
industrious alchemist strangling an assembly of prominent
citizens in order to use their cadavers in her laboratory,
where she stews them up with serpent's oil, mummies, and
skulls, concocting therefrom a powerful potion. Vathek
has an uncurbed curiosity that leads him into various
experiments, to peer into the secrets of astrology, alchemy,
sorcery, and kindred sciences. He uses a magic drink
that gives the semblance of death, like that used later in
The Monk, as earlier, of course, in *Romeo and Juliet*, and
elsewhere.

The Moor in *Zofloya* is well versed in dæmonic science.
He tells of chemical experiments where he forces everyone to do his will or die. By his potions he can change
hate into love or love into hate, and can give a drug which
produces semi-insanity. Under the influence of this a man
weds a dæmonic temptress thinking her the woman he
loves, then commits suicide when he wakes to the truth.

This reminds us of Sax Rohmer's Fu-Manchu stories of diabolic hypodermics that produce insanity.

In *Ankerwich Castle* a woman lying at the point of death is miraculously cured by a drug whose prescription the author neglects to state. In the same story a child is branded in a peculiar fashion. A new-born babe whose birth must remain secret yet who must be recognizable in emergency, is marked on its side with letters burnt in with a strange chemical, which will remain invisible till rubbed with a certain liquid. Matilda in *The Monk* dabbles in satanic chemistry and compounds evil potions in her subterranean experiments.

Mary Shelley uses the idea of supernatural biology in her story of the man-monster, *Frankenstein*, the story of the young scientist who after morbid study and experiment, constructs a human frame of supernatural size and hideous grotesqueness and gives it life. But the thing created appalls its creator by its dreadful visage, its more than human size, its look of less than human intelligence, and the student flees in horror from the sight of it. Mrs. Shelley describes the emotions of the lonely, tragic thing thrust suddenly into a world that ever recoils shuddering from it. She reveals the slow hate distilled in its heart because of the harsh treatment it meets, till at last it takes diabolic revenge, not only on the man who has created it but on all held dear by him. The struggles that rend his soul between hate and remorse are impressive. The wretched being weeps in an agony of grief as it stands over the body of Frankenstein whom it has harried to death, then goes away to its own doom. The last sight of it, as the first, is effective, as, in tragic solitude, towering on the ice-floe, it moves toward the desolate North to its death.

In the characterization of this being, as in the unusual conception, Mrs. Shelley has introduced something poignantly new in fiction. It was a startling theme for the mind of a young girl, as were *Vathek* and *The Monk* for youths of twenty years, and only the abnormal psychological conditions she went through could have produced it. There is more curdling awfulness in Frankenstein's monster than in the museum of armored ghosts, Bleeding Nuns, and accompanying horrors of the early Gothic novels. The employment of the Frankenstein motif in a play produced recently in New York,[1] illustrates anew the vitality of the idea.

The search for the philosopher's stone appears in various novels of the period. *St. Leon*, by William Godwin, relates the story of a man who knew how to produce unlimited gold by a secret formula given him by a mysterious stranger who dies in his home. Shelley[2] brings in this power incidentally with the gift of endless life. There is an awe-inspiring use of ventriloquism in Charles Brockden Brown's novel, *Wieland*, while *Arthur Mervyn* gives a study in somnambulism. *Zofloya* suggests hypnotism or mesmerism by saying that Victoria's thought summoned the Moor to her,—that they could have brought him had he been "at the further extremity of this terrestrial globe." This seems a faint foreshadowing of Ibsen's idea in *The Master Builder*. These may illustrate the use of science in Gothicism.

The elixir of life is brewed in divers Gothic novels. Dramatic and intense as are the psychological experiences connected with the discovery of the magic potion, the effects of the success are more poignant still. The thought that endless mortality, life that may not be laid down, becomes a burden intolerable has appeared in fiction since Swift's account of the Struldbrugs, and perhaps before. Godwin's *St. Leon* is a story of the secret of perpetual life. The tiresome Godwinistic hero is visited

[1] *The Last Laugh.*   [2] In *St. Irvyne.*

by a decrepit old man who wishes to tell him on a pledge
of incommunicability what will give him the power of
endless life and boundless wealth. The impoverished
nobleman accepts with consequences less enjoyable than
he has anticipated.

Shelley's hectic romance,[1] whose idea, as Shelley ad-
mitted to Stockdale, came from Godwin's book, uses the
same theme. The young student with burning eyes, who
has discovered the elixir of life, may be compared with
Mary Shelley's later picture of Frankenstein. Events
are rather confused here, as the villain falls dead in the
presence of the devil but comes to life again as another
character later in the story,—Shelley informing us of
their identity but not troubling to explain it.

The most impressive instance of the theme of fleshly
immortality in the early novels is found in *Melmoth*.
Here the mysterious wanderer possesses the power of
endless life, but not the right to lay it down when existence
becomes a burden. Melmoth can win the boon of death
only if he can find another mortal willing to change destinies with him at the price of his soul. He traverses
the world in his search and offers the exchange to persons in direst need and suffering the extreme torments,
offering to give them wealth as well as life eternal. Yet
no man nor woman will buy life at the price of the
soul.

Aids to Gothic Effect. Certain themes appear recur-
ringly as first aids to terror fiction. Some of them are
found equally in later literature while others belong more
particularly to the Gothic. An interesting aspect of the
supernatural visitants is gigantism, or the superhuman
size which they assume. In *The Castle of Otranto*, the sensational ghost is of enormous size, and his accouterments
are colossal. In the last scene he is astounding:

[1] *St. Irvyne or the Rosicrucian.*

A clap of thunder shook the castle to its foundations; the earth rocked and the clank of more than mortal armor was heard behind. . . . The walls of the castle behind Manfred were thrown down with a mighty force, and the form of Alfonso, dilated to an immense magnitude, appeared in the center of the ruins. "Behold the true heir of Alfonso!" said the vision.

This reminds one of an incident in F. Marion Crawford's *Mr. Isaacs*, where the Indian magician expands to awful size, miraculously draws down a mist and wraps it round him as a cloak. Zofloya is frequently spoken of as immense, and it is said that "common objects seem to sink in his presence." In the last scene the wicked Victoria sees the Moor change from a handsome youth to a fierce gigantic figure. A diabolic apparition eight or nine feet high pursues a monk,[1] and the knight[2] engages in combat with a dæmonic giant who slays him. The devil in *The Monk* is represented as being of enormous stature, and much of the horror excited by the man-monster that Frankenstein created arises from the creature's superhuman size. In most cases gigantism connotes evil power and rouses a supernatural awe in the beholder. The giant is an Oriental figure and appears in *Vathek*, along with genii, dwarfs, and kindred personages, but the Gothic giant has more diabolism than the mere Oriental original. He seems to fade out from fiction, appearing only occasionally in later stories, while he has practically no place in the drama, owing doubtless to the difficulties of stage presentation.

Insanity as contributing to the effect of supernaturalism affords many gruesome studies in psychiatry. Madness seems a special curse of the gods or torment from the devil and various instances of its use occur in Gothic fiction. The devil in *Zofloya*, at Victoria's request, gives Henrique

[1] In *The Spirit of the Castle.* [2] In *The Spirit of Turrettville.*

an enchanted drug which renders him temporarily insane, during which time he marries Victoria, imagining her to be Lilla whom he loves.   When he awakes to the realization of what he has done, real madness drives him to suicide. In *The Castle of Caithness* the wicked misanthrope goes mad from remorse.   He imagines that the different ones he has murdered are hurling him into the pit of hell, until, in a maniac frenzy, he dashes his brains out against the prison walls.   In *Ethelwina* the father who has sold his daughter to dishonor flies shrieking in madness through the corridors of the dungeon to escape the sight of his child's accusing specter.   Poor Nanny in Hogg's *Brownie of Bodbeck* is described as having "a beam of wild delight in her eye, the joy of madness."   She sings wild, unearthly songs and talks deliriously of incomprehensible things, of devilish struggles.

Melmoth uses the idea with special effectiveness.   The insanity of the young husband whose bride is mysteriously slain on their wedding day by the supernatural power accompanying Melmoth, may be compared with the madness of the wife in Scott's *Bride of Lammermoor*.   Maturin also shows us a scene in a mad-house, where a sane man, Stanton, is confined, whom Melmoth visits to offer exchange of destinies.   Melmoth taunts him cruelly with his hopeless situation and prophecies that he, too, will go mad from despair.   We hear Stanton's wild cry, echoed by a hundred yells like those of demons, but the others are stilled when the mad mother begins her lamentation,—the mother who has lost husband, home, children, reason, all, in the great London fire.   At her appalling shrieks all other voices are hushed.   Another impressive figure in the mad-house is the preacher who thinks himself a demon and alternately prays and blasphemes the Lord

Charles Brockden Brown rivals Maturin in his terrible use of insanity for supernatural effect.   The demented

murderer in *Edgar Huntley* gives an impression of mystery
and awe that is unusual, while *Wieland* with its religious
mania produced by diabolic ventriloquism is even more
impressive.   Brown knew the effect of mystery and dread
on the human mind and by slow, cumulative suggestion
he makes us feel a creeping awe that the unwieldy machinery of pure Gothicism never could achieve.   In studies of
the morbid mentality he has few equals.   For psychologic
subtlety, for haunting horror, what is a crashing helmet or
a dismembered ghost compared with Brown's Wieland?
What are the rackings of monkish vindictiveness when set
against the agonies of an unbalanced mind turned in upon
itself?   What exterior torture could so appeal to our sympathies as Wieland's despair, when, racked with religious
mania, he feels the overwhelming conviction that the
voice of God—which is but the fiendish trick of a ventrilo-
quist—is calling him to murder his wife and children as a
sacrifice to Deity?   Such a tragedy of dethroned reason is
intolerably powerful; the dark labyrinths of insanity, the
gloom-haunted passages of the human mind, are more
terrible to traverse than the midnight windings of Gothic
dungeons.   We feel that here is a man who is real, who is
human, and suffering the extremity of anguish.

Perhaps the most hideous aspect of insanity in the terror
novel is that of the lycanthrope in *The Albigenses*.   The
tragic wolf-man imagines himself to be a mad wolf and
cowers in his lair, glaring with gleaming, awful eyes at all
who approach him, gnawing at a human head snatched
from the graveyard.   There are various other uses of
insanity in the novel of the period, but these will serve to
illustrate.   The relation between insanity and the supernatural has been marked in later literature.

The use of portents is a distinct characteristic of the
horror romance.   Calamity is generally preceded by some

sign of the supernatural influence at work, some present-
ment of dread.   Crime and catastrophe are forefelt by
premonition of woe and accompaniment of horror.   In
The Accusing Spirit supernatural thunder heralds the
discovery of the corpse in its winding-sheet, and the monk
says, "Yes, some dread discovery is at hand.   These
phenomena are miraculous; when the common laws of
nature are violated, the awful portents are not sent in
vain."   In *The Romance of the Castle*, an anonymous story,
a woman hears the clock strike two and announces that
she will be dead at three.

This night an awful messenger sent from that dread tri-
bunal from whose power there is no appeal, by signs terrific
foretold my fate approached—foretold my final moment.
"Catherine, behold!" was all that issued from the specter's
lips, but in its hand it held a scroll which fixed my irrevocable
doom, in letters which fascinated while they appalled my
sight.

She keeps her appointment promptly.   Her experience
might be compared with the vision which revealed his date
of death to Amos Judd in James Mitchell's novel of that
name, and to the foreknowledge in George Eliot's *The
Lifted Veil*.

In *The Spirit of the Castle*,[1] the ghost of the old marquis
knocks three times on the door preceding the arrival of the
heir, and a black raven flies away as he enters.   At the
approach of the true heir to the estate from which he has
been kept by fraud in *The Old English Baron*, the doors of
the ancient castle fly open, upon which the servants cry,
"The doors open of themselves to receive their master!"
When Walpole's usurping Manfred sees the plumage on the
miraculous casque shaken in concert with the brazen
trumpet, he exclaims, "What mean these portents?   If

[1] By W. C. Proby.

I have offended——" At this point the plumes are shaken still more strenuously, and the helmet is equally agitated when the great sword leaps in. Manfred cries to the apparition, "If thou art a true knight, thou wilt scorn to employ sorcery to carry thy power. If these omens be from heaven or hell, Manfred trusts to righteousness to protect his cause." But the omens bring bad luck to Manfred.

There is much use of portent in *Melmoth*. The specter of the Wanderer appearing just before the old man's death predicts the spiritual doom of the dying. As the old uncle is almost breathing his last, he cries out, "What the devil brings you here?" at which the servants cross themselves and cry, "The devil in his mouth!" Melmoth, the Wanderer, is a walking portent of evil, for the priest is unable to pray in his presence, the communion bread turns viperous when he is there and the priest falls dead in the attempt to exorcise the fiendish power. Mysterious strains of music sound as heralds of disaster in several Gothic novels, as[1] where the inexplicable strains are heard only by the bride and groom preceding the strange tragedy that befalls them.

At the approach of a supernatural visitant in the terror novel the fire always burns blue,—where there is a fire, and the great hearth usually affords ample opportunity for such portentous blaze. The thermometer itself tends to take a downward path when a ghost draws near. The three drops of blood shed from the statue's nose in *Otranto*, while ridiculed by the critics, are meant simply as a portent of evil. Prof. William Lyon Phelps points out[2] that the idea did not originate with Walpole, but was familiar as a superstition regarding premonition of ill, as referred to in Dryden's *Amboyna*, IV., 1. This instance may be com-

[1] In *Melmoth*.
[2] In his *Beginnings of the English Romantic Movement*, p. 108.

pared with the much more skillfully handled omens in later drama, as Maeterlinck's and Ibsen's, particularly in *The Emperor and Galilean*. Various other portents of ill appear in Gothic fiction. [1]

The symbols of dread and the ghostly are used to good effect in the terror romance. The cumulative effects of supernatural awe are carefully built up by the use of gruesome accompaniments and suggestions. The triple veil of night, desolation, and silence usually hangs over the haunter and the haunted, predisposing to an uncanny psychosis. The Gothic ghost does not love the garish day, and the terror castle, gloomy even under the brightest sun, is of unimaginable darkness at night. Certain houses add especially to the impression of fear. At crucial moments the stroke of twelve or one o'clock is sure to be sounded appallingly by some abbey bell or castle clock or other rusty horologue. In addition to its services as timekeeper, the bell has a predisposition to toll.

Melancholy birds fly freely through these medieval tales, their dark wings adding to the general gloom. The principal specimens in the Gothic aviary are the common owl, the screech or "screeching" owl, the bat and the raven, while the flock is increased by anonymous "birds of prey," "night birds," "gloomy birds" and so forth. In *St. Oswyth*, as the murderer steals at midnight through the corridor toward his helpless victim, "the ill-boding bird of night that sat screeching on the battlement of the prison

[1] Eliza Heywood's romance, *Lasselia: or, the Self-Abandoned*, shows a similar portent, as Dr. George Frisbee Whicher notes in his *The Life and Romances of Mrs. Eliza Heywood.*

Professor Ashley H. Thorndike, in his *Tragedy*, in speaking of the plays of the Restoration dramatist John Banks (p. 273), says: "Even the portents are reduced to a peculiar decorum:—

"Last night no sooner was I laid to rest
Than just three drops of blood fell from my nose!"

These three drops of blood probably have a much more extended history in romance and the drama, which it would be interesting to trace out.

tower, whose harsh, discordant notes were echoed by the
hoarse croaking of the ominous raven" terrifies but does
not deter the villain.

The "moping, melancholy screech owl" is one of the
prominent personages in *The Accusing Spirit*, emphasizing
the moments of special suspense, as in *St. Oswyth* as the
wicked baron lies quaking in remorse for having caused a
nun to be buried alive, the condemning cry of the doleful
birds increases his mental anguish. Similar instances,
with or without special nomenclature, occur in countless
Gothic novels. Much use is also made of the dark ivy
in its clambering over medieval architecture, shutting out
the light and adding to the general gloom. The effect
of horror is increased frequently by the location of the
scenes in vaults and graveyards with all their gruesome
accessories, and skulls are used as mural ornaments elsewhere, or as library appointments by persons of morbid
temperament. Enough skeletons are exhumed to furnish
as large a pile of bones as may be seen in certain antique
churches in Italy and Mexico.

The element of mystery and mystification is another
family feature of the novel of suspense. There is no
proper thrill without the suspense attained by supernatural mystery. Even the novels that in the end carefully
explain away all the ghostly phenomena on a natural basis
strive with care to build up plots which shall contain
astounding discoveries. Mrs. Radcliffe and Regina Maria
Roche are noted in this respect. They have not the
courage of their ghosts as such but, after they have thrilled
the reader to the desired extent, they tear down the fabric
of mystification that they have constructed and meticu-
lously explain everything.

The black veil constitutes a favorite method of suspense
with Mrs. Radcliffe. On various occasions Emily pales

and quivers before a dark velvet pall uncannily swaying in the midnight wind, and on one such ramble she draws aside the curtain and finds a hideous corpse, putrid and dropping to decay, lying on a couch behind the pall. Many chapters further on she learns that this is a wax figure made to serve as penance for an ancient sinner. Again she shivers in front of the inky curtain, watching its fold move unaccountably, when a repulsive face peers out at her. She shrieks and flees, thinking she has seen a ghost, but discovers later that it is *only* one of a company of bandits that have taken up their secret abode in the house. Black veils are in fashion in all of Mrs. Radcliffe's romances and she drapes them very effectively, while the arras waves likewise in other tales as well.

Mysterious manuscripts are another means of mystification. Mrs. Radcliffe's novels also abound in such scripts. In *The Romance of the Forest* Adeline discovers a decaying paper which reads, "Oh, ye, whoever ye are, that chance or misfortune may direct to this spot, to you I speak, to you reveal the story of my wrongs and ask you to avenge them." This injunction to avenge wrongs is a frequent assignment, though rather much to ask in most cases. *The Spirit of the Castle* has its dusty document that starts off: "Already my hand brandishes the dagger that shall close my eyes forever. (Mysterious manuscripts are not strong on grammar and make slight attempt to avoid mixed figures.) I will expire by the side of the clay-cold corpse of my Antoinette." In *St. Oswyth* the paper says, "Beneath the deep foundations of the ruin the recorded mystery of the house of Oswyth lies buried from all mortal discovery." But the most impressive manuscript is the one in *Melmoth* that records the wanderings of the agonized fate-harried man and those whose tortures he witnesses. A codicil to the old uncle's will advises his nephew against reading the document, but of course he does read it, since what are mouldy manuscripts in Gothic novels for, but to be deciphered by the hero or heroine?

Reference to dread secrets occur otherwise than in written form. In one favored tale,[1] we are told of "a mystery whose elucidation I now have a presentiment would fill me with horror!" In another,[2] Vincent on his death-bed speaks of "a horrid secret which labors at my breast," and the Abate speaks to the marquis of "a secret which shall make your blood run cold!" In *St. Oswyth* we hear that "an impenetrable cloud of cureless sorrow hung over Sir Alfred and there was a dreadful mystery in his life destiny, unknown, as it should seem, to any one, and which he was unwilling should be questioned." The dungeoned prisoner in *Bungay Castle* cries, "Were I at liberty to speak I could a tale unfold would tempt you to curse the world and even detest those claims which bind man to man. You would be ready to forego the ties of nature and shun society. Time must, it will develop the whole of this mystery!" And so on.

Inexplicable music forms one of the commonest elements of mystification in these romances. Its constant recurrence suggests that there must have been victrolas in medieval times. The music is chiefly instrumental, sometimes on a harp, sometimes on a violin, though occasionally it is vocal. Mrs. Radcliffe and Regina Maria Roche accompany the heroine's musings at all hours with doleful strains suspected to be of supernatural performance. The appearance of the devil masquerading as the Moor[3] is heralded by flute-like sounds, and in *The Spirit of Turrettville* the specter plays on the harp and sings. The recurrence of the theme is so constant that it acquires the monotony of a tantalizing refrain.

Groans and wails of unexplained origin also aid in build-

[1] Regina Maria Roche's *Clermont*.
[2] *A Sicilian Romance*, by Mrs. Radcliffe.   [3] In *Zofloya*.

ing up suspense. In fact, a chorus of lugubriousness arises so that the Gothic pages groan as they are turned. Mysterious disappearances likewise increase the tension. Lights appear and vanish with alarming volition, doors open and close with no visible human assistance, and various other supernatural phenomena aid in Gothic mystery and mystification.

Although the ghosts and devils occupy the center of interest in the horrific romance, the human characters must not be lightly passed over. There are terror temperaments as well as Gothic castles, tempests, and scenes. The interfering father or other relative, brutal in threats and breathing forth slaughter, comes in frequently to oppress the hero or heroine into a loathed marriage. The hero is of Radcliffian gloom, a person of vague past and saturnine temper, admired and imitated by Byron. Sir Walter Raleigh,[1] says, "The man that Byron tried to be was the invention of Mrs. Radcliffe." The officials of the Inquisition and the dominant figures in convents and monasteries show fiendish cruelty toward helpless inmates, gloating in Gothic diabolism over their tortures. There are no restful human shades of gray, only unrelieved black and white characters. The Romantic heroine is a peculiar creature, much given to swooning and weeping, yet always impeccably clad in no matter what nocturnal emergency she is surprised. She tumbles into verse and sketching on slight provocation, but her worst vice is that of curiosity. In her search for supernatural horrors she wanders at midnight through apartments where she does not belong, breaks open boxes, desks, and secret hiding-places to read whatever letters or manuscripts she can lay her hands on, behaving generally like the yellow journalist of fiction.

The pages of the Gothic novel are smeared with gore

[1] In *The English Novel*, p. 228.

and turn with ghostly flutter. The conversation is like nothing on land or sea or in the waters under the earth, for the tadpoles talk like Johnsonian whales and the reader grows restless under Godwinistic disquisitions. The authors are almost totally lacking in a sense of humor, yet the Gothic novel, taken as a whole, is one of the best specimens of unconscious humor known to English literature.

Conclusion. Perhaps the most valuable contribution that the Gothic school made to English literature is Jane Austen's inimitable satire of it, *Northanger Abbey*. Though written as her first novel and sold in 1797, it did not appear till after her death, in 1818. Its purpose is to ridicule the Romanticists and the book in itself would justify the terroristic school, but she was ahead of her times, so the editor feared to publish it. In the meantime she wrote her other satires on society and won immortality for her work which might never have been begun save for her satiety of medieval romances. The title of the story itself is imitative, and the well-known materials are all present, yet how differently employed! The setting is a Gothic abbey tempered to modern comfort; the interfering father is not vicious, merely ill-natured; the pursuing, repulsive lover is not a villain, only a silly bore. The heroine has no beauty, nor does she topple into sonnets nor snatch a pencil to sketch the scene, for we are told that she has no accomplishments. Yet she goes through palpitating adventures mostly modelled on Mrs. Radcliffe's incidents. She is hampered in not being supplied with a lover who is the unrecognized heir to vast estates, since all the young men in the county are properly provided with parents.

The delicious persiflage in which Jane Austen hits off the fiction of the day may be illustrated by a bit of conversation between two young girls.

"My dearest Catherine, what have you been doing with yourself all the morning? Have you gone on with *Udolpho*?"

"Yes; I have been reading it ever since I woke, and I have got to the black veil."

"Are you, indeed? How delightful! Oh, I would not tell you what is behind that black veil for the world! Are you not wild to know?"

"Oh, yes, quite! What can it be? But do not tell me—I would not be told on any account. I know it must be a skeleton; I am sure it is Laurentina's skeleton. Oh, I am delighted with the book! I should like to spend my whole life reading it, I assure you. If it had not been to meet you, I would not have come away from it for the world."

"Dear creature! How much obliged I am to you; and when you have finished *Udolpho*, we will read *The Italian* together; and I have made out a list of ten or twelve more of the same kind for you."

"Have you, indeed? How glad I am! What are they all?"

"I will read you their names directly; here they are, in my pocket-book: *Castle of Wolfenbach*, *Clermont*, *Mysterious Warnings*, *Necromancer of the Black Forest*, *Midnight Bell*, *Orphan of the Rhine*, and *Horrid Mysteries*. These will last us some time."

"Yes, pretty well; but are they all horrid? Are you sure they are all horrid?"

"Yes, quite sure; for a particular friend of mine, a Miss Andrews—a sweet girl, one of the sweetest creatures in the world—has read every one of them!'"

Mr. George Saintsbury[1] expresses himself as sceptical of this list as a catalogue of actual romances, stating that he has never read one of them and should like some other authority than Miss Andrews for their existence. He is mistaken in his doubt, however, since during the progress of this investigation four out of the eight have been identified as to authorship, and doubtless the others are lurk-

[1] In his introduction to his pocket volume of *Tales of Mystery*.

ing in some antique library. *Clermont* is by Maria Regina
Roche; *Mysterious Warnings* by Mrs. Parsons, in London,
1796; *Midnight Bell* by Francis Latham; and *Horrid
Mysteries* by Marquis Grosse, London, 1796.

Jane Austen's stupid bore, John Thorpe, and Mr.
Tilney, the impeccable, pedantic hero, add their comment
to Gothic fiction, one saying with a yawn that there hasn't
been a decent novel since *Tom Jones*, except *The Monk*,
and the other that he read *Udolpho* in two days with his
hair standing on end all the time.

But the real cleverness of the work consists in the burlesque of Gothic experiences that Catherine, because of
the excited condition of her mind induced by excess of
romantic fiction, goes through with on her visit to Northanger Abbey. She explores secret wings in a search for
horrors, only to find sunny rooms, with no imprisoned wife,
not a single maniac, and never skeleton of tortured nun.
Mr. Tilney's ironic jests satirize all the elements of Gothic
romance. Opening a black chest at midnight, she finds
a yellowed manuscript, but just as she is about to read it
her candle flickers out. In the morning sunshine she
finds that it is an old laundry list. The only result of
her suspicious explorings is that she is caught in such
prowlings by the young man whose esteem she wishes to
win. He sarcastically assures her that his father is not
a wife-murderer, that his mother is not immured in a
dungeon, but died of a bilious attack. These delicately
tipped shafts of ridicule riddle the armor of medievalism
and give it at the same time a permanency of interest
because of Jane Austen's treatment of it. The Gothic
novel will be remembered, if for nothing else, for her
parody of it.

But Miss Austen is not the only satirist of the *genre*.
In *The Heroine*, Eaton Stannard Barrett gives an amusing
burlesque of it. It is interesting to note in this connec-

tion that while *Northanger Abbey* was written and sold in 1797 it was not published till 1818, and Barrett's book, while written later, was published in 1813.

In the introduction, an epistle, supposed to be endited by one Cherubina, says:

MOON, May 1, 1813.

Know that the moment that a mortal manuscript is written in a legible hand and the word End or Finis attached thereto, whatever characters happen to be sketched therein acquire the quality of creating a soul or spirit which takes flight and ascends immediately through the regions of the air till it arrives at the moon, where it is embodied and becomes a living creature, the precise counterpart of the literary prototype.

Know farther that all the towns, villages, rivers, hills, and valleys of the moon also owe their origin to the descriptions which writers give of the landscapes of the earth.

By means of a book, *The Heroine*, I became a living inhabitant of the moon. I met with the Radclyffian and Rochian heroines, and others, but they tossed their heads and told me pertly that I was a slur on the sisterhood, and some went so far as to say that I had a design on their lives.

Cherry, an unsophisticated country girl, becomes Cherubina after reading romantic tales. She decides that she is an heiress kept in unwarranted seclusion, and tells her father that he cannot possibly be her father since he is "a fat, funny farmer." She rummages in his desk for private papers, discovering a torn scrap that she interprets to her desires. She flies, leaving a note to tell the fleshy agriculturist that she is gone "to wander over the convex earth in search of her parents," with what comic experiences one may imagine. There is much discussion of the Gothic heroine, particularly those from Mrs. Radcliffe's and Regina Maria Roche's pages. The girl sprinkles her letters with verse. She passes through storms, explores deserted houses, and comes to what she thinks is her ancestral castle in London, but is told that it is Covent Garden Theatre. She decides that she is Nell Gwynne's niece and goes to that amiable person to demand all her property. She pokes around in the cellar to find her captive mother, and discovers an enormously fat woman playing with frogs, who drunkenly insists that she is her mother. Leaving that place in disgust she takes possession of somebody else's castle and orders it furnished in Gothic style, according to romance. She has the fat farmer shut up in the madhouse.

The book is very amusing, and a more pronounced parody on Gothicism than *Northanger Abbey* because the whole story turns round that theme,—but, of course, it is not of so great literary value. It seems strange, however, that it is so little known. It burlesques every feature of terror fiction, the high-flown language, the excited oaths, the feudal furniture, the medieval architecture, the Gothic weather, the supernatural tempers, the spectral apparitions —one of which is so muscular that he struggles with the heroine as she locks him in a closet, after throwing rapee into his face, which makes him sputter in a mortal fashion. Cherubina finds a blade bone of mutton in some Gothic garbage and takes it for a bone of an ancestor. Radcliffian adjectives reel across the pages and the whole plays up in a delightful parody the ludicrous weaknesses and excesses of the terror fiction.

Likewise the Anti-Jacobin parodies the Gothic ghost and there is considerable satire directed at the whole Gothic *genre* in Thomas Love Peacock's novel *Nightmare Abbey*.

In general, Gothicism had a tonic effect on English literature, and influenced the continental fiction to no small degree. By giving an interest and excitement gained from ghostly themes to fiction, the terror writers made romance popular as it had never been before and immensely extended the range of its readers. The novel has never lost the hold on popular fancy that the Gothic ghost gave to it. This interest has increased through the various aspects of Romanticism since then and in every period has found some form of supernaturalism on which to feed. True, the machinery of Gothicism creaks audibly at times, some of the specters move too mechanically, and there is a general air of unreality that detracts from the effect. The supernaturalism often lacks the naturalness which is necessary. Yet it is not fair to apply to these early efforts the same standards by which we judge the novels of to-day. While their range is narrow they do achieve certain impressive effects. Though the class became conventionalized to an absurd degree and the later examples are laughable, while a host of imitations made the type ridiculous, the Gothic novel has an undeniable force.

Besides the bringing of supernaturalism definitely into fiction, which is a distinct gain, we find other benefits as well. In Gothicism, if we examine closely, we find the beginnings of many forms of supernaturalism that are crude here, but that are to develop into special power in later novels and short stories. The terror novel excites our ridicule in some respects, yet, like other things that arouse a certain measure of laughter, it has great value. It seems a far cry from the perambulating statue in *Otranto* to Lord Dunsany's jade gods that move with measured, stony steps to wreak a terrible vengeance on mortals who have defied them, but the connection may be clearly enough seen. The dreadful experiments by which Frankenstein's monster is created are close akin to the revolting vivisections of Wells's Dr. Moreau, or the operations described by Arthur Machen whereby human beings lose their souls and become diabolized, given over utterly to unspeakable evil. The psychic elements in *Zofloya* are crudely conceived, yet suggestive of the psychic horrors of the work of Blackwood, Barry Pain, and Theodore Dreiser, for example. The animal supernaturalism only lightly touched on in Gothic novels is to be elaborated in the stories of ghostly beasts like those by Edith Wharton, Kipling, Ambrose Bierce, and others. In fact, the greater number of the forms of the supernatural found in later fiction and the drama are discoverable, in germ at least, in Gothic romance. The work of this period gave a tremendous impetus to the uncanny elements of romanticism and the effect has been seen in the fiction and drama and poetry since that time. Its influence on the drama of its day may be seen in Walpole's *Mysterious Mother* and Lewis's *Castle Specter*. Thomas Lovell Beddoe's extraordinary tragedy, *Death's Jest Book*, while largely Elizabethan in materials and method, is closely related to the Gothic as well. It would be impossible to understand or appreciate the supernatural in the nineteenth-century literature and that of our own day without a knowledge of the Gothic to which most of it goes back. Like most beginnings, Gothicism is crude in its earlier forms, and conventional in the flood of imitations that followed the successful attempts. But it is really vital and most of the ghostly fiction since that time has lineally descended from it rather than from the supernaturalism of the epic or of the drama.

CHAPTER II

Later Influences

THE Gothic period marked a change in the vehicle of supernaturalism. In ancient times the ghostly had been expressed in the epic or the drama, in medievalism in the romances, metrical and prose, as in Elizabethan literature the drama was the specific form. But Gothicism brought it over frankly into the novel, which was a new thing. That is noteworthy, since supernaturalism seems more closely related to poetry than to prose; and as the early dramas were for the most part poetic, it did not require such a stretch of the imagination to give credence to the unearthly. The ballad, the epic, the drama, had made the ghostly seem credible. But prose fiction is so much more materialistic that at first thought supernaturalism seems antagonistic to it. That this is not really the case is evidenced from the fact that fiction since the terror times has retained the elements of awe then introduced, has developed, and has greatly added to them.

With the dying out of the *genre* definitely known as the Gothic novel and the turning of Romanticism into various new channels, we might expect to see the disappearance of the ghostly element, since it had been overworked in terrorism. It is true that the prevailing type of fiction for the succeeding period was realism, but with a large admixture of the supernormal or supernatural. The super-

natural machinery had become so well established in prose
fiction that even realists were moved by it, some using
the motifs with bantering apology—even Dickens and
Thackeray, some with rationalistic explanation, but practically all using it. Man must and will have the supernatural in his fiction. The very elements that one might
suppose would counteract it,—modern thought, invention,
science,—serve as feeders to its force. In the inexplicable
alchemy of literature almost everything turns to the unearthly in some form or other.

We have seen the various sources from which the Gothic
novel drew its plots, its motifs for ghostly effect. The
supernatural fiction following it still had the same sources
on which to draw, and in addition had various other
influences and veins of literary inspiration not open to
Gothicism. Modern science, with the new miracles of its
laboratories, proved suggestive of countless plots; the new
study of folk-lore and the scholarly investigations in that
field unearthed an unguessed wealth of supernatural
material; Psychical Research societies with their patient
and sympathetic records of the forces of the unseen;
modern Spiritualism with its attempts to link this world
to the next; the wizardry of dreams studied scientifically,
—all suggested new themes, novel complications, hitherto
unknown elements continuing the supernatural in fiction.

With the extension of general reading, and the greater
range of translations from other languages, the writers of
England and America were affected by new influences
with respect to their use of the supernatural. Their work
became less insular, wider in its range of subject-matter
and of technical methods, and in our fiction we find the
effect of certain definite outside forces.

The overlapping influences of the Romantic movement
in England and America, France and Germany, form an
interesting but intricate study. It is difficult to point out

marked points of contact, though the general effect may be evident, for literary influences are usually very elusive. It is easy to cry, "Lo, here! lo, there!" with reference to the effect of certain writers on their contemporaries or successors, but it is not always easy to put the finger on anything very tangible. And even so, that would not explain literature. If one could point with absolute certainty to the source for every one of Shakespeare's plots, would that explain his art? Poe wrote an elaborate essay to analyze his processes of composition for *The Raven*, but the poem remains as enigmatic as ever.

As German Romanticism had been considerably affected by the Gothic novel in England, it in turn showed an influence on later English and American ghostly fiction. Scott was much interested in the German literature treating of evil magic, apparitions, castles in ruins, and so forth, and one critic says of him that his dealings with subjects of this kind are midway between Meinhold and Tieck. He was fascinated with the German ballads of the supernatural, especially Burger's ghostly *Lenore*, which he translated among others. De Quincey likewise was a student of German literature, though he was not so accurate in his scholarship as Scott. His horror tale, *The Avengers*, as well as *Klosterheim*, has a German setting and tone.

There has been some discussion over the question of Hawthorne's relation to German Romanticism. Poe made the charge that Hawthorne drew his ideas and style from Ludwig Tieck, saying in a criticism:

The fact is, he is not original in any sense. Those who speak of him as original mean nothing more than that he differs in his manner or tone, and in his choice of subjects, from any author of their acquaintance—their acquaintance not extending to the German Tieck, whose manner in *some*

of his works is absolutely identical with that *habitual* to Hawthorne. . . . The critic (unacquainted with Tieck) who reads
a single tale by Hawthorne may be justified in thinking him
original.

Various critics have discussed this matter with no very
definite conclusions. It should be remembered that Poe
was a famous plagiary-hunter, hence his comments may be
discounted. Yet Poe knew German, it is thought, and
in his writings often referred to German literature, while
Hawthorne, according to his journal, read it with difficulty
and spoke of his struggles with a volume of Tieck.

Hawthorne and Tieck do show certain similarities, as in
the use of the dream element, the employment of the
allegory as a medium for teaching moral truths, and the
choice of the legend as a literary form. Both use somewhat the same dreamy supernaturalism, yet in style as in
subject-matter Hawthorne is much the superior and improved whatever he may have borrowed from Tieck.
Hawthorne's vague mystery, cloudy symbolism, and deep
spiritualism are individual in their effect and give to his
supernaturalism an unearthly charm scarcely found elsewhere. Hawthorne's theme in *The Marble Faun*, of the attaining to a soul by human suffering, is akin to the idea in
Fouqué's *Undine*. There the supernaturalism is franker,
while that of Hawthorne's novel is more evasive and delicate, yet the same suggestion is present in each case.
Lowell in his *Fable for Critics* speaks of Hawthorne as
"a John Bunyan Fouqué, a Puritan Tieck."

There are still more striking similarities to be pointed
out between the work of Poe and that of E. T. A. Hoffmann. As Hawthorne was, to a slight extent, at least,
affected by German legends and wonder tales, Poe was
influenced by Hoffmann's horror stories. Poe has been
called a Germanic dreamer, and various German and

English critics mention the debt that he owes to Hoffmann. Mr. Palmer Cobb[1] brings out some interesting facts in connection with the two romanticists.   He says:

The verification of Poe's indebtedness to German is to be sought in the similarity of the treatment of the same motives in the work of both authors. The most convincing evidence is furnished by the way in which Poe has combined the themes of mesmerism, metempsychosis, dual existence, the dream element, and so forth, in exact agreement with the grouping employed by Hoffmann. Notable examples of this are the employment of the idea of double existence in conjunction with the struggle of good and evil forces in the soul of the individual, and the combination of mesmerism and metempsychosis as leading motives in one and the same story.

Mr. Cobb points out in detail the similarities between Poe's stories of dual personality and the German use of the theme as found in Fouqué, Novalis, and Hoffmann, particularly the last.   Hoffmann's exaggerated use of this idea is to be explained on the ground that he was obsessed by the thought that his double was haunting him, and he, like Maupassant under similar conditions of mind, wrote of supernaturalism associated with madness.   Hoffmann uses the theme of double personality.[2]   In Poe's *William Wilson* the other self is the embodiment of good, a sort of incarnate conscience, as in Stevenson's Markheim, while Hoffmann's *Elixière* represents the evil.   Poe has here reversed the idea.   In Hoffmann's *Magnetiseur* we find the treatment of hypnotism and metempsychosis and the dream-supernaturalism in the same combination that Poe uses.[3]   Hoffmann[4] and Poe[5] relate the story of a superna-

[1] *The Influence of E. T. A. Hoffmann on Edgar Allan Poe.*
[2] In the *Doppelganger, Kater Murr,* and *Elixière des Teufels.*
[3] In his *Tale of the Ragged Mountains.*
[4] In *Die Jesuit-kirche in G.*   [5] In *The Oval Portrait.*

tural portrait, where the wife-model dies as the sacrifice
to the painting.

Both Hoffmann and Poe use the grotesquerie of supernaturalism, the fantastic element of horror that adds to
the effect of the ghostly. Even the generic titles are almost
identical.[1]   But in spite of these similarities in theme and
in grouping, there is no basis for a charge that Poe owes
a stylistic debt to Hoffmann.   In his manner he is original
and individual.   He uses his themes with much greater
art, with more dramatic and powerful effect than his
German contemporary.   Though he employs fewer of the
crude machineries of the supernatural, his ghostly tales
are more unearthly than Hoffmann's.   His horrors have a
more awful effect because he is an incomparably greater
artist.   He knows the economy of thrills as few have done.
His is the genius of compression, of suggestion.   His dream
elements, for instance, though Hoffmann uses the dream
to as great extent as Poe—are more poignant, more unbearable.

The cult of horror in German literature, as evidenced in
the work of Hoffmann, Kleist, Tieck, Arnim, Fouqué,
Chamisso, had an influence on English and American
literature of supernaturalism in general.   The grotesque
diablerie, the use of dream elements, magnetism, metempsychosis, ghosts, the elixir of life—which theme appears
to have a literary elixir of life—are reflected to a certain
degree in the English ghostly tales of the generation following the Gothic romance.

A French influence is likewise manifest in the later
English fiction.   The Gothic novel had made itself felt in
France as well as in Germany, a proof of which is the fact
that Balzac was so impressed by Maturin's novel that he
wrote a sequel to it.[2]   The interrelations of the English,

[1] Compare Poe's definition of his type as phantasy pieces with Hoffmann's
title Phantasie Stücke.   [2] *Melmoth Réconcilié.*

French, and German supernatural literature are nowhere better illustrated than in the work of Balzac. He admits Hoffmann's inspiration of his *Elixir of Life*, that horrible story of reanimation, where the head is restored to life and youth but the body remains that of an old man, dead and decaying, from which the head tears itself loose in the church and bites the abbot to the brain, shrieking out, "Idiot, tell me now if there is a God!" Balzac's influence over Bulwer-Lytton is seen in such stories as *The Haunters and the Haunted, or the House and the Brain*, and *A Strange Story*, in each of which the theme of supernaturally continued life is used. Balzac's *Magic Skin* is a symbolic story of supernaturalism that suggests Hawthorne's allegoric symbolism and may have influenced it in part. It is a new application of the old theme, used often in the drama as in Gothic romance, of the pledge of a soul for earthly gratification. A magic skin gives the man his heart's desires, yet each granted wish makes the talisman shrink perceptibly, with an inexorable decrease. This theme, symbolic of the truth of life, is such a spiritual idea used allegorically as Hawthorne chose frequently and doubtless influenced Oscar Wilde's *Picture of Dorian Grey*. Balzac's *Unknown Masterpiece* is another example of his supernaturalism that has had its suggestive effect on English ghostly fictions.

Guy de Maupassant has doubtless influenced English tales of horror more than any foreign writer since Hoffmann. As a stylist he exercised a definite and strong influence over the short-story form, condensing it, making it more economical, more like a fatal bullet that goes straight to the mark, and putting into a few hundred words a story of supernatural horror relentless in its effect. O. Henry's delicately perfect ghost story, *The Furnished Room*, is reminiscent of Maupassant's technique as seen in *The Ghost*. And surely F. Marion Crawford's *Screaming Skull* and Ambrose Bierce's *Middle Toe of the Right Foot* are from the same body as Maupassant's *Hand*. What a terrible corpus it must be! There is the same gruesome mystery, the same implacable horror in each story of a mutilated ghost.

Maupassant's stories of madness, akin to Poe's analyses of mental decay, of the slow corruption of the brain, are among his most dreadful triumphs of style, and have influenced various English stories of insanity. In Maupassant's own tottering reason we find the tragic explanation of his constant return to this type of story. Such tales as *Mad*, where a husband goes insane from doubt of his wife; *Madness*, where a man has a weird power over human beings, animals, and even inanimate objects, making them do his will, so that he is terrified of his own self, of what his horrible hands may do mechanically; *Cocotte*, where the drowned dog, following its master a hundred miles down the river, drives him insane; *The Tress*, a curdling story of the relation between insanity and the supernatural, so that one is unable to say which is cause and which effect, illustrate Maupassant's unusual association between madness and uncanny fiction. Who but Maupassant could make a story of ghastly hideousness out of a parrot that swears? As Maupassant was influenced by Poe, in both subject matter and technique, so he has affected the English writers since his time in both plot material and treatment of the supernatural. And as his *La Horla* strongly reflects FitzJames O'Brien's *What Was It? A Mystery* that anticipated it by a number of years, so it left its inevitable impress on Bierce's *The Damned Thing* and succeeding stories of supernatural invisibility. A recent story by Katherine Fullerton Gerould, *Louquier's Third Act*, seems clearly to indicate the De Maupassant influence, reflecting the method and motifs of *La Horla* and *The Coward*. Maupassant's tales have a peculiar horror possessed by few, partly because of his undoubted genius and partly the result of his increasing madness.

Other French writers have also influenced the uncanny story in English. Théophile Gautier has undoubtedly inspired various tales, such as *The Mummy's Foot*, by Jessie Adelaide Weston, which is the match, though not in beauty or form, to his little masterpiece of that title. A. Conan Doyle's *Lot No. 249*, a horrible story of a re-animated mummy, bears an unquestionable resemblance to Gautier's *The Romance of the Mummy* as well as *The Mummy's Foot*, though Poe's *A Word with a Mummy*, a fantastic story emphasizing the science of miraculous embalming of living persons so that they would wake to life after thousands of years, preceded it. Something of the same theme is also used by F. Marion Crawford,[1] where the bodies in the old studio awake to menacing life. This motif illustrates the prevalence of the Oriental material in recent English fiction. Gautier's *La Morte Amoureuse* has exercised suggestive power over later tales, such as Crawford's vampire story,[2] though it is significant to recall that Poe's *Berenice* preceded Gautier's story by a year, and the latter must have known Poe's work.

The fiction of Erckmann-Chatrian appears to have suggested various English stories. *The Owl's Ear* obviously inspired another,[3] both being records of supernatural acoustics the latter dealing with spiritual sounds. *The Invisible Eye*, a fearsome story of hypnotism, has an evident parental claim on Algernon Blackwood's story,[4] though the latter is psychically more gruesome. *The Waters of Death*, an account of a loathsome, enchanted crab, suggests H. G. Wells's story of the plant vampire.[5]

[1] In *Khaled*.   [2] *For the Blood Is the Life*.
[3] *The Spider's Eye*, by Lucretia P. Hale.
[4] *With Intent to Steal*.   [5] *The Flowering of the Strange Orchid*.

Likewise Anatole France's *Putois*, the narrative of the man who came to have an actual existence because some-one spoke of him as an imaginary person, is associated with the drolleries of supernaturalism, such as are used by Thomas Bailey Aldrich in the story of an imagined per-son, *Miss Mehitabel's Son*, and by Frank R. Stockton.[1] Anatole France has several delicately wrought idylls of the supernatural, as *The Mass of Shadows*, where the ghosts of those who have sinned for love may meet once a year to be reunited with their loved ones, and in the church, with clasped hands, celebrate the spectral mass, or such tender miracles as *The Juggler of Notre Dame*, where the juggler throws his balls before the altar as an act of worship and is rewarded by a sight of the Virgin, or *Scholasticus*, a symbolic story much like one written years earlier by Thomas Bailey Aldrich,[2] where a plant miraculously springs from the heart of a dead woman. *Amycus and Celestine*, the story of the faun and the hermit, of whom he tells us that "the hermit is a faun borne down by the years" is suggestive of the wonderful little stories of Lord Dunsany. Lord Dunsany, while startlingly original in most respects, seems a bit influenced by Anatole France. His *When the Gods Slept* seems reminiscent of *The Isle of the Penguins*. In France's satire the gods change pen-guins into men whose souls will be lost, because the priest has baptized them by mistake, while in Dunsany's story the baboons pray to the Yogis, who promise to make them men in return for their devotion.

And the baboons arose from worshipping, smoother about the face and a little shorter in the arms, and went away and hid themselves in clothing and herded with men. And men could not discern what they were for their bodies were bodies

---

[1] In *The Transferred Ghost* and *The Spectral Mortgage*.
[2] *Père Antoine's Date Palm*.

of men though their souls were still the souls of beasts and the worship went to the Yogis, spirits of ill.

Maeterlinck, influenced by his fellow-Belgian, Charles Van Lerberghe, whose *Flaireurs* appeared before Maeterlinck's plays of the uncanny and to whom he acknowledges his indebtedness, has strongly affected ghostly literature since his rise to recognition. In his plays we find an atmospheric supernaturalism. The settings are of earth, yet with an unearthly strangeness, with no impression of realism, of the familiar, the known. In Maeterlinck's plays we never breathe the air of actuality, never feel the footing of solid earth, as we always do in Shakespeare, even in the presence of ghosts or witches. Shakespeare's visitants are ghostly enough, certainly, but the scenes in which they appear are real, are normal, while in the Belgian's work there is a fluidic supernaturalism that transforms everything to unreality. We feel the grip of fate, as in the ancient Greek tragedies, the inescapable calamity that approaches with swift, silent pace. Yet Maeterlinck's is essentially static drama. There is very little action, among the human beings, at least, for Fate is the active agent. In *The Blind*, *The Intruder*, and *Interior* the elements are much the same, the effects wrought out with the same unearthly manner. But in *Joyzelle*, which shows a certain similarity to *Midsummer Night's Dream* and *The Tempest*, we have a different type of supernaturalism, the use of enchantment, of fairy magic that comes to a close happily. In the dream-drama[1] there is a mixture of realism and poetic symbolism, the use of the dream as a vehicle for the supernormal, and many aspects of the weird combined in a fairy play of exquisite symbolism.

The influence of Maeterlinck is apparent in the work of English writers, particularly of the Celtic school. W. B.

[1] *The Blue Bird.*

Yeats's fairy play, *The Land of Heart's Desire*, with its pathetic beauty, *Countess Cathleen*, his tragedy of the countess who sells her soul to the devil that her people may be freed from his power, as well as his stories, show the traces of Maeterlinck's methods. William Sharp, in his sketches and his brief plays in the volume called *Vistas*, reflects the Belgian's technique slightly, though with his own individual power. Sharp's other literary self, Fiona McLeod, likewise shows his influence, as does Synge in his *Riders to the Sea*, and Gordon Bottomley in his *Crier by Night*, that eerie tragedy of an unseen power. Maeterlinck's supernaturalism seems to suggest the poetry of Coleridge, with its elusive, intangible ghostliness. The effect of naïveté observable in Coleridge's work is in Maeterlinck produced by a child-like simplicity of style, a monosyllabic dialogue, and a monotonous, unreasoning repetition that is at once real and unreal. The dramatist has brought over from the poet the same suggestive use of portents and symbols for prefiguring death or disaster that lurks just outside. The ghostliness is subtle, rather than evident, the drama static rather than dynamic.

Ibsen, also, has strongly influenced the supernatural in both our drama and our fiction. His own work has a certain kinship with that of Hawthorne, showing a like symbolism and mysticism, a like transfusion of the unreal with the natural, so that one scarcely knows just how far he means our acceptance of the unearthly to extend. He leaves it in some cases an open question, while in others he frankly introduces the supernatural. The child's vision of the dead heroes riding to Valhalla, with his own mother who has killed herself, leading them,[1] the ghost that tries to make an unholy pact with the king,[2] the apparition and the supernatural voice crying out "He is the God of Love!"[3]

[1] In *The Vikings of Helgeland.*   [2] In *The Pretenders.*
[3] In *Brand.*

illustrate Ibsen's earlier methods. The curious, almost inexplicable *Peer Gynt*, with its mixture of folk-lore and symbolism, its ironic laughter and satiric seriousness, seems to have had a suggestive influence on other works, such as *Countess Eve*,[1] where the personification of temptation in the form of committed sin reflects Ibsen's idea of Peer Gynt's imaginary children. The uncanny power of unspoken thought, the haunting force of ideas rather than the crude visible phantasms of the dead, as in the telepathy, or hypnotism, or what you will, in *The Master Builder*, the evasive, intangible haunting of the living by the dead as in *Rosmersholm*, the strange powers at work as in *The Lady from the Sea*, have had effect on the numerous psychic dramas and stories in English. The symbolic mysticism in *Emperor and Galilean*, showing the spirits of Cain and of Judas, with their sad ignorance of life's riddles, the vision of Christ in person, with His unceasing power over men's souls, foreshadowed the plays and stories bringing in the personality of Christ, as *The Servant in the House*, and *The Passing of the Third Floor Back*.

Modern Italian literature, as represented by Fogazzaro and D'Annunzio, introduces the ghostly in fiction and in the drama, and has had its effect on our literature. Fogazzaro's novels are essentially realistic in pattern, yet he uses the supernatural in them, as in miraculous visions,[2] and metempsychosis and madness associated with the supernatural.[3] D'Annunzio's handling of the unearthly is more repulsive, more psychically gruesome, as the malignant power of the ancient curse in *La Città Morta*, where the undying evil in an old tomb causes such revolting horror in the action of the play. This has a counterpart in a story,[4] by Josephine Daskam Bacon, where a

[1] By J. H. Shorthouse.   [2] In *The Sinner* and *The Saint*.
[3] In *The Woman*.   [4] *The Unburied*.

packet of letters from two evil lovers lie buried in a hearth and by their subtle influence corrupt the soul of every woman who occupies the room. D'Annunzio uses the witch motive powerfully,[1] madness that borders on the supernatural,[2] and the idea of evil magic exorcised by melting an image of wax to cause an enemy's death[3] which suggests Rossetti's poem using that incident, the unforgettable *Sister Helen*.

Likewise a new force in the work of the Russian school has affected our fiction of the ghostly in recent years. Russian literature is a new field of thought for English people, since it is only of late years that translations have been easily accessible, and, because of the extreme difficulty of the language, very few outsiders read Russian. As German Romanticism began to have its definite power over English supernatural fiction in the early part of the nineteenth century by the extension of interest in and study of German literature, and the more frequent translation of German works, so in this generation Russian literature has been introduced to English people and is having its influence.

A primitive, still savage race like the Russians naturally shows a special fondness for the supernatural. Despite the fact that literature is written for the higher classes, a large peasant body, illiterate and superstitious, will influence the national fiction. In the Russian works best known to us there is a large element of the uncanny, of á type in some respects different from that of any other country. Like the Russian national character, it is harsh, brutal, violent, yet sentimental. One singular thing to be noted about it is the peculiar combination of supernaturalism with absolute realism. The revolting yet dreadfully effective realism of the Russian literature is never

[1] In *The Daughter of Jorio.*   [2] In *Sogno d'un Mattino di Primavera.*
[3] In *Sogno d'un Tramonto d'Autunno.*

more impressive than in its union with ghostly horror, which makes the impossible appear indubitable. In Gogol's *The Cloak*, for instance, the fidelity to homely details of life, the descriptions of pinching poverty, of tragic hopes that waited so long for fulfillment, are painful in themselves and give verisimilitude to the element of the unearthly that follows. You feel that a poor Russian clerk who had stinted himself from necessity all his life *would* come back from the dead to claim his stolen property and demand redress. The supernatural gains a new power, a more tremendous thrill when set off against the every-day-ness of sordid life. We find something of the same effect in the stories of Algernon Blackwood and Ambrose Bierce and F. Marion Crawford.

Tolstoi's symbolic story of *Ivan the Fool* is an impressive utterance of his views of life, expressed by the allegory of man's folly and wisdom and the schemes of devils.

Turgeniev's pronounced strain of the unearthly has had its influence on English fiction. He uses the dream elements to a marked degree, as in *The Song of Love Triumphant*, a story of Oriental magic employed through dreams and music, and *The Dream*, an account of a son's revelatory visions of his unknown father. The dream element has been used considerably in our late fiction, some of which seems to reflect Turgeniev. Another motive that he uses effectively is that of suggested vampirism,[1] and of psychical vampirism,[2] where a young man is "set upon" by the spirit of a dead woman he has scarcely known, till he dies under the torment. This seems to have affected such stories as that of psychical vampirism in *The Vampire*, by Reginald Hodder. We find in much of Turgeniev's prose the symbolic, mystical supernaturalism besides his use of dreams, visions, and a distinct Oriental element. In *Knock! Knock! Knock!* the treatment of

[1] As in *Phantoms*.　　　　　　　[2] As in *Clara Militch*.

whose spiritualism reminds one somewhat of Browning's,[1] in its initial skepticism and later hesitation, the final effect of which is to impress one with a sense of supernaturalism working extraordinarily through natural means, so that it is more powerful than the mere conventional ghostly could be, we see what may have been the inspiration for certain spiritualistic novels and stories in English. The same tone is felt in Hamlin Garland's treatment of the subject, for instance. The mystical romanticism of Turgeniev is less brutally Russian than that of most of his compeers.

Like Maupassant and Hoffman and Poe, the Russian writers use to a considerable extent the association between insanity and the supernatural to heighten the effect of both. They may have been influenced in this by Poe's studies of madness, as by Maupassant's, and they appear to have an influence over certain present-day writers. It would be difficult to say which is the stronger influence in the treatment of abnormal persons, Maupassant or the Russian writers. One wonders what type of mania obsesses certain of the Russian fictionists of to-day, for surely they cannot be normal persons. Examples of such fiction are: Alexander Pushkin's story of mocking madness resulting from a passion for cards, whose ghostly motif has a sardonic diabolism,[2] Tchekhoff's story of abnormal horror,[3] a racking account of insanity,[4] and *The Black Monk*, a weird story of insanity brought on by the vision of a supernatural being, a replicaed mirage of a black monk a thousand years old. But it is in the work of Leonidas Andreyev that we get the ultimate anguish of madness. *The Red Laugh*, an analysis of the madness of war, of the insanity of nations as of individuals, seems to envelop the world in a sheet of flame. Its horrors go be-

[1] In *Sludge, the Medium.*   [2] *The Queen of Spades.*
[3] *Sleepyhead.*   [4] *Ward No. 6.*

yond words and the brain reels in reading.   There are in
English a number of stories of insanity associated with the
supernatural which may have been influenced by the
Russian method, though Ambrose Bierce's studies in the
abnormality of soldier life preceded Andreyev by years.
F. Marion Crawford's *The Dead Smile* and various stories
of Arthur Machen have a Russian horror, and other
instances might be mentioned.

The Russian fiction with its impersonality of pessimism,
its racial gloom, its terrible sordid realism forming a basis
for awesome supernaturalism, is of a type foreign to our
thought, yet, as is not infrequently the case, the radically
different has a strange appeal, and the effect of it on our
stories of horror is undoubted.   English and American
readers are greatly interested in Russian literature just
now and find a peculiar relish in its terrors, though the
harsher elements are somewhat softened in transference
to our language.

Other fields of thought have been opened to us within
this generation by the widening of our knowledge of
the literature of other European countries.   Books are
much more freely translated now than formerly and no
person need be ignorant of the fiction of other lands.
From the Spanish, the Portuguese, the Chinese, Japanese,
and other tongues we are receiving stories of supernaturalism that give us new ideas, new points of view.   The
greater ease of travel, the opportunity to study once-
distant lands and literatures have been reflected in our
fiction.   Some one should write a monograph on the
literary influence of Cook's tours!   Our later work has
a strong touch of the Oriental,—not an entirely new
thing, since we find it in Beckford's *Vathek* and the pre-
Gothic tales of John Hawkesworth,—but more noticeable
now.   Examples are Stevenson's *New Arabian Nights*,
Bottle Imp, and others, F. Marion Crawford's *Khaled*

and *Mr. Isaacs*, Blackwood's stories of Elementals, George Meredith's fantasy, *The Shaving of Shagpat*, though many others might be named. The Oriental fiction permits the use of magic, sorcery, and various elements that seem out of place in ordinary fiction. The popularity of Kipling's tales of Indian native life and character illustrates our fondness for this aspect of supernaturalism.

Apart from the foreign influences that affect it we notice a certain change in the materials and methods of ghostly fiction in English. New elements had entered into Gothic tales as an advance over the earlier forms, yet conventions had grown up so that even such evasive and elusive personalities as ghosts were hidebound by precedent. While the decline of the *genre* definitely known as the Gothic novel in no sense put an end to the supernatural in English fiction, it did mark a difference in manner. The Gothic ghosts were more elementary in their nature, more superficial, than those of later times. Life was, in the days of Walpole and Mrs. Radcliffe, more local because of the limitations of travel and communication, it being considered astounding in Gothic times that a ghost could travel a thousand miles with ease while mortals moved snail-like. Scientific investigation was crude compared with the present and had not greatly touched fiction. Scientific folk-lore investigations were as unknown as societies of psychical research, hence neither had aided in the writing of ghostly fiction.

The mass of ghostly stuff which has appeared in English since the Gothic period, and which will be classified and discussed under different motifs in succeeding chapters, shows many of the same characteristics of the earlier, yet exhibits also a decided development over primitive, classical and Gothic forms. The modern supernaturalism is more complex, more psychological than the terroristic, perhaps because nowadays man is more intellectual, his thought-processes more subtle. Humanity still wants ghosts, as ever, but they must be more cleverly presented to be convincing. The ghostly thrill is as ardently desired by the reading public, as eagerly striven for by the writers as ever, though it is more difficult of achievement now than formerly. Yet when it is attained it is more poignant and lasting in its effects because more subtle in its art. The apparition that eludes analysis haunts the memory more than do the comparatively simple forms of the past. Compare, for instance, the spirits evoked by Henry James and Katherine Fullerton Gerould with the crude clap-trap of cloistered spooks and armored knights of Gothic times. How cheap and melodramatic the earlier attempts seem!

The present-day ghost is at once less terrible and more terrible than those of the past. There is not so much a sense of physical fear now, as of psychic horror. The pallid specters that glide through antique castles are ineffectual compared with the maleficent psychic invasions of modernity. On the other hand, the recent ghostly story frequently shows a strong sense of humor unknown in Gothicism, and only suggested in earlier forms, as in the elder Pliny's statement that ghosts would not visit a person afflicted with freckles, which shows at least a germinal joviality in classical spooks.

One feature that distinguishes the uncanny tales of to-day from the Gothic is their greater range of material. The early terror story had its source in popular superstition, classical literature, medieval legends, or the Elizabethan drama, while in the century that has elapsed since the decay of the Gothic novel as such, new fields of thought have been opened up, and new sources for ghostly plots have been discovered which the writers of modern stories are quick to utilize. Present-day science with its

wonderful development has provided countless plots for
supernatural stories. Comparative study of folk-lore,
with the activities of the numerous associations, has
brought to light fascinating material. Modern Spiritualism, with its seances, its mediumistic experiments, has
inspired many novels and stories. The Psychical Research Society, with branches in various parts of the
world and its earnest advocates and serious investigations,
has collected suggestive stuff for many ghostly stories.
The different sources for plot material and mechanics
for awesome effect, added to these from which the terror
novel drew its inspiration, have incalculably enriched
the supernatural fiction and widened the limits far beyond
the restrictions of the conventionalized Gothic.

Science has furnished themes for many modern stories
of the supernatural. Modern science itself, under normal
conditions, seems like necromancer's magic, so its incursion into thrilling fiction is but natural. Every aspect
of research and discovery has had its exponent in fictive
form, and the skill with which the material is handled
constitutes one point of difference between the present
ghostly stories and the crude scientific supernaturalism
of the early novels. The influence of Darwin, Spencer,
Huxley, and other scientists of the last century did much
to quicken fiction as well as thought, and the effects can
be traced in the work of various authors.

The widespread interest in folk-lore in recent years
has had an appreciable influence on the stories of the
supernatural. While the methods of investigation followed by the serious students of folk-lore are scientific
and the results are tabulated in an analytic rather than a
literary style, yet the effect is helpful to fiction. Comparative studies in folk-lore, by the bringing together of a
mass of material from diverse sources, establishes the fact
of the universal acceptance of supernaturalism in some

form. Ethnic superstitions vary, yet there is enough similarity between the ideas held by tribes and races so widely separated as to discredit any basis of imitation or conscious influence between them, to be of great interest to scientists. No tribe, however low in the social scale, has been found that has no belief in powers beyond the mortal.

Folk-lore associations are multiplying and the students of literature and anthropology are joining forces in the effort to discover and classify the variant superstitions and legends of the past and of the races and tribes still in their childhood. Such activities are bringing to light a fascinating wealth of material from which the writers of ghostly tales may find countless plots. Such studies show how close akin the world is after all. A large number of books relating stories of brownies, bogles, fairies, banshees, wraiths, hobgoblins, witches, vampires, ghouls, and other superhuman personages have appeared. I am not including in this list the fairy stories that are written for juvenile consumption, but merely the folkloristic or literary versions for adults.

The most marked instance of the influence of folk-lore in supplying subject matter for literature is shown in the recent Celtic revival. The supernatural elements in the folk-tales of Ireland, Scotland, and Wales have been widely used in fiction, poetry, and the drama. In this connection one is reminded of Collins's *Ode on the Popular Superstitions of the Highlands Considered as the Subject for Poetry*. The Irish National School, with W. B. Yeats, John Synge, and Lady Gregory as leaders, have made the folk-tales of Ireland live in literature and the ghostly thrill of the old legends comes down to us undiminished. Lord Dunsany's work is particularly brilliant, going back to ancient times and re-creating the mythologic beings for us, making us friendly with the gods, the centaurs, the giants, and divers other long-forgotten characters. Kipling has made the lore of the Indian towns and jungles live for us, as Joel Chandler Harris has immortalized the legends of the southern negro. Thomas A. Janvier in his tales of old Mexico calls back the ghosts of Spanish conquerors and Aztec men and women, repeopling the ancient streets with courtly specters. The fondness for folk-loristic fiction is one of the marked aspects of Romanticism at the present time.

The activities of the Society for Psychical Research have had decided effect in stimulating ghostly stories. When so many intelligent persons turn their attention to finding and classifying supernatural phenomena the currents of thought thus set up will naturally influence fiction. Nowadays every interest known to man is reflected in literature. The proceedings of the association have been so widely advertised and so open to the public that persons who would not otherwise give thought to the supernatural have considered the matter. Such thinkers as W. T. Stead and Sir Oliver Lodge, to mention only two, would inevitably influence others. In this connection it is interesting to note the recent claims by Stead's daughter that her father has communicated with the living, and Lodge's book, just published, *Raymond, or Life and Death*, that gives proof of what he considers incontrovertible messages from his son killed in battle. The collection of thousands of affirmative answers to the question as to whether one had ever felt a ghostly presence not to be explained on natural grounds brought out a mass of material that might serve for plot-making. Haunted houses have been catalogued and the census of specters taken.

The investigations in modern Spiritualism have done much to affect ghostly literature. The terrors of the later apparitions are not physical, but psychical, and probably the stories of the future will be more and more allied to Spiritualism. Hamlin Garland, John Corbin, William Dean Howells, Algernon Blackwood, Arnold Bennett, and others have written novels and stories of this material, though scarcely the fringe of the garment of possibilities has yet been touched. If one but grant the hypothesis of Spiritualism, what vistas open up for the novelist! What thrilling complications might come from the skillful manipulation of astrals alone,—as aids in establishing alibis, for instance! Even the limitations that at present bind ghost stories would be abolished and the effects of the dramatic employment of spiritualistic faith would be highly sensational. If the will be all powerful, then not only tables but mountains may be moved. The laws of physics would be as nothing in the presence of such powers. A lovelorn youth bent on attaining the object of his desires could, by merely willing it so, sink ocean liners, demolish skyscrapers, call up tempests, and rival German secret agents in his havoc. Intensely dramatic psychological material might be produced by the conflict resulting from the double or multiple personalities in one's own nature, according to spiritualistic ideas. There might be complicated crossings in love, wherein one would be jealous of his alter ego, and conflicting ambitions of exciting character. The struggle necessary for the model story might be intensely dramatic though altogether internal, between one's own selves. One finds himself so much more interesting in the light of such research than one has ever dreamed. The distinctions between materializations and astralizations, etherealizations and plain apparitions might furnish good plot structure. The personality of the "sensitives" alone would be fascinating material and the cosmic clashes of will possible under these conceived conditions suggest thrilling stories.

Dreams constitute another definite source for ghostly plots in modern literature. While this was true to a certain extent in the Gothic novel, it is still more so in later fiction. Lafcadio Hearn[1] advances the theory that all the best plots for ghost stories in any language come from dreams. He advises the person who would write supernatural thrillers to study the phases of his own dream life. It would appear that all one needs to do is to look into his own nightmares and write. Hearn says: "All the great effects produced by poets and story writers and even by religious teachers, in the treatment of the supernatural fear or mystery, have been obtained directly or indirectly from dreams." Though one may not literally accept the whole of that statement, one must feel that the relation between dreams and supernatural impressions is strikingly close. The feeling of supernatural presence comes almost always at night when one is or has been asleep. The guilty man, awaking from sleep, thinks that he sees the specters of those he has wronged—because his dreams have embodied them for him. The lover beholds the spirit of his dead love, because in dreams his soul has gone in search of her. Very young children are unable to distinguish between dreams and reality, as is the case of savages of a low order, believing in the actuality of what they experience in dreams. And who can say that our dream life is altogether baseless and unreal?

The different nightmare sensations, acute and vivid as they are, can be analyzed to find parallelisms between them and the ghostly plots. For example, take the sensation, common in nightmares, of feeling yourself falling from immeasurable height. The same thrill of suspense is communicated by the climax in Lewis's and Mrs. Dacre's Gothic novels, where the devil takes guilty mortals to the mountain top and hurls them down,

[1] In his *Interpretations of Literature.*

down. The horrible potentialities of shadows suggested frequently in dreams is illustrated by Mary Wilkins Freeman's story where the accusing spirit comes back as a haunting shadow on the wall, rather than as an ordinary ghost, tormenting the living brother till *his* shadow also appears, a portent of his death.[1] The awful grip of causeless horror, of nameless fear which assails one so often in nightmares is represented in *The Red Room*,[2] where black Fear, the Power of Darkness, haunts the room rather than any personal spirit. It is disembodied horror itself. Wilkie Collins illustrates the presaging vision of approaching disaster in *The Dream Woman*. The nightmare horror of supernaturalism is nowhere better shown than in Maupassant's *La Horla* where the sleeper wakes with a sense of leaden weight upon his breast, and knows that night after night some dreadful presence is shut in with him, invisible yet crushing the life out of him and driving him mad.

The nightmare motifs are present to a remarkable degree in Bulwer-Lytton's *The Haunted and the Haunters, or the House and the Brain*. There we have the gigantism of the menacing Thing, the supernatural power given to inanimate objects, the ghostly chill, the darkness, and the intolerable oppression of a nameless evil thing beside one. Vampirism might easily be an outcome of dreams, since based on a physical sensation of pricking at the throat, combined with debility caused by weakness, which could be attributed to loss of blood from the ravages of vampires. F. Marion Crawford's story, *For the Blood Is the Life*, is more closely related to dreams than most of the type, though probably Bram Stoker's *Dracula* is the most horrible.

The curious side of supernaturalism as related to dreams is illustrated by *The Dream Gown of the Jap-*

[1] *The Shadows on the Wall.*   [2] By H. G. Wells.

anese Ambassador,[1] and the more beautiful by Simeon Solomon's *Vision of Love Revealed in Sleep*. Mary Wilkins Freeman has a remarkable short story, *The Hall Bedroom*, which is one of the best illustrations of the use of dream imagery and impressions. Here the effects are alluring and beautiful, with the horror kept in the background, but perhaps the more effective because of the artistic restraint. Odors, sights, sounds, feelings, are all raised to an intensity of sensuous, slumbrous enjoyment, all subliminated above the mortal. The description of the river in the picture, on which the young man floats away to dreamy death, similar to the Japanese story referred to by Hearn, helps to give the impression of infinity that comes only in dreams. Algernon Blackwood in numerous stories not only uses the elements of dreams and nightmares but explicitly calls attention to the fact. Dream supernaturalism is employed in Barry Pain's stories, in Arthur Machen's volume,[2] and in many others. Freud's theory of dreams as the invariable result of past experiences or unconscious desires has not been stressed in fiction, though doubtless it will have its inning presently. A. Conan Doyle's *The Secret of Goresthorpe Grange* is an amusing story of the relation of definite wishes and dreams of the ghostly.

These are some of the sources from which the later writers of occultism have drawn their plots. They represent a distinct advance over the Gothic and earlier supernaturalism in materials, for the modern story has gained the new elements without loss of the old. The ghostly fiction of to-day has access to the animistic or classical or medieval themes, yet has the unlimited province of present thought to furnish additional inspiration. There never was a time when thinking along general lines was more spontaneously reflected in fiction than now, and

[1] By Brander Matthews. [2] *The Hill of Dreams*.

supernatural literature claims all regions for its own.
Like every other phase of man's thought, ghostly fiction
shows the increasing complexity of form and matter, the
wealth of added material and abounding richness of
style, the fine subtleties that only modernity can give.

CHAPTER III

MODERN GHOSTS

THE ghost is the most enduring figure in supernatural fiction. He is absolutely indestructible. He glides from the freshly-cut pages of magazines and books bearing the date of the year of our Lord nineteen hundred and seventeen as from the parchment rolls of ancient manuscripts. He appears as unapologetically at home in twentieth century fiction as in classical mythology, Christian hagiology, medieval legend, or Gothic romance. He changes with the styles in fiction but he never goes out of fashion. He is the really permanent citizen of this earth, for mortals, at best, are but transients. Even the athlete and the Methusaleh must in the end give up the flesh, but the wraith goes on forever, In form, too, he wears well. Ghostly substance of materialization, ethereal and vaporous as it appears to be, is yet of an astonishing toughness. It seems to possess an obstinate vitality akin to that attributed to the boll weevil in a negro ballad, that went on undaunted by heat or cold, rain or drought, time or tide. The ghost, like death, has all seasons for its own and there is no closed season for spooks. It is much the case now as ever that all the world loves a ghost, yet we like to take our ghosts vicariously, preferably in fiction. We'd rather see than be one.

One point of difference between the ghostly fiction of the past and of the present is in the matter of length. The

Gothic novel was often a three- or four-decker affair in
whose perusal the reader aged perceptibly before the ghost
succeeded or was foiled in his haunting designs.   There
was obviously much more leisure on the part of spooks
as well as mortals then than now.   Consequently the
ghost story of to-day is told in short-story form for the
most part.   Poe knew better than anybody before him
what was necessary for the proper economy of thrills
when he gave his dictum concerning the desirable length
for a story, which rule applies more to the ghostly
tale than to any other type, for surely there is needed
the unity of impression, the definiteness of effect which
only continuity in reading gives.   The ghostly narrative
that is too long loses in impressiveness, whether it is
altogether supernatural or mixed with other elements.
In either case, it is less successful than the shorter, more
poignant treatment possible in the compressed form.
The tabloid ghost can communicate more thrills than the
one in diluted narration.

The apparitions in later English fiction fall naturally
into several distinct classes with reference to the reality
of their appearance.   There are the mistaken apparitions,
there are the purely subjective specters, evoked by the
psychic state of the percipients, and there are the objective
ghosts, independent of the mental state of the witnesses,
appearing to persons who are not mentally prepared
to see them.

The mistaken ghost is an old form, for most of Mrs.
Radcliffe's interesting apparitions belong to this class
and others of the Gothic writers used subterfuge to
cheat the reader.   In the early romance there was frequently deliberate deception for a definite purpose, the
ghosts with the histrionic temperament using a make-up
of phosphorus, bones, and other contrivances to create
the impression of unearthly visitation.   Recent fiction

is more cleverly managed than that. Rarely now does one find a story where the ghost-seer is deliberately imposed upon, for in most modern cases the mistake occurs by accident or misapprehension on the part of the percipient, for which nobody and nothing but his own agitation is responsible. Yet there are occasional hoax ghosts even yet, for example, *The Ghost of Miser Brimpson*,[1] where a specter is rigged up as the scheme of a clever girl to win over an obdurate lover, and *The Spectre Bridegroom*, which is a well-known example of the pseudo-spook whose object is matrimony. *His Unquiet Ghost*[2] is a delightful story of a fake burial to evade the revenue officials. Watt, the "corp," says: "I was a powerful onchancy, onquiet ghost. I even did my courtin' whilst in my reg'lar line o' business a'harntin' a graveyard!" His sweetheart sobs out her confession of love to "his pore ghost," an avowal she has denied the living man. Examples of the apparitions that unwittingly deceive mortals are found in *The Ghost at Point of Rock*,[3] where the young telegraph operator, alone at night on a prairie, sees a beautiful girl who enters and announces that she is dead,—how is he to know that she is in a somnambulistic stupor, and has wandered from a train? Another is[4] a story where the young man falls in love with what he thinks is a wraith of the water luring him to his death, but learns that she is a perfectly proper damsel whose family he knows. *The Night Call*[5] is less simple than these, a problematic story that leaves one wondering as to just what is meant.[6]

The subjective ghosts are legion in modern fiction.

[1] By Eden Phillpotts.   [2] By Charles Egbert Craddock.
[3] By F. H. Spearman.
[4] *By the Waters of Paradise*, by F. Marion Crawford.
[5] By Henry Van Dyke.
[6] As Dr. Blanche Williams points out in her discussion of the short story.

They are those evoked by the mental state of the percipients so that they become realities to those beholding
them. The mind rendered morbid by grief or remorse
is readily prepared to see the spirits of the dead return in
love or with reproach. The apparitions in animistic
beliefs, as in classical stories and Gothic romance, were
usually subjective, born of brooding love or remorse
or fear of retribution, appearing to the persons who
had cause to expect them and coming usually at night
when the beholders would be alone and given over to
melancholy thought or else to troubled sleep. Shakespeare's ghosts were in large measure subjective, "selective
apparitions." When Brutus asked the specter what he
was, the awful answer came, "Thy evil genius, Brutus!"
Macbeth saw the witches who embodied for him his own
secret ambitions, and he alone saw the ghost of Banquo,
because he had the weight of murder on his heart.

The subjective ghost story is difficult to write, as the
effect must be subtly managed yet inescapably impressive.
If done well it is admirable, and there are some writers
who, to use Henry James's words concerning his own work,
are "more interested in situations obscure and subject to
interpretation than the gross rattle of the foreground."
The reader, as well as the writer, must put himself in the
mental attitude of acceptance of the supernatural else the
effect is lacking, for the ghostly thrill is incommunicable
to those beyond the pale of at least temporary credulity.

Kipling's *They* is an extraordinary ghost story of suggestion rather than of bald fact. It is like crushing the
wings of a butterfly to analyze it, but it represents the
story of a man whose love for his own dead child enabled
him to see the spirits of other little children, because he
loved. As the blind woman told him, only those who were
spiritually prepared could see them, for "you must bear
or lose!" before glimpsing them. Thomas Bailey Al-

drich's *Miss Mehitabel's Son* is a humorously pathetic
account of the subjective spirit of a child that was never
born. Algernon Blackwood's ghosts are to a great
extent subjective. As John Silence, the psychic doctor,
says to the shuddering man who has had a racking experience: "Your deeply introspective mood had already
reconstructed the past so intensely that you were *en rap-
port* at once with any forces of those past days that
chanced to be still lingering. And they swept you up all
unresistingly." In *The Shell of Sense*, [1] the woman who is
about to accept her dead sister's husband feels such a sense
of disloyalty that she sees the sister's spirit reproaching
her. Her conscience has prepared her for the vision.
Juliet Wilbur Tompkins shows us the spirit of a mother
returning to comfort the daughter who has in life misunderstood and neglected her, but now, realizing the truth,
is grieving her heart out for her. [2] Ambrose Bierce tells
of a prisoner who murders his jailer to escape, but is
arrested and brought back by the spirit of the dead man. [3]
Any number of instances might be given of ghosts appearing to those who are mentally prepared to be receptive
to supernatural visions, but these will serve to illustrate
the type.

Objective ghosts are likewise very numerous in modern
fiction. The objective spirits are those that, while they
may be subjective on the part of the persons chiefly
concerned, to begin with, are yet visible to others as well,
appearing not only to those mentally prepared to see them
but to others not thinking of such manifestations and
even sceptical of their possibility. The objective ghosts
have more definite visibility, more reality than the purely
subjective spirits. They are more impressive as haunters.
There is a plausibility, a corporeality about the later

[1] By Olivia Howard Dunbar.
[2] *They That Mourn.*   [3] *An Arrest.*

apparitions that shows their advance over the diaphanous phantoms of the past. Ghosts that eat and drink, play cards, dance, duel, and do anything they wish, that are so lifelike in their materialization that they would deceive even a medium, are more terrifying than the helpless specters of early times that could only give orders for the living to carry out. The modern ghost has lost none of his mortal powers but has gained additional super-mortal abilities, which gives him an unsportsmanlike advantage over the mere human being he may take issue with.

Henry James's *The Turn of the Screw* is a remarkable example of the objective ghost story. It is one of the best ghostly stories in English, because more philosophical, showing more knowledge of the psychology not only of the adult but of the child, not only of the human being but of the ghost, than most fiction of the type. Peter Quint and Miss Jessel with their diabolical conspiracy of evil against the two children are so real that they are seen not only by the children they hound but by the unsuspecting governess as well. She is able to describe them so accurately that those who knew them in life—as she did not at all—recognize them instantly. In *The Four-fifteen Express*,[1] John Derringer's ghost is seen by a man that does not know he is dead, and who has not been thinking of him at all. The ghost reveals incontrovertible proof of his presence, even leaving his cigar-case behind him,—which raises the question as to whether ghosts smoke in the hereafter in more ways than one. The ghastly incident in Emily Brontë's *Wuthering Heights* where the agonized ghost comes to the window, gashing its wrist on the broken pane, is strikingly objectified, for she comes to a person who never knew her and is not thinking of any supernatural manifestation. *Shadows on the Wall*,[2] that

---

[1] By Amelia B. Edwards.   [2] By Mary Wilkins Freeman.

story of surpassing power of suggestion, is objective in its
method, for not only the man who has wronged his dead
mother sees his spirit returning, not in the ordinary way
but as an accusing shadow on the wall, but the sisters
see it as well.

In *John Inglesant*,[1] the spirit of Lord Strafford is
seen by the young lad in the vestibule as well as by the
king whose conscience burns for having left him to die
undefended. Frank R. Stockton's transferred ghost
is an objective apparition, for surely the guest in the
upper chamber was not expecting to see the shade of a
living man perch itself on the foot of his bed at midnight.
The horrible specter in *The Messenger*,[2] is seen by various persons at different times, some of whom are totally
unprepared for such exhibition. And many similar
instances might be given.

Whether ghosts be mistaken, subjective or objective,
their appearance has always elicited considerable interest
on the part of humanity. Their substance of materialization, their bearing, dress, and general demeanor are
matters of definite concern to those who expect shortly
to become ghosts themselves. In some instances the
modern ghost sticks pretty closely to the animistic
idea of spirit material, which was that the shade was
a sort of vapory projection of the body, intangible, impal-
pable, yet easily recognized with reference to previous
personality. Chaucer describes some one as being "nat
pale as a forpyned goost," which illustrates the conception
in his day, and the Gothic specimen was usually a pallid
specter, though Walpole furnished one robust haunter of
gigantic muscle. Yet for the most part the Gothic ghosts
were misty wraiths, through which the sword could
plunge without resistance. They were fragile and helpless as an eighteenth-century heroine when it came to a

[1] By J. H. Shorthouse.   [2] By Robert W. Chambers.

real emergency, and were useful chiefly for frightening
the guilty and consoling the innocent. In some stories
of the present we have a similar materialization. The
spirit woman in Kipling's *Phantom Rickshaw* is so ethereal
that the horse and its rider plunge through her without
resistance, and Dickens's Mr. Marley is of such vapory
substance that Scrooge can see clear through him to count
the coat-tail buttons at his back. In a recent story,
The Substitute,[1] the spirit is said to evade her friend like
a mist.

The Gothic ghost frequently walked forth as a skeleton,
clad in nothing but his bones and a lurid scowl. Skeletons still perambulate among us, as in *The Messenger*,
where the stripped-off mask shows a hideous skull.

The skeleton burst from out the rotting robes and collapsed
on the ground before us. From between the staring ribs and
the grinning teeth spurted a torrent of black blood, showering
the shrinking grasses, and then the thing shuddered and fell
over into the black ooze of the bog.

The ghost of Zuleika[2] is described as "a skeleton woman robed in the ragged remains of a black mantle.
Near this crumbling earth body there lay the spirit of
Zuleika attached to it by a fine thread of magnetic ether.
Like the earthly body it was wrapped in a robe of black
of which it seemed the counterpart." Elliott O'Donnell
has a story of a mummy that in a soldier's tent at night
sobs, breathes, moves, sits up, and with ghastly fingers
unfolds its cere-cloth wrappings, appearing to him as
the counterpart of his long-dead mother, looking at
him with the eyes he had worshiped in his boyhood.

I fell on my knees before her and kissed—what? Not the
feet of my mother but those of the long-buried dead! Sick

[1] By Georgia Wood Pangborne.   [2] In *Ahrinziman*, by Anita Silvani.

with repulsion and fear I looked up and there bending over
me and peering into my eyes was the face, the fleshless,
mouldering face of the foul corpse!

But on the whole, though skeletons do appear in later
fiction, the rattle of bones is not heard as often as in
Gothic times.

Ghostly apparitions are more varied in form than in
early times. The modern ghost does not require a whole
skeleton for his purposes, but he can take a single bone
and put the hardiest to flight with it. It is a dreadful thing
to realize that a ghost can come in sections, which in-
definitely multiplies its powers of haunting. F. Marion
Crawford has a story of a diabolical skull, one of the most
rabid revenge ghosts on record. A man has murdered his
wife by pouring melted lead into her ear while she slept,
in accordance with a suggestion from a casually told story
of a guest. The dead woman's skull—the husband cut the
head off for fear people would hear the lead rattle, and
buried it in the garden—comes back to haunt the husband,
with that deadly rattle of the lump of lead inside. The
teeth bite him, the skull rolls up a hill to follow him, and
finally kills him, then sets in to haunt the visitor who told
the suggestive story.[1] Elsewhere as well Crawford shows
us skulls that have uncanny powers of motion and emotion. In Wilkie Collins's *Haunted Hotel* the specter is seen
as a bodiless head floating near the ceiling of the room
where the man was murdered and his body concealed.
Thackeray[2] describes a ghost with its head on its lap,
and of course every one will remember the headless horseman with his head carried on the pommel of his saddle that
frightened poor Ichabod Crane out of his wits.

We get a rabble of headless apparitions in *Brissot's
Ghost*, one of the Anti-Jacobin parodies (ridiculing Richard
Glover's ballad of Hosier's Ghost):

[1] *The Screaming Skull.*   [2] In *A Notch on the Axe.*

Sudden up the staircase sounding
  Hideous yells and shrieks were heard;
Then, each guest with fear confounding,
  A grim train of ghosts appeared;
Each a head in anguish gasping
  (Himself a trunk deformed with gore)
In his hand, terrific clasping,
  Stalked across the wine-stained floor.

In Bulwer-Lytton's *The Haunters and the Haunted* a woman's hand without a body rises up to clutch the ancient letters, then withdraws, while in his *Strange Story* the supernatural manifestation comes as a vast Eye seen in the distance, moving nearer and nearer, "seeming to move from the ground at a height of some lofty giant." Then other Eyes appear. "Those Eyes! Those terrible Eyes! Legions on legions! And that tramp of numberless feet! *they* are not seen, but the hollows of the earth echo to their tread!" The supernatural phenomena in Ambrose Bierce's stories have an individual horror. In *A Vine on the House* he shows a hideous revenge ghost manifested in a peculiar form. A couple of men take refuge in a deserted house and note a strange vine covering the porch that shakes unaccountably and violently. In mystification they dig it up, to find the roots in the form of a woman's body, lacking one foot, as had been the case with the woman who had lived there and whose husband had killed her secretly and buried her beside the porch.

The revenge ghost in modern fiction frequently manifests itself in this form, mutilated or dismembered, each disfigurement of the mortal body showing itself in a relentless immortality and adding to the horror of the haunting. There seems to be no seat of ghostly mind or soul, for the body can perform its function of haunting in whole or in part, unaided by the head or heart, like a section of a snake that has life apart from the main body.

And this idea of detached part of the form acting as a determined agent for revenge adds a new horror to fiction. I haven't as yet found an instance of a woman's heart, bleeding and broken, coming up all by itself to haunt the deserting lover, but perhaps such stories will be written soon. And think what terrors would await the careless physician or surgeon if each outraged organ or dismembered limb came back to seek vengeance on him!

Ghosts of modern fiction are more convincing in their reality than the specters of early times. They are stronger, more vital; there seems to be a strengthening of ghostly tissue, a stiffening of supernatural muscle in these days. Ghosts are more healthy, more active, more alive than they used to be. There is now as before a strong resemblance to the personality before death, the same immortality of looks that is discouraging to the prospects of homely persons who have hoped to be more handsome in a future state. Fiction gives no basis for such hope. Peculiarities of appearance are carried over with distressing faithfulness to detail, each freckle, each wrinkle, each gray hair showing with the clearness of a photographic proof. Note the lifelikeness of the governess's description of Peter Quint in *The Turn of the Screw.*

He has red hair, very red, very close-curling, and a pale face, long in shape, with straight, good features and little queer whiskers that are as red as his hair. His eyebrows are somehow darker and particularly arched as if they might move a good deal. His eyes are sharp, strange, awful. His mouth is wide, his lips thin.

This seems an unspectral description, for red hair is not wraith-like, yet a red-headed ghost that lifted its eyebrows unnaturally would be alarming. She says of him:

"He was absolutely, on this occasion, a living, dangerous, detestable presence."

Each minor disfigurement is retained, as the loss of the tooth in Crawford's screaming skull, the missing toe in Bierce's *Middle Toe of the Right Foot*, the lacking foot in the ghostly vine, and so forth. Nothing is neglected to make identification absolute in present tales of horror. The spirits described by Bram Stoker have red, voluptuous lips and pink cheeks, and the spirit of Sir Oliver's mother, in De Morgan's *An Affair of Dishonor*, that comes to meet him as he passes her mausoleum on his way to the shameful duel, limps as in life, so that he recognizes her, though the cloaked and hooded figure has its face turned from him. Jessie Adelaide Middleton shows us one ghost with half a face.

Ghostly apparel constitutes an interesting feature of supernaturalism in literature. There seem to be as definite conventions concerning spectral clothes as regarding the garb of the living fashionables. It is more difficult to understand the immortality of clothes than of humanity, for bodily tissue even of ghosts might quite conceivably renew itself, but not so with the ghostly garments. Of what stuff are ghost-clothes made? And why do they never wear out?

In olden times when people wore clothes of less radical styles than now and fewer of them, masculine spirits were in part identified by their familiar armor. Armor is so material and heavy that it seems incongruous to the ghostly function, yet shields and accouterments were necessary accompaniments of every knightly spook. He must be ever ready to tilt with rival ghost. The Gothic phantoms were well panoplied and one remembers particularly the giant armor in Walpole's novel. Nowadays the law forbids the carrying of weapons, which restriction seems to have been extended to ghostdom as well.

Specters are thus placed at a disadvantage, for one would scarcely expect to see even the wraith of a Texas cow-boy toting a pistol.

Specters usually appear in the garments in which the beholder saw them last in life. Styles seem petrified at death so that old-time ghosts now look like figures from the movies or guests at a masquerade ball. One other point to be noted is that women phantoms are frequently seen in black or in white. White seems reminiscent of the shroud, as well as of youth and innocence, so is appropriate, while black connotes gloom, so is suitable, yet the really favored color is gray. Most of the specters this season are dressed in gray. I scarcely know why this is affected by shades, yet the fact remains that many wraiths both men and women are thus attired. Gray is the tone that witches of modern tastes choose also, whereas their ancient forbears went in black and red. Modern ghosts are at a disadvantage in the matter of clothes compared with the earlier ones, since the styles now change so quickly and so decidedly that a ghost is hopelessly *passé* before he has time to materialize at all in most instances.

Examples of ghostly garments in later fiction evidence their variety. Katherine Fullerton Gerould[1] shows us three ghosts, one of a woman in a blue dress, one of a rattle-snake, and one of a Zulu warrior wearing only a loin-cloth, a nose-ring, and a scowl. (We do not often see the nude in ghosts, perhaps because they have a shade of modesty.) *Co-operative Ghosts*[2] depicts a man clad in the wraith of a tweed suit, mid-Victorian, "with those familiar Matthew Arnold side-whiskers." In addition to Mr. Morley's coat-tail buttons which we glanced through him to see, we observe that he wears ghostly spectacles, a pig-tail, tights and boots, and a prim waist-coat. In Kipling's *They* we see the glint of a small boy's blue blouse,

[1] In *On the Stairs.*   [2] By F. Converse.

while another Kipling youngster, a war-ghost,[1] struts
around in his comical first trousers which he would not be
robbed of even by the German soldiers that murdered him.
Other children in the same story are said to have on "dis-
gracefully dirty clothes." I do not recall any soilure on
Gothic garments, save spectral blood-stains and the
mold of graves. Neither did I discover any child wraith
in Gothicism save the pitiful spirits of baby victims in
The Albigenses and the baby wraiths in Hogg's *The Wool-
gatherer*. The Englishman driven mad by the apparition
of the woman he has wronged in Kipling's story[2] is described by him as "wearing the dress in which I saw her last
alive; she carried the same tiny handkerchief in her right
hand and the same card-case in her left." (A woman eight
months dead with a card-case!) Blackwood shows us a
ghost in purple knee-breeches and velvet coat; in *The Gray
Guest*[3] the returning Napoleon wears a long military cloak
of gray and military boots, while Crawford has one dreadful ghost coming back to wreak revenge in wet oil-skins.
The eccentric spook in Josephine Daskam Bacon's *The
Heritage* is dressed in brown and sits stolidly and silently
on the side of the bed with its back turned. Think of
being haunted by an unbudging brown back! No wonder
it drove the young husband to spend his wedding night
huddled on the stairs. We have instances of a ghost
in a red vest, a relentless revenge spirit that hounds
from ocean to ocean his murderer and the betrayer of his
daughter, and another of a ghost in a red shirt. There
is on the whole as much variety and appropriateness
of costume in modern ghost fiction as in Broadway
melodrama.

Another point of difference between the specters of to-
day and those of the past is in the extension of their ave-

[1] In *Swept and Garnished*.　　　　[2] *Phantom Rickshaw*.
[3] By Laurence Clarke.

nues of approach to us. Ghostly appeal to the senses is
more varied now than in earlier times. The classical as
well as the Gothic ghosts appealed in general only to the
sight and hearing, as well as, of course, to the sixth sense
that realizes the presence of a supernatural being. Ghosts
were seen and heard and were content with that. But
nowadays more points of contact are open to them and
they haunt us through the touch, the smell, as well as sight
and hearing. The taste as a medium of impression has
not yet been exploited by fiction writers though doubtless it will be worked out soon. There is a folk-tale of the
Skibos that wolves eat ghosts and find them very appetiz-
ing and the devil in Poe's *Bon Bon* says he eats the spirits
of mortals. One might imagine what haunting dyspepsia
could result if an ill-tempered spook were devoured against
his will. It is conceivable, too, that gastronomic ghosts
might haunt cannibals; and who knows that the dark
brown taste in the mouths of riotous livers is not some
specter striving to express itself through that medium
instead of being *merely* riotous livers?

The appeal of ghosts to the sight has already been
discussed so need not be mentioned here. But the element of invisibility enters in as a new and very terrible
form of supernatural manifestation in later fiction. In
spite of the general visibility, some of the most horrible
tales turn on the fact that the haunter is unseen. H. G.
Wells's *Invisible Man* is a human being, not a ghost; yet
the story has a curdling power that few straight ghost
stories possess. Maupassant's *La Horla* is a nightmare
story of an invisible being that is terrific in its effect. The
victim knows that an unseen yet definite and determined
something is shut in his room with him night after night,
eating, drinking, reading, sitting on his chest, driving him
mad. Ambrose Bierce's *The Damned Thing* is a gruesome
story of invisibility, of a something that is abroad with

unearthly power of evil, whose movements can be measured by the bending of the grasses, which shuts off the
light from other objects as it passes, which struggles with
the dogs and with men, till it finally kills and horribly
mangles the man who has been studying it, but is never
seen. Another[1] has for its central figure a being that
violently attacks men and is overpowered and tied only by
abnormal strength, that struggles on the bed, showing its
imprint on the mattress, that is imprisoned in a plaster
cast to have its mold taken, that is heard breathing
loudly till it dies of starvation, yet is absolutely never
visible. Blackwood's Fire Elemental may be seen moving along only by the bending of the grass beneath it and
by the trail it leaves behind, for though it is audible yet it
is never seen. As a brave man said of it, "I am not afraid
of anything that I can *see!*" so these stories of supernatural invisibility have a chilling horror more intense than
that of most ghostly tales. The element of invisibility
of unmistakably present spirits is shown in other stories.

One tender story of an invisible ghost is told in *In No
Strange Land*,[2] of a man killed suddenly in a wreck while
on his way home to the birthday dinner his wife is prepar-
ing for him. He does not know that he has been hurt; but
while his dead body lies mangled under the wreckage his
spirit hurries home. He swears whimsically under his
breath at some interruption and thinks with joy of the
happy little group he will meet. But when he enters his
home he cannot make them see or hear him. They are
vaguely aware of some strange influence, are awed by it,
and the little son with the poet's heart whispers that he
hears something, but that is all. The man stands by,
impotently stretching out his arms to them till he hears
the messenger tell them that he is dead.

[1] *What Was It? A Mystery*, by Fitz-James O'Brien.
[2] By Katherine Butler.

Ghosts are variable with respect to sounds as well as appearance. The early ghosts were for the most part silent, yet could talk on occasion, and classical apparitions were sometimes vocal and sometimes silent.   The Gothic ghost sometimes had an impediment in his speech while at other times he could converse fluently. The Gothic specter, real as well as faked, frequently lifted voice in song and brought terror to the guilty bosom by such strains. Yet when he spoke he was usually brief in utterance. Perhaps the reason for that lay in the lack of surety on the part of the writers as to the proper ghostly diction.   Gothic authors were not overstrong on technique and they may have hesitated to let their specters be too fluent lest they be guilty of dialectic errors.   It would seem incongruous for even an illiterate ghost to murder the king's English, which presents a difficulty in the matter of realism, so perchance the writers dodged the issue by giving their ghosts brevity of speech, or in some cases by letting them look volumes of threats but utter no word. This may explain the reason for the non-speaking ghosts in classical and Elizabethan drama.   There is a similar variation in the later fiction, for many of the ghosts are eloquently silent, while other phantoms are terrifyingly fluent. All this goes to prove the freedom of the modern ghost for he does what he takes a notion to do. The invisible ghosts are as a rule voiceless as well.

The Gothic romance was fond of mysterious music as an accompaniment of supernatural visitation, but ghostly music is less common than it used to be. Yet it does come at times, as in *A Far-away Melody*,[1] where two spinster sisters living alone hear heavenly music as portent of their death. Ghostly song is heard in another case,[2] where a woman's spirit comes back to sing in a duet at her funeral, and Crawford's ghost[3]

[1] By Mary Wilkins Freeman.   [2] *Two Voices*.   [3] In *Man Overboard*.

constantly whistles a tune he had been fond of during life. In *Co-operative Ghosts* the wraith of the young girl who in Cromwellian times betrayed her father's cause to save her lover's life sings sadly,

> "I could not love thee, dear, so much,
> Loved I not honor more!"

In Crawford's *A Doll's Ghost*, that peculiar example of preternatural fiction, not a children's story as one might think, nor yet humorous, the mechanical voice of the doll and the click of its tiny pattering feet occur as strange sounds. Lord Strafford[1] walks with a firm, audible tread on his way to appall the king, and in Blackwood's *Empty House* the ghosts move with sounds of heavy, rushing feet, followed by a noise of scuffling and smothered screams as the ancient murder is re-enacted, then the thud of a body thrown down the stairs,—after which is a terrible silence. The awful effect of a sudden silence after supernatural sounds is nowhere shown more tensely than in *The Monkey's Paw*,[2] that story of superlative power of suggestion. When the ghostly visitant knocks loudly at the outer door, we feel the same thrill of chilling awe as in the knocking at the gate in Macbeth, and more, for the two who hear are sure that this is a presence come back from the dead. Then when the last magic wish has been breathed, utter silence comes, a silence more dreadful in its import than the clamor has been.

New sounds are introduced in modern ghostly tales, such as the peculiar hissing that is a manifestation of the presence of the ancient spirit[3] followed by the crackling and crashing of the enchanted flames. In Blackwood's *Keeping His Promise* the heavy, stertorous breathing of the invisible Thing is heard, and the creaking of the bed

---

[1] In *John Inglesant*.   [2] By W. W. Jacobs.
[3] In *A Nemesis of Fire*, by Blackwood.

weighted down by the body. Mary Wilkins Freeman brings in ghostly crying in a story, while Blackwood speaks of his Wendigo as having "a sort of windy, crying voice, as of something lonely and untamed, wild and of abominable power." Kipling introduces novel and touching sounds in his stories of ghostly children. The child-wraiths are gay, yet sometimes near to tears. He speaks of "the utterly happy chuckle of a child absorbed in some light mischief," "sudden, squeaking giggles of childhood," "the rustle of a frock and the patter of feet in the room beyond," "joyous chuckles of evasion," and so forth. These essentially childlike and lifelike sounds are deeply pathetic as coming from the ghosts of little ones that hover, homesick, near the earth they dread to leave. The little ghost boy in Richard Middleton's story,[1] manifests himself, invisibly, through the little prancing steps, the rustling of the leaves through which he runs, and the heart-breaking imitations of an automobile. Later ghostly fiction introduces few of the clankings of chains and lugubrious groans that made the Gothic romance mournful, and the modern specters are less wailful than the earlier, but more articulate in their expression. There are definite ghostly sounds that recur in various stories, such as the death-rap above the bed of the dying, the oft-mentioned mocking laughter in empty places, the cry of the banshee which is the presage of death not only of the body but of the soul, as well. On the whole, the sounds in modern supernatural stories are more varied in their types, more expressive of separate and individual horror, and with an intensified power of haunting suggestion than was the case with the earlier forms.

The sense of smell was not noticeably exploited in the ancient or Gothic ghost stories, though certain folk-tales,

[1] *The Passing of Edward.*

as Hawaiian stories of the lower world, speak of it. The
devil was supposed to be in bad odor, for he was usually accompanied by sulphurous scents, as we notice in
Calderon's drama,[1] and some of the Gothic novels, but
that seems to be about the extent of the matter. But
moderns, while not so partial to brimstone, pay considerable attention to supernatural odors. The devil has been
dry-cleaned, but the evil odors of later fiction are more
objectionable than the fumes of the pit, are more variant, more individual and distinctive. Odors seem less
subjective than sights or sounds, and are not so conventionalized in ghostly fiction, hence when they are cleverly
evoked they are unusually effective. These supernatural
scents have a very lasting quality too, for they linger on
after the other manifestations of the preternatural are
past. In *The Haunted Hotel*,[2] the ghost manifests itself
through the nostrils. In room number thirteen there is
an awful stench for which no one can account, and which
cannot be removed by any disinfectants. Finally when
a woman especially sympathetic to a man mysteriously
dead is put in the room, the ghost appears as a decaying
head, floating near the ceiling and emitting an intolerable
odor. *The Upper Berth*[3] tells of a strange, foul sea odor
that infests a certain stateroom and that no amount of
fumigating or airing will remove. As the Thing comes out
of the sea to carry its victim away with it, the man in the
lower berth gets the full force of the unearthly smell.
There are definite foul supernatural odors associated with
supernatural animals in recent ghostly tales, as that "ghost
of an unforgettable strange odor, of a queer, acrid, pungent
smell like the odor of lions," which announces the presence
of the awful out-door something called by the Indians,
the Wendigo. In Kipling's story[4] of a man whose

[1] *El Magico Prodigioso.*   [2] By Wilkie Collins.
[3] By F. Marion Crawford.   [4] *The Mark of the Beast.*

soul has been stolen by Indian magic through the curse of a leper priest and a beast's soul put in its place,—his companions are sickened by an intolerable stench as of wild beasts, and when the curse is removed and he comes back to himself, he sniffs the air and asks what causes "such a horrid doggy smell in the air."

Sometimes the ghastly presence comes as a whiff of perfume,[1] where the spirit of the dead woman brings with it flowers in masses, with a heavenly perfume which lingers after the spirit in visible form has departed. The subtlest and most delicately haunting story of this type is O. Henry's,[2] where the loved, dead girl reveals herself to the man who is desperately hunting the big city over for her, merely as a whiff of mignonette, the flower she most loved.

But it is through the sense of touch that the worst form of haunting comes. Seeing a supernatural visitant is terrible, hearing him is direful, smelling him is loathsome, but having him touch you is the climax of horror. This element comes in much in recent stories. The earlier ghosts seemed to be more reserved, to know their spectral place better, were not so ready to presume on unwelcome familiarities as those in later fiction, but spooks have doubtless followed the fashion of mortals in this easy, relaxed age and have become a shade too free in their manners. Of course, one remembers the crushing specter in Otranto castle that flattened the hapless youth out so effectually, and there are other instances less striking. But as a general thing the Gothic ghost was content to stand at a distance and hurl curses. Fortunately for our ancestors' nerves, he did not incline much to the laying on of hands. Modern ghosts, however, have not been taught to restrain their impulses and they venture on

[1] As in *Here and There*, by Alice Brown.
[2] *The Furnished Room*.

liberties that Radcliffian romance would have disapproved of.

The Damned Thing gives an example of muscular supernaturalism, for the mysterious being kills a dog in a stiff fight, then later slays the master after a terrible struggle in which the man is disfigured beyond words to describe. O'Brien shows a terrible being of abnormal power that is tied only after a tremendous effort, and which fights violently to free itself. And the Thing in the upper berth had an awesome strength.

It was something ghostly, horrible, beyond words, and it moved in my grasp. It was like the body of a man long dead and yet it moved, and had the strength of ten men living, but I gripped it with all my might, the slippery, oozy, horrible thing. I wrestled with the dead thing; it thrust itself upon me and nearly broke my arms; it wound its corpselike arms around my neck, the living death, and overpowered me, so that at the last I cried aloud and fell and left my hold.

As I fell the thing sprang across me and seemed to throw itself upon the captain. When I last saw him on his feet his face was white and his lips set. It seemed to me that he struck a violent blow at the dead being, and then, he, too, fell forward on his face.

The ghostly touch is frequently described, not only in fiction but in reports of the Psychical Society as well, as being of supernatural chill or of burning heat. *Afterwards*,[1] brings in the icy touch of the spirit hand. In certain cases the ghost touch leaves a burn or mark that never goes away.

Yet the touch of horror is not the only one introduced in fiction of the supernatural. There are tender and loving touches as well, expressing yearning love and a longing to communicate with the living. What could be more beautiful than the incident in *They?* "I felt

[1] By Fred C. Smale.

my relaxed hand taken and turned softly between the soft hands of a child. The little brushing kiss fell in the center of my palm—as gift on which the fingers were *once* expected to close—a fragment of a mute code devised very long ago." And in a similar story,[1] the woman says, "I will swear to my dying day that two little hands stole and rested—for a moment only—in mine!" Wilkie Collins speaks of his story, *The Ghost's Touch*, as follows:

The course of this narrative leads the reader on new and strange ground. It describes the return of a disembodied spirit to earth—not occurring in the obscurity of midnight but in the searching light of day; neither seen as a vision nor heard as a voice—revealing itself to mortal knowledge through the sense that is least easily self-deceived, the sense that feels.

The widow feels the clasp of her husband's hands, not only psychically but physically, and when she asks for a further sign, the ghost kisses her unmistakably on the lips. Another widow[2] feels her hand clasped by the hand of her husband who has mysteriously disappeared after having presumably absconded with trust funds—and knows that he is dead and seeking to give her some message. His hand gently leads her to the edge of the cliff where he has fallen over and been killed, so that she may know the truth. The lover in Poe's *Eleonora* feels a "spiritual kiss" from the lips of his beloved. The ghost touch is an impressive motif of strength in recent fiction and marks an advance over the earlier forms, showing an access of imaginative power and psychological analysis.

Another point of contrast between the modern and the older ghosts is in the greater freedom enjoyed by those of to-day. The ghosts of our ancestors were weak and helpless creatures in the main and the Gothic specter was

[1] *A Pair of Hands*, by Quiller-Couch.
[2] In *Our Last Walk*, by Hugh Conway.

tyrannized over to such an extent that he hardly dared
call his shade his own. The spook of to-day has acquired a
latchkey and asserted his independence. He may have a
local habitation but he isn't obliged to stay there. Now-
a-days even the spectral women are setting up to be
feminists and have privileges that would have caused the
Gothic wraiths to swoon with horror. Ghosts are not so
sensitive to the barometer now as they used to be, nor do
they have such an active influence over the weather as did
the Gothic phantoms. They do not need a tempest for their
materialization nor a supernatural play of lightning for
their wild threats, and comparatively few storms occur
in later fiction. Yet there is certainly no lessening of the
ghostly thrill in consequence.

Neither are the spirits of to-day limited to any set hours
as was the rule in Gothicism. The tyranny of the dark,
the autocratic rule of twelve or one o'clock as the arbitrary
hour for apparitions, has been removed. Katherine Fullerton Gerould shows an interesting collection of ghosts that
come at eleven o'clock in the morning, Georgia Wood
Pangborne brings one out on the seashore in mid-after-
noon, and Kipling has various ghosts that appear in daylight and in the open air.

Ghosts in modern fiction are not dependent upon a setting of sullen scenery as in Gothicism, but may choose any
surroundings they like. Since modern household arrange-
ments do not include family vaults as a general thing, and
since cemeteries are inconveniently located, there is a
tendency on the part of haunters to desert such quarters.
Mary Wilkins Freeman and Charles Egbert Craddock
each has one ghost story located in a graveyard, and
The Last Ghost in Harmony[1] is set in a burying-ground,
but the specter complains loudly of the unsentimental
mind of the town which has lost interest in ghosts, and

[1] By N. M. Lloyd.

leaves in disgust. Likewise the domination of the Gothic castles, those "ghaist-alluring edifices," has passed away and modern spooks are not confined to any one locality as in the past. They appear where they will, in the most prosaic places, in cheap lodging-houses, in hall bedrooms, in bungalows, in the staterooms of steamers, on tramp ships, and so forth. Algernon Blackwood has set a number of thrilling ghost stories out in the open, in the woods, in the desert sand wastes, and similar places. One effect of such realistic and unspectral setting is to give a greater verisimilitude to the events described, and the modern tale bears out Leigh Hunt's suggestion that "a ghost story, to be a good one, should unite, as much as possible, objects as they are in life, with a preternatural spirit." Yet here are ghosts that do haunt certain rooms as relentlessly as ever Gothic specter did.

The modern ghost has power over certain localities rather than mere houses or apartments. If the house he calls his own is torn down, he bides his time and haunts the new structure built on the same spot. Or if no new house goes up, he hangs around and haunts the vacant lot, which is a more reprehensible procedure than the ordinary habits of spooks. One story concerns a house so persistently ghosted that its owner took it down section by section, trying to arrive at the location of the curse, but to no avail. When the whole building had been razed and the site plowed over, the ghost undiscouraged haunted merrily on. Then the owner left in disgust. Algernon Blackwood is fond of situations where localities are haunted by evil spirits,[1] where a whole village is inhabited by the ghosts of long-dead witches, or *Secret Worship* that relates the experience of a man who wanders within the limits of a place made horrible by devil-worshipers, long-dead, but life-like, and inhabiting a house

[1] As in *Ancient Sorceries*.

that has been torn down years before but appears as usual, where they entrap the souls of the living for their fiendish sacrifice. Another[1] is the record of a spirit of frightful evil that haunts a house built on the spot where an older house once stood, whose diabolism lingers on to curse the living. The spirit that haunts a locality rather than one room or house has a more malignant power than the more restricted ghost and this adds a new element of definite supernaturalism to modern fiction. But as houses are so much less permanent now than formerly, ghosts would be at a terrible disadvantage if they had to be evicted every time a building was torn down.

Ghostly psychology is a fascinating study. The development of spectral personality is one of the evident facts gained from a historical survey of supernatural fiction. The modern ghost has more individuality, more distinctiveness, in the main, than his forbears. The ghosts of medievalism, of ancient superstition, and the drama were for the most part pallid, colorless beings in character as in materialization. The ancient ghosts were more mournful than the moderns, since the state of the dead in early times was by no means enviable. The most one could hope for then was Hades, while the spirits who hadn't been buried couldn't find entrance even there but were forced by relentless spectral police to keep forever moving. The Christian religion furnishes a more cheerful outlook, so in later manifestations the gloom is considerably lightened. Yet even so the Gothic ghosts were morbid, low-minded specters not much happier than the unlucky wights they felt it their business to haunt. Their woe-begone visages, their clanking chains, and other accompaniments of woe betokened anything but cheer.

There are some unhappy spirits in recent fiction, but

[1] *A Psychic Invasion.*

not such a large proportion as in the past. And there is
usually some basis for their joylessness; they don't have
general melancholia with no grounds for it. The ghost of
the dead wife in *Readjustment*[1] is miserable because she
has never understood her husband, either in life or in
death, and she comes back seeking an explanation. Another spectral woman[2] is wretched because she has the
double crime of murder and suicide on her soul. Poor
Marley grieves because he is doomed to see the opportuni-
ties that life has offered him to serve others and that he
has neglected, being forced to see with the clear vision of
the other world the evil results of his own neglect, which is
enough to make any one wretched. A guilty conscience is
like the burning heart that each spirit in the Hall of Eblis
bore in his breast. In *The Roll-call of the Reef*,[3] the troop
of drowned soldiers, infantry, and horsemen, come rising
out of the surf to answer to their names. Each man is
asked by name, "How is it with you?" and answers with
the deadly sin that has damned him. In Wilkie Collins's
gruesome tale[4] there is one spirit that is unhappy because
his body lies unburied, a recurrence of a theme frequent
in classical stories and Gothic romance, but rare in later
fiction. For the most part the later ghosts are something
more than merely unhappy spirits. They are more positive,
more active, more individualistic, too philosophical to
waste time in useless grieving.

Nor are there many simply happy spirits, perhaps because the joyous souls are likely to seek their paradise and
forget about the earth. Yet there are instances, such as
the light-hearted spirits of children in various stories, that
with the resilience of childhood shake off gloom and are
gay; Rosamond,[5] that comes back to tell her friend how

---

[1] By M. H. Austin.
[2] In *The Closed Cabinet*.
[3] By A. T. Quiller-Couch.
[4] *The Queen of Hearts*.
[5] In *Here and There*.

happy the other life is, the peacefully content mother,[1] and others.

The ghosts that are actively vicious are the most vivid and numerous in later fiction. The spirits of evil seem to have a terrible cumulative force, being far more maleficent than the earlier ones, and more powerful in carrying out their purposes. Every aspect of supernaturalism seems to be keyed up to a higher pitch of terror. Evil seems to have a strangely greater power of immortality over that of good, judging from the proportion employed in modern fiction. Has evil so much more strength of will, so much more permanence of power that it lives on through the years and centuries, while good deeds perish with the body? It would appear so from fiction. The ghosts of good actions do not linger round the abode of the living to any noticeable extent, but evil deeds are deathless. We have many stories of places and persons haunted by the embodied evil of the past, but few by the embodied good. The revenge ghosts outnumber the grateful dead by legions.

Modern specters have a more complex power than the old. They are more awful in their import, for they haunt not merely the body, but the soul. The wicked spirits will to work dreadful harm to the soul as well as the body, and drive the victim to spiritual insanity, seeking to damn him for the life everlasting, making him, not merely their victim, but through eternity their co-worker in awful evil. The victim of the vampire, for instance, who dies as a result of the attack, has to become in his turn a loathsome vampire to prey on other souls and bodies. Blackwood's Devil-worshipers seek to kill the soul as well as the body of their victim. The deathlessness of evil is shown in Lytton's[2] and in many of Blackwood's stories, as where the psychic doctor says to a man, "You are now in touch with certain violent emotions,

[1] In *They That Mourn*.   [2] *The Haunters and the Haunted.*

passions, purposes, still active in this house, that were
produced in the past by some powerful and evil personality that lived here.''

Few writers have equaled F. Marion Crawford in the
modern ghost story. His tales have a curdling intensity,
a racking horror that set them far above the ordinary
supernatural fiction. They linger in the mind long after
one has tried in vain to forget them, if indeed one ever does
forget their sense of evil power. There is in each of his
stories an individual horror that marks it as distinct from
its fellows, a power chiefly won by delineation of this
immortality of evil, as in *The Dead Smile*, with its description of the hideous smile that pollutes the lips of the living
and of the dead. ''Nurse McDonald said that when Sir
Hugh Ockram smiled, he saw the faces of two women in
hell, two dead women he had betrayed.'' His vicious
impulses last after death and from his grave he reaches
out to curse his own children, seeking to drive them to
awful, though unconscious sin.

Henry James has drawn for us two characters of unmiti-
gated evil in Peter Quint and Miss Jessel, who, he says,
are ''hovering, prowling, blighting presences.'' They are
agents on whom is laid the dire duty of causing the air to
reek with evil. He says, ''I recognize that they are not
ghosts at all, as we now know the ghost, but goblins, elves,
imps, demons. The essence of the matter was the villainy
of the motive in the evoked predatory creature.'' What
he wishes to do in this story is to express a general sense of
spiritual infamy, not specialized, as the hot breath of the
Pit usually confines itself to some one particular psychical
brutality, but as capable of everything, the worst that can
be conceived. How well he has succeeded in his effort,
those who know the story can testify.

Ambrose Bierce's stories are in many instances remarkable examples of this psychic horror. *The Death of Hal-*

pin Frazer has a touch of almost unbearable dreadfulness. Frazer is assaulted by an evil spirit in a wood at night and choked to death, the spirit inhabiting the dead body of the man's own mother who has idolized him. His dead mother's face, transfixed with diabolical hate, is thrust upon him, and the loved hands that have caressed him strangle him. This is similar to the situation of an evil spirit occupying the body of a loved dead mother in *The Mummy's Tale*, by Elliot O'Donnell. Bierce's stories beat upon the mind like bludgeons and his morbid plots are among the most dreadful in our literature. One wonders what abnormality of mind conceives such themes, evolves such situations. If it be true, as Macaulay suggests, that not only every poet but every person who appreciates poetry is slightly unbalanced mentally, surely every writer of such extreme and horrific stories must be abnormal. There is more than one writer of modern ghostly fiction of whom it might be said that "his soul is open on the Hell side."

Another temperament found distinctively in the later fiction is the humorous ghost. He is a recent development, and as might be supposed, is characteristically American. There were a few burlesque ghosts in Elizabethan drama, the Ghost of Jack,[1] for instance, and one colored ghost that would seem to connote mirth, but the really humorous specter did not come till later. It remained for the Yankee to evoke the spook with a sense of humor. Ghosts are not essentially laughable, and to make them comic without coarseness or irreverence is an achievement. Numerous writers have busied their pens with the funny spook and now we have ghostly laughter that is mirthful and not horrisonous as in other types. Specters now laugh with us instead of at us, and instead of the mocking laughter heard in lonely places we have

[1] In Peele's *Old Wives Tales*.

"heart-easing mirth." Washington Irving evokes several humorous hoax ghosts, such as the headless horseman that created excitement in Sleepy Hollow and the serenading phantom in *The Specter Bridegroom*.

Richard Middleton in his *Ghost Ship* shows some very informal humorous ghosts. The girls and boys rise from their graves to flirt over their tombstones on moonlight nights, and the children play with the village specters as companions, their favorite being the man that sits on the wellcurbing with his severed head held in his hands. The cottagers rebuke the spooks overhead when they grow too noisy, and a general good-fellowship prevails. Into this setting the ghost ship sails one night, anchoring itself in the middle of a turnip patch, and the riotous captain demoralizes the men of the village, ghosts and all, with his rum and his jokes. After a stay of some time, one night in a storm the villagers look out.

Over our heads, sailing very comfortably through the windy stars, was the ship that had passed the summer in landlord's field. Her portholes and her windows were ablaze with lights and there was a noise of singing and fiddling on her decks. . . . They do say that since then the turnips on landlord's field have tasted of rum.

Olive Harper tells[1] of a reporter who is invited by a cordial spook—who has been a New York social leader—to a spectral banquet and ball underneath Old Trinity. She satirizes human foibles and weaknesses, showing ghosts that gossip and gormandize, simper and swear as they did in life. They learn to play poker, dance, and kill time as they used to do. Frank R. Stockton has written several delicious drolleries of supernaturalism, as *The Transferred Ghost*, where the spook of a living man, the irascible

[1] In *The Sociable Ghost*.

uncle of the charming Madeline, terrifies the young suitor
who lacks courage to propose.   The audacious and ever-
present ghost swings his feet from the porch railing, invisible to the girl as inaudible by her, and breaks in on the
conversation in a most disconcerting way.   The young
man at last cries out in desperation, "What are you waiting for? I have nothing to say to you?" whereat the girl,
who has been undoubtedly waiting to hear the proposal
the embarrassed youth was trying to make, thinks he is
speaking to her and departs in high dudgeon.   On a later
occasion the specter comes to announce to him that he has
got his transfer and may be somebody else's ghost instead
of that of the man who was expected to die and didn't,
when the lover cries out, "I wish to Heaven you were
mine!"   And Madeline, melting in a sigh, whispers, "I
am yours!"   The sequel to this is also comic. [1]

Brander Matthews has several stories of humorous supernaturalism, *Rival Ghosts* being the account of ancestral
spooks belonging to a young bridegroom, and who resent
being brought into enforced companionship by his sudden
elevation to a title, since one ghost must haunt the house
and one the heir.   The ingenious groom, at last harassed
to invention by the continual squabbling of the ghosts,
brings about a wedding between them.   This is the only
instance I have found of a wedding between two specters,
though there are various cases on record of marriage
between one living and one spectral personage.   John
Kendrick Bangs devotes several volumes to the doings
and sayings of spooks, describing parties in a house-boat
on the Styx, where the shades of the departed great gather
together and engage in festivities and discussions, and
showing types of water-ghosts and various kinds of spooks.
The humorous ghost is a more frequent person than one
would suppose without giving some thought to the subject,

[1] *The Spectral Mortgage.*

for many writers have sharpened their wits on the comic haunt.

As may be seen from the examples mentioned, the ghost has made perceptible progress in psychology. The modern apparition is much more complex in personality than the crude early type, and shows much more variety. The up-to-date spook who has a chance to talk things over with William James, and knows the labyrinths of the human mind is much better adapted to inflict psychal terrors than the illiterate specter of the past. He can evolve mental tortures more subtle and varied than ever, or he can amuse a downcast mortal by his gambols.

Stories of to-day show a decided advance over the Gothic in the matter of motives for spectral appearance. There are, it is true, certain motives in common between them, but the present-day spirit is less limited, for he has gained the new without loss of the old, if he wishes to keep the old. The principal impulse that impelled classical shades to walk the earth was to request burial, since lacking that he could not enter into the abode of the dead. This appears frequently also in Gothic romance. It is shown but little in recent fiction, perhaps because the modern ghost is reconciled to cremation or is blithely indifferent to what becomes of his body since it no longer rules him. *The Queen of Hearts* is one of the few instances of its use in modern fiction, for it is a vanishing motive for the most part. Gothic ghosts were also wont to return to show the hiding-place of treasure, but that, too, is dying out as an incentive to haunting. The prosaic explanation here may be that now persons put their treasure in safety deposits, hence there is scant occasion for mystery concerning its location after death. Gothic spooks came back on occasion to reveal parentage, for parents, like valuables, were frequently mislaid in terror romance. This is not so important now, since vital statistics usually keep such matters duly recorded, yet instances do sometimes occur.

Ghosts in the terror romance came to make requests, apart from the petition for burial, which tendency is still observed on the part of later spooks, though not to the same extent as formerly. The requests are psychologically interesting, as they usually relate to simple ties of affection, illustrated by the mother-spirit[1] who asks her friend to take her children. Gothic spirits came back often to make revelations concerning the manner of their death, which is not often the case now, though it does sometimes happen. And Dickens shows us one ghost returning to influence the jury that is trying a man for murder. Specters used to appear to forewarn the living against impending danger, which impulse is rather lacking in later fiction though it still occurs. The curious element of futurity enters into several of these ghostly warnings, as in Dickens's *The Signal Man* where the apparition presages the man's death, as in Algernon Blackwood's story[2] is related the incident of a man who saw the two Indians scalp a white man and drag his body away, at last crying out, "I saw the body, and *the face was my own.*" Warning spirits of futurity are seen in *On the Stairs*, where each man beholds his own destiny,— one seeing the spectral snake that afterwards kills him in a hunting expedition, one the ghost of a Zulu, the savage that almost destroys him some time afterwards, and the last the ghost of a young woman in a blue dress, the woman whom he marries and who hounds him to his death. She presently sees her own fate, too, but what it is the author does not tell us. One curious incident in the story is the instantaneous appearance on the stairs of the woman herself and her ghostly double, one in a white dress, one in the fatal blue. This sort of spectral warning,

[1] In *The Substitute.*   [2] In *A Haunted Island.*

this wireless service for the conveyance of bad news and hint of threatening danger, serves to link the ghost story of the present with those of the past. The records of the Psychical Society show hundreds of such instances, and much use is made in fiction of plots hinging on such motif. Scott's White Lady of Avenel appears as a death portent, as also the "Bahr-geist" in another novel.

The revenge ghost looms large in fiction as in the drama. He was the most important figure in Elizabethan as in classical drama, and Shakespeare's ghosts are principally of that class. A terrible example of the type is in Robert Lovell Beddoes' *Death's Jest-Book*, that extraordinary example of dramatic supernaturalism, where the ghost of the murdered man comes back embodied from the grave and is an active character to the end of the play. He is summoned to life through a hideous mistake, the murderer having asked the magician to call up the spirit of his dead wife, but the body of his victim having been secretly buried beside her so that the murderer may have no rest even in the grave, the awful accusing spirit rises to confront him, instead of his wife's phantom. The revenge ghost is both objective and subjective in his manifestation and his impelling motive adds a touch of frozen horror to his appearance. He appears in various forms, as dismembered parts of the body—illustrated in the stories above referred to,— in a horrific invisibility, in a shape of fear visible only to the guilty, or in a body so objectified as to seem absolutely real and living to others beside the one haunted. The apparently casual, idle figure that strolls about the docks and streets in *The Detective*, seen by different persons and taken for a man interested only in his own pursuits, is a revenge ghost so relentless that he hounds his victim from country to country, at last killing him by sheer force of terror as he sits on his bed at night, leaving the imprint of his body on the mattress beside the

dead man whose face is rigid with mad horror. He has
come back in physical embodiment to avenge the betrayal
of his daughter. Ambrose Bierce shows us many spirits
animated by cold and awful revenge, sometimes visible
and sometimes unseen, as where a soldier killed for striking an officer answers, "Here!" to the roll-call, just at
which moment a mysterious bullet from nowhere strikes
the officer through the heart.[1] Crawford sends a drowned
sailor back in wet oil-skins to slay his twin brother who has
impersonated him to win the girl they both loved. When
the two bodies wash ashore one is a newly dead corpse,
the other a skeleton in oil skins; while the dreadful rattle
of the accusing lump of lead in the wife's skull in another
story is a turn of the screw of her horrid revenge. The
revenge ghost in modern fiction is more varied in forms of
manifestation, at times more subtle in suggestion and
ghostly psychology, than the conventionalized type of the
drama and remains one of the most dreadful of the forms
of fear.

In general, the modern stories show a greater intensity
of power in employing the motives that earlier forms had
used as well as far greater range of motivation. The
earlier ghosts were limited in their impulses, and their
psychology was comparatively simple. Not so with the
apparitions of to-day. They have a far wider range of
motives, are moved by more complex impulses and mixed
motivation in many cases difficult to analyze.

The Gothic ghost had some conscience about whom he
haunted. He had too much reserve to force himself
needlessly upon those that had no connection with his
past. If he knew someone that deserved punishment for
wrong done him or his, he tried to haunt him and let
others alone. The modern ghost is not so considerate.
He is actuated in many cases by sheer evil that wreaks it-

[1] In *His Two Military Executions*.

self upon anyone in range. Death gives a terrible immortality and access of power to those whose lives have been particularly evil, and the results are dangerous to society. Dark discarnate hate manifests itself to those within reach. Algernon Blackwood would have us believe that all around us are reservoirs of unspeakable horror and that any moment of weakness on our part may bring down the hosts of damnation upon us. This is illustrated in such stories as *With Intent to Steal*, where the spirit of a man who has hanged himself comes back with hypnotic power forcing others to take their lives in the same way, or in another,[1] showing power exerted viciously against human beings in a certain building, or still another[2] where the witchcraft holds the village in thrall, and elsewhere. Ambrose Bierce, Bram Stoker, F. Marion Crawford, and Arthur Machen have written a number of stories bringing out this side of ghostly psychology, showing the bands of outlawed spirits that prey on society. There are spectral bandits and bravos that answer the call of any force hostile to man, or act of their own accord from an impulse of malicious mischief.

The jealous ghost is somewhat common of late, showing that human emotions are carried over into the life beyond. In various stories we find the dead wife interfering to prevent a second marriage, or to make life wretched for the interloper even after the ceremony. But the most extreme case of jealousy—even exceeding the instance of the man whose wife and physician conspired to give him an overdose to put him out of the way and who is frantic to prevent their marriage—is found in Arnold Bennett's novel, *The Ghost*. Here the spirit of a man who has madly loved an opera-singer haunts every suitor of hers and either drives him to abandon his courtship or kills him, till finally the singer begs the ghost to spare the man she

[1] *The Empty House.*   [2] *Secret Worship.*

loves, which he sadly does, and departs. This is reminiscent of one of Marie de France's *lais*.

The varying motives for appearance may be illustrated by reference to a few ghosts in modern fiction, such as the woman[1] who comes to drive away a writer's sense of humor,—than which there could be no greater spiritual brutality,—and set him to writing vile, debased tragedies. Perhaps she has transferred her attentions to other authors than the one in the story! Other instances are the little Gray Ghost in Cornelia A. P. Comer's story by that name, who impels a stranger to take her child from an orphan asylum and adopt it, much against his will; the immortal lovers that haunt a woman who has made a marriage of convenience—which has turned out to be a marriage of inconvenience for her husband[2]; the talkative spook in Andrew Lang's *In Castle Perilous*, that discourses learnedly on its own materialization, speaking in technical terms, pokes fun at Shakespeare for the glow-worm on a winter night, and the cockcrow in his *Hamlet*, and—but these are perhaps enough. If one may judge from ghostly fiction, death subtracts nothing from human emotion but rather adds to it, so that the spectral impulses are more poignant and intense. The darker passions are retained with cumulative power, and there is a terrible immortality of hate, of jealousy and revenge.

There is no more impressive revenant than one Coleridge gives in his *Wanderings of Cain*, the mournful phantom of Abel appearing to Cain and his little son, Enos. The child says to his father, "I saw a man in unclean garments and he uttered a sweet voice, full of lamentations." Cain asks the unhappy spirit, "But didst thou not find favor in the sight of the Lord thy God?" to which the shape answers, "The Lord is God of the living only. The dead have another God!"

[1] In *A Psychic Invasion*.   [2] In *The Long Chamber*.

" Cain ran after the shape and the shape fled shrieking over the sands, and the sands rose like white mists behind the steps of Cain but the feet of him that was like Abel disturbed not the sands. "

One of the most interesting phases of comparative ghost-lore is the study of the intricate personality of specters. With respect to dual personality the late supernatural stories are curiously reminiscent of the animistic belief that a ghost is a double of the mortal, a vapory projection of his actual body, to be detached at will during life and permanently at death. I do not know of any instances of doubles in classical literature, nor is the idea used in Gothic romance. Likewise Shakespeare's ghosts are all spirits of persons safely dead. It remained for the modern writer with his expertness in psychology and psychiatry to evoke the ghosts of the living persons, the strange cases of dual personality and of separate personalities supernaturally merged into one, and those inexplicable ghosts of subliminal memories. All these forms appear in elusive analysis, in complex suggestiveness, in modern uncanny stories, and constitute one of the distinct marks of advance over the earlier types.

The double, a frequent figure in English fiction, bears a resemblance to the Doppelgänger of German folk-tales. Numerous examples of dual personality, of one being appearing in two forms, are seen, with different twists to the idea, yet much alike. It has been suggested that these stories have their germinal origin in Calderon's play,[1] where a man is haunted by himself. Poe's *William Wilson* is a tense and tragic story of a man pursued by his double, till in desperation he kills him, only to realize that he has slain his better self, his conscience. His duplicate cries out, "Henceforward thou art also dead,

[1] *El Embozado.*

dead to the world, to Heaven and to hope! In me thou didst exist and in my death, see by this thine image, which is thine own, how utterly thou hast murdered thyself!'' Stevenson's *Markheim* shows in the person of the stranger the incarnate conscience, an embodiment of a man's nobler self that leads him through the labyrinth of self-examination to the knowledge of the soul's truth. The stranger tests the murderer by offering him a way of escape, by suggesting further crime to him, by showing him relentlessly what the consequence of each act will be, till in despair Markheim, realizing that his life is hopelessly weak and involved, decides to surrender it rather than to sin further. Step by step the nameless visitor leads him, Markheim shuddering back from the evil that is suggested, thinking the stranger is a demonic tempter, till at last the transfigured face shows him to be the nobler angel. Stevenson's *Dr. Jekyll and Mr. Hyde* is, of course, the best-known instance of this sort of dual personality, this walking forth in physical form of the evil in one's own nature, with a separate existence of its own. No writer could hope to express this idea more powerfully than has been done in this chemical allegory, this biological dissection of the soul. The thrill of suspense, the seemingly inexplicable mystery, the dramatic tenseness of the closing scenes make this sermon in story form unforgettable. Kipling has given a striking story of a man haunted by his own phantom body, in *At the End of the Passage.* His own figure slipped silently before him as he went through his lonely house. ''When he came in to dinner he found himself seated at the table. The vision rose and walked out hastily. Except that it cast no shadow it was in all respects real.'' The horror of this haunting specter of himself, this double of his own body and soul, drives the man to suicide, after which a peculiar twist of horror is given by the detail at the close, of the discovery by his comrade, of the man's own photograph imprinted on the dead retina and reproduced by the camera hours after his death. In Julian Hawthorne's allegory,[1] the dead man's spirit meets the devil, who is his own evil self incarnate.

Edith Wharton's *Triumph of Night* reveals a ghost of a living man standing behind his double's chair, visible to the person opposite and showing on the ghostly face the evil impulses that the living countenance cleverly masks. John Kendrick Bangs has his hero say,[2] "I came face to face with myself, with that other self in which I recognized, developed to the fullest extent, every bit of my capacity for an evil life," and Blackwood[3] relates the meeting of a musician and his ghostly double in an opera hall. Mr. Titbottom,[4] through the power of his magic spectacles reflecting his image in a mirror, sees himself as he really is, as he looks to God, and flees horror-stricken from the sight. This symbolic representation is akin to the *Prophetic Pictures* of Hawthorne, where a woman's griefs and marks of age are shown in her pictured face before they are revealed in her actual experience, a pictured futurity. The most impressive instance of this relation between a human being and his portrait is in Oscar Wilde's *Picture of Dorian Grey*, that strange study of a man's real nature expressing itself on his painted likeness, while the living face bears no mark of sin or shame or age, until the tragic revelation at the end. Edith Wharton[5] also represents a supernatural dualism, the woman's statue showing on its marble face the changing horror of her own stricken countenance. *The White Sleep of Auber Hurn* is a curious story of a spiritual double, a psychological study of a man who was in two places at once, seen by various persons who

---

[1] *Lovers in Heaven.*   [2] In *Thurlow's Christmas Story.*
[3] In *The Man from the Gods.*
[4] In George William Curtis's *Prue and I.*
[5] In her *Duchess at Prayer.*

knew him in each case, being killed in a train wreck many
miles away from his room where he was lying asleep in his
bed,—a sleep that knows no waking.[1]

Distinct from the expression of one personality in two
bodies, the supernatural merging of two separate personalities into one appears in recent ghostly fiction. It forms
a subtle psychologic study and is uncannily effective.
H. G. Wells's *Story of the Late Mr. Elvesham* is a peculiar
narrative of a transfer of personality as the result of a
mysterious drink, by which an old man takes possession
of a young man's body, leaving the youth to inhabit the
worn-out shell of the dotard. Algernon Blackwood in
The Terror of the Twins describes a supernatural merging
of two natures into one by the power of a dead father's
insane curse. The younger son loses his vitality, his
mind, his personality, all of which is supermortally given
to his older brother, while the deprived son dies a drivel-
ling idiot of sheer inertia and utter absence of vital
power. Mary Heaton Vorse[2] describes a neurotic woman
who comes back from the grave to obsess and possess the
interloper in her home, through the immortal force of her
jealousy, making the living woman actually become the

---

[1] Other stories of double personality are *The Ivory Gate*, by Walter
Besant; *The Man with a Shadow*, by George M. Fenn; *The Jolly Corner*, by
Henry James; *The Transferred Ghost*, by Frank R. Stockton; *On the Stairs*,
by Katherine Fullerton Gerould; *Elixire des Teufels*, by E. T. A. Hoffmann;
Howe's Masquerade, by Hawthorne; *The Recent Carnival of Crime in Con-
necticutt*, by Mark Twain; *The Queen of Sheba*, by Thomas Bailey Aldrich;
The Doppelgänger, by Elizabeth Bisland Wetmore.

Georg Brandes, in his article, "Romantic Reduplication and Psychology,"
in *Main Currents of Nineteenth Century Literature*, points out the prevalence of this motif in German fiction. He says: "It finds its first
expression in Jean Paul's *Leibgeber Schappe*, and is to be found in almost all
of Hoffmann's tales, reaching its climax in *Die Elixire des Teufels*. It crops
up in the writings of all the Romanticists, in Kleist's *Amphitryton*, in
Achim von Arnim's *Die Beiden-Waldemar*, in Chamisso's *Erscheinung*.
Brentano treats it comically in *Die Mehreren Wehmüller*.

[2] In *The Second Wife*.

reincarnation of the dead wife. This story naturally suggests Poe's *Ligeia* which is the climax of ghostly horror of this motif, with its thesis that "man doth not yield himself to the angels nor unto death utterly save through the weakness of his own feeble will" expressed in a terrible crescendo of ghastly horror. Poe's *Morella* is a similar study of the supernatural merging of an exterior personality into a living body, where the dead mother and her child are literally one flesh and one spirit. Blackwood's *The Return* is an example of the compact-ghost, that comes back at the hour of death to reveal himself to his friend as he long ago promised he would. The dead artist manifests himself through a sudden and wonderful realization of the beauty of the world to which the materialistic friend has heretofore been blinded and indifferent. Feeling this sudden rapturous sweep of beauty through his soul, the living man knows that his artist friend is dead and that his spirit has become a part of his own being. In the same manner the little lonely soul in Granville Barker's wonderful piece of symbolism, *Souls on Fifth*, enters into the being of the man who has the understanding heart and continues her existence as a part of him.

An essentially modern type of ghost story is that which has its explanation on the basis of subliminal memories. It seems that all around us are reservoirs of ancestral memories, records of the vital thoughts and actions of the long dead, psychical incarnations of their supreme moments, their striking hours, into which the living at times stumble and are submerged. Some slight spiritual accident may bring down upon mortals the poignant suffering and bliss of the dead in whose personality they are curiously duplicated. These ghosts of dead selves from the past are different from the doubles that are projections of the living, or prophetic specters of the

future, and are clearly distinguished. *The Borderland*,
by Francis Parsons, tells of a young army officer who is
obsessed by subliminal self, the ghost of his grandfather.
He feels that he *is* his grandfather, living another existence,
yet he lacks the pluck, the manhood, that the old pioneer
possessed. At a crisis in his military affairs, the old
frontiersman comes visibly forward to give him the
courage that is needed, after which he manifests himself
no more. The scene of this subliminal haunting is a
Texas prairie, during a border fight, rather an unghostly
setting yet one which makes the supernatural seem more
actual. Arthur Johnson[1] presents the case of a man who
sees the ghosts of ancestral memory in a vivid form. He
sees and hears his own double wildly accuse his wife—
who is the double of his own—betrothed, after having
killed her lover. His hand is wounded and the fingers
leave bloodstains as they snatch at the gray chiffon
round his wife's throat. After a fit of unconsciousness
into which he falls is over, the modern man awakes to
find his hand strangely wounded, and on the floor of the
upper room he picks up a scrap of bloodstained gray
chiffon! Blackwood's *Old Clothes* shows a little girl
obsessed by subliminal memories. She is haunted by
terrible experiences in which she says that she and some
of those around her have been concerned. She goes into
convulsions if anything is fastened around her waist, and
she cries out that some cruel man has shut her up in the
wall to die and has cut off Philip's hands so that he cannot
save her. Investigations bring to light the facts that a
long-dead ancestress, living in the same house, had been
walled up alive by her husband after he had cut off her
lover's hands before her face. The skeleton is found
chained by the waist inside the ancient wall. Blackwood's *Ancient Sorceries* depicts the ghosts of buried

[1] In *Mr. Eberdeen's House.*

life, of a whole village enchanted by the past and living over again the witchcraft of the long ago. As John Silence, the psychic doctor, tells of the Englishman who drops casually into the village and is drawn into the magic:

Vesin was swept into the vortex of forces arising out of the intense activities of a past life and lived over again a scene in which he had often played a part centuries ago. For strong actions set up forces that are so slow to exhaust themselves that they may be said in a sense never to die. In this case they were not complete enough to render the illusion perfect, so the little man was confused between the present and the past.

That story of unusual psychical experience, *An Adventure*, by two Oxford women, can be explained on no other basis than some such theory as this. The book claims to be a truthful account of a happening at Versailles, where two English women, teachers and daughters of clergymen, saw in broad daylight the ghosts of the past, the figures of Marie Antoinette and her court. The writers offer the explanation that they stumbled into a sort of pocket of the unhappy queen's memories and saw the past relived before their eyes because she had felt it so keenly and vividly long ago. Other instances might be given, but these are sufficient to illustrate the type. Such stories have a curious haunting power and are among the most effective narratives. The idea is modern and illustrates the complexity of later thought as compared with the simplicity of earlier times.

A comparative study of ghost stories leads one to the conclusion that the ghost is the most modern of ancients and the most ancient of moderns. In some respects the present specter is like and in some unlike the previous forms. Ghosts, whether regarded as conjective or purely subjective, are closely related to the percipients' thoughts.

Primitive times produced a primitive supernaturalism and the gradual advance in intellectual development has brought about a heightening and complexity of the weird story. 'Tis in ourselves that ghosts are thus and so!

The spook of to-day is of a higher nervous organization than his forbears. In many instances the latter-day ghost is so distracted by circumstances that he hardly knows where he's at, as for instance, the ghost in such case as *The Tryst*, by Alice Brown, where a man is thought to be drowned and his ghost comes out to comfort his sweetheart, only to have the drowned man brought back to life presently; and in *The Woman from Yonder*, by Stephen French Whitman, where a scientist with impertinent zeal brings life back to the body of a woman who had bled to death while Hannibal was crossing the Alps and been buried in a glacier till the glacier spat her out. Now, what was the status of those ghosts? Was there a ghost if the person wasn't really dead? But if a woman isn't dead after she has been in an ice-pack for two thousand years or thereabouts what surety is there for the standing of any ghost?

The apparitions of to-day have more lines of interest than the ancient ghosts. The Gothic specter was a one-idea creature, with a single-track brain. He was not a ghost-of-all-work as are some of the later spooks. He was a simple-souled being who felt a call to haunt somebody for some purpose or other, so he just went and did it. The specters of to-day are more versatile,—they can turn their hand to any kind of haunting that is desired and show an admirable power of adaptability, though there are highly developed specialists as well. The psychology of the primitive ghost and of the Gothic specter was simple. They knew only the elemental passions of love and hate. Gothic spooks haunted the villain or villainess to foil them in their wicked designs or punish them for past misdeeds, or hovered over the hero or heroine to advise, comfort, and chaperon them. But the modern ghosts are not satisfied with such sit-by-the-fire jobs as these. They like to keep in the van of activity and do what mortals do. They run the whole scale of human motions and emotions and one needs as much handy psychology to interpret their hauntings as to read George Meredith. They are actuated by subtle motivations of jealousy, ardent love, tempered friendship, curiosity, mischief, vindictiveness, revenge, hate, gratitude, and all other conceivable impulses. The Billy Sunday sort of ghost who wants to convert the world, the philanthropic spirit who wants to help humanity, the socialist specter that reads the magazine, the friendly visitor that sends its hands back to wash the dishes, the little shepherd lad that returns to tend the sheep, are among the new concepts in fiction of the supernatural. The ghost of awful malice, to be explained only on the basis of compound interest of evil stored up for many years, is a new force.

Though the ghostly narrative has shifted its center of gravity from the novel to the short story since Gothic times, and many more of the modern instances are in that form, the supernatural novel has recently taken on a new lease of life. Honors are almost even between the English and the American ghost story, as most of the representative writers on each side turn their pen at some time to write terror tales. The ghost has never lost his power over the human mind. Judging from the past, one may say that the popularity of the ghost story will continue undiminished and will perhaps increase. Certainly there has been a new influx of stories within later times. What mines of horror yet remain untouched for writers of the future, it would be hard to say, yet we do not fear for the exhaustion of the type. On the contrary, ghosts in

fiction are becoming so numerous that one wonders if the
Malthusian theory will not in time affect them.   We are
too fond of being fooled by phantoms to surrender them,
for "the slow touch of a frozen finger tracing out the
spine" is an awesome joy.   For ourselves, we are content
for the present to function on one plane, but we love to
adventure on another plane through spectral substitutes.
We may give up the mortal but we'll not willingly give
up the ghost.   We love him.   We believe in him.   Our attitude towards specters is much like that of the little black
boy that Ellis Parker Butler tells about in *Dey Ain't No
Ghosts*, who sees a terrifying array of "all de sperits in de
world, an' all de ha'nt in de world, an' all de hobgoblins
in de world, an' all spicters in de world, an' all de ghostes
in de world," come out to bring a fearsome message to a
frightened pickaninny.

De king ob de ghostes, whut name old Skull-an'-Bones, he
place he hand on de head ob li'l black Mose, an' de hand feel
like a wet rag, an' he say:
"Dey ain'no ghosts!"
An' one ob de hairs on de head ob li'l black Mose turn' white.
An' de monstrous big ha'nt what he name Bloody Bones he
lay he hand on de head ob li'l black Mose, an' he hand feel
like a toad-stool in de cool ob de day, an' he say:
"Dey ain' no ghosts!"
An' anudder one ob de hairs whut on de head ob li'l black
Mose turn' white.
An' a heejus sperit whut he name Moldy Pa'm place he
hand on de head ob li'l black Mose, an' he hand feel like de
yunner side ob a lizard, an' he say:
"Dey ain' no ghosts!"

And so on through the assembly.   Small wonder that
the terrified youngster is loath to go up to the loft to bed
alone that night and demurs to the demand.

So he ma she say, "Git erlong wid you! Whut you skeered ob when dey ain' no ghosts?"

An' li'l black Mose he scrooge an' he twist an' he pucker up he mouf an' he rub he eyes an' prisintly he say right low:

"I ain' skeered ob de ghosts whut am, ca'se dey ain' no ghosts."

"Den whut *am* you skeered ob?" ask he ma.

"Nuffin," say de li'l black boy whut he name am Mose, "but I jes' feel kinder oneasy 'bout de ghosts whut ain't!"

Jes' lack white folks. Jes' lack white folks.

CHAPTER IV

The Devil and His Allies

"GHOSTS are few but devils are plenty," said Cotton Mather, but his saying would need to be inverted to fit present-day English fiction. Now we have ghosts in abundance but devils are scarce. In fact, they bid fair to become extinct in our romances, at least in the form that is easily recognizable. Satan will probably soon be in solution, identified merely as a state of mind. He has been so Burbanked of late, with his dæmonic characteristics removed and humanities added that, save for sporadic reversion to type, the old familiar demon is almost a vanished form. The modern mind seems to cling with a new fondness to the ghost but has turned the cold shoulder to the devil, perhaps because many modernists believe more in the human and less in the supernatural —and after all, ghosts are human and devils are not. The demon has disported himself in various forms in literature, from the scarlet fiend of monkish legend, the nimble imp and titanic nature-devil of folk-lore to Milton's epic, majestic Satan, and Goethe's mocking Mephistopheles, passing into allegoric, symbolic, and satiric figures in later fiction. He has been an impressive character in the drama, the epic, the novel, in poetry, and the short story. We have seen him as a loathly, brutish demon in Dante, as a superman, as an intellectual satirist, and as a human being appealing to our sympathy. He

has gradually lost his epic qualities and become human.
He is not present in literature now to the extent to which
he was known in the past, is not so impressive a figure as
heretofore, and at times when he does appear his personality is so ambiguously set forth that it requires close
literary analysis to prove his presence.

In this chapter the devil will be discussed with reference
to his appearances on earth, while in a later division he
will be seen in his own home.   It would be hard to say
with certainty when and where the devil originated, yet
he undoubtedly belongs to one of our first families and is
said to have been born theologically in Persia about the
year 900 B.C.   He has appeared under various aliases, as
Ahriman of the Zoroastrian system, Pluto in classical
mythology, Satan, Beelzebub, Prince of Darkness, and by
many other titles.   In his *Address to the De'il* Burns
invokes him thus:

> "Oh, Thou! whatever title suit thee,—
> Auld Hornie, Satan, Nick or Cloutie!"

He has manifested himself in fiction under diverse names,
as Demon, Lucifer, Satan, Mephistopheles, Prince Lucio,
The Man in Black, and so forth, but whatever the name he
answers to, he is known in every land and has with
astonishing adaptability made himself at home in every
literature.

The devil has so changed his form and his manner of
appearance in later literature that it is hard to identify
him as his ancient self.   In early stories he was heralded
by supernatural thunder and lightning and accompanied
by a strong smell of sulphur.   He dressed in character
costume, sometimes in red, sometimes in black, but always
indubitably diabolic.   He wore horns, a forked tail, and
cloven hoofs and was a generally unprepossessing creature
whom anyone could know for a devil.   Now his rôle is

not so typical and his garb not so declarative. He wears an evening suit, a scholar's gown, a parson's robe, a hunting coat, with equal ease, and it is sometimes difficult to tell the devil from the hero of a modern story. He has been deodorized and no longer reeks warningly of the Pit.

The mediæval mind conceived of the devil as a sort of combination of mythologic satyr and religious dragon. It is interesting to note how the pagan devil-myths have been engrafted upon the ideas of Christianity, to fade out very slowly and by degrees. In monkish legends the devil was an energetic person who would hang round a likely soul for years, if need be, on the chance of nabbing him. Many monkish legends have come down to us.

The diabolic element in English folk-lore shows a rich field for study. The devil here as in the monkish legendry appears as an enemy of souls, a tireless tempter. He lies in wait for any unwary utterance, and the least mention of his name, any thoughtless expletive, such as "The devil take me if—" brings instant response from him to clinch the bargain. Yet the devil of rustic folk-lore is of a bucolic dullness, less clever than in any phase of literature, more gullible, more easily imposed on. English folk-lore, especially the Celtic branches, shows the devil as very closely related to nature. He was wont to work off his surplus energy or his wrath by disturbing the landscape, and many stories of his prankish pique have come down to us. If anything vexed him he might stamp so hard upon a plain that the print of his cloven hoof would be imprinted permanently. He was fond of drinking out of pure springs and leaving them cursed with sulphur, and he sometimes showed annoyance by biting a section out of a mountain, Devil's Bit Mountain in Ireland being one of the instances. In general, any peculiarity of nature might be attributed to the activities of Auld Hornie.

The devil has always been a pushing, forward sort of person, so he was not content with being handed round by word of mouth in monkish legend or rustic folk-lore, but must worm his way into literature in general. Since then many ink-pots have been emptied upon him besides the one that Luther hurled against his cloister wall. The devil is seen frequently in the miracle plays, showing grotesquerie, the beginnings of that sardonic humor he is to display in more important works later. In his appearance in literature the devil is largely anthropomorphic. Man creates the devil in his own image, one who is not merely personal but racial as well, reflecting his creator. In monkish tradition an adversary in wait for souls, in rustic folk-lore a rollicking buffoon with waggish pranks, in miracle plays reflecting the mingled seriousness and comic elements of popular beliefs, he mirrors his maker. But it is in the great poems and dramas and stories that we find the more personal aspects of devil-production, and it is these epic and dramatic concepts of the devil that have greatly influenced modern fiction. While the Gothic romance was but lightly touched by the epic supernaturalism, the literature since that time has reflected it more, and the Satanic characters of Dante, Milton, Calderon, Marlowe, and Goethe have cast long shadows over modern fiction. The recent revival of interest in Dante has doubtless had its effect here.

Burns in his *Address to the De'il* shows his own kindly heart and honest though ofttimes misdirected impulses by suggesting that there is still hope for the devil to repent and trusting that he may do so yet. Mrs. Browning, in her *Drama of Exile*, likewise shows in Lucifer some appeal to our sympathies, reflecting the pitying heart of the writer,—showing a certain kinship to Milton's Satan yet with weakened intellectual power. She makes Gabriel say to him:

"Angel of the sin,
Such as thou standest,—pale in the drear light
Which rounds the rebel's work with Maker's wrath—
Thou shalt be an Idea to all souls,
A monumental, melancholy gloom,
Seen down all ages whence to mark despair
And measure out the distances from good."

Byron's devil in *A Vision of Judgment* is, like Caliban's ideas of Setebos, "altogether such an one" as Byron conceived himself to be. He is a terrible figure, whose

"Fierce and unfathomable thoughts engraved
Eternal wrath on his immortal face."

He shows diabolical sarcasm when he says, "I've kings enough below, God knows!" And how like Oscar Wilde is the devil he pictures to us in his symbolic story, *The Fisherman and his Soul*. The prince of darkness who appears to the young fisherman that wishes to sell his soul to the devil is "a man dressed in a suit of black velvet cut in Spanish fashion. His proud face was strangely pale, but his lips were like a proud red flower. He seemed weary and was leaning back toying in a listless manner with the pommel of his saddle." When the fisherman unthoughtedly utters a prayer that baffles the fiend for the time, the demon mounts his jennet with the silver harness and rides away, still with the proud, disdainful face, sad with a *blasé* weariness unlike the usual alertness of the devil. He has a sort of Blessed Damozel droop to his figure, and the bored patience of a lone man at an afternoon tea. Wilde shows us some little mocking red devils in another of his stories,[1] and *The Picture of Dorian Grey* is a concept of diabolism.

Scott in *The Talisman* puts a story of descent from the

[1] *A Legend of Sharp.*

Evil One in the mouth of the Saracen, the legend of the spirits of evil who formed a league with the cruel Zohauk, by which he gained a daily sacrifice of blood to feed two hideous serpents that had become a part of himself. One day seven sisters of wonderful beauty are brought, whose loveliness appeals to the immortals. In the midst of supernatural manifestations the earth is rent and seven young men appear. The leader says to the eldest sister:

I am Cothreb, king of the subterranean world. I and my brethren are of those who, created out of elementary fire, disdained even at the command of Omnipotence, to do homage to a clod of earth because it is called man. Thou mayest have heard of us as cruel, unrelenting, and persecuting. It is false. We are by nature kind and generous, vengeful only when insulted, cruel only when affronted. We are true to those that trust us; and we have heard the invocations of thy father the sage Mithrasp, who wisely worships not only the Origin of Good, but that which is called the Source of Evil. You and your sisters are on the eve of death; but let each give to us one hair from your fair tresses in token of fealty, and we will carry you many miles to a place of safety where you may bid defiance to Zohauk and his ministers.

The maidens accept the offer and become the brides of the spirits of evil.

The devil in Scott's *Wandering Willie's Tale*,[1] also speaks a good word for himself. When the gudesire meets in the woods the stranger who sympathizes with his obvious distress, the unknown offers to help him, saying, "If you will tell me your grief, I am one that, though I have been sair miscaa'd in the world, am the only hand for helping my freends." The gudesire tells his woes and says that he would go to the gates of hell, and farther, to get the receipt due him, upon which the hos-

[1] In *Red Gauntlet*.

pitable stranger conducts him to the place mentioned. The canny Scot obtains the document, outwits the devil, and wins his way back to earth unscathed.

One marked aspect of recent devil-fiction is the tendency to gloze over his sins and to humanize him. This is shown to a marked degree in Marie Corelli's sentimental novel, *The Sorrows of Satan*, where she expends much anxious sympathy over the fiend. To Miss Corelli's agitated mind Satan is a much maligned martyr who regretfully tempts mortals and is grieved when they yield to his beguilements. Her perfervid rhetoric pictures him as a charming prince, handsome, wealthy, yet very lonesome, who warns persons in advance that he is not what he seems and that they would do well to avoid him. But the fools rush in crowds to be damned. According to her theory, the devil is attempting to work out his own salvation and could do so save for the weakness of man. He is able to get a notch nearer heaven for every soul that resists his wiles, though in London circles his progress is backward rather than forward. How is Lucifer fallen! To be made a hero of by Marie Corelli must seem to Mephisto life's final indignity! Her characterization of the fiend shows some reminiscence of a hasty reading of Milton, Goethe, and the Byronic Cain.

The devil has a human as well as dæmonic spirit in Israel Zangwill's *They that Walk in Darkness*, where he appears as Satan Maketrig, a red-haired hunchback, with "gigantic marble brow, cold, keen, steely eyes, and handsome, clean-shaven lips." He seems a normal human being in this realistic Ghetto setting, though he bears a nameless sense of evil about with him. In his presence, or as he passes by, all the latent evil in men's souls comes to the surface. He lures the rabbi away from his wife, from God, and from all virtue, yet to see him at the end turn away again in spirit to the good, spurning the tempter whom he recognizes at last as dæmonic. There is a human anguish in the eyes of Satan Maketrig, that shows him to be not altogether diabolic, and he seems mournful and appealing in his wild loneliness. His nature is in contrast to that of the fiend in Stanley J. Weyman's *The Man in Black*. Here his cold, sardonic jesting that causes him to play with life and death, so lightly, his diabolic cunning, his knowledge of the human heart and how to torture it, remind us of Iago. The dark shade extends to the skin as well as to the heart in the man in black in Stevenson's *Thrawn Janet*, for he exercises a weird power over his vassal, the old servant, and terrifies even the minister. And *War Letters from a Living Dead Man*, written by Elsa Parker but said to be dictated by a correspondent presumably from somewhere in hell, shows us His Satanic Majesty with grim realism up to date.

The devil appears with mournful, human dignity, yet with superhuman gigantism in Algernon Blackwood's *Secret Worship*, where the lost souls enter into a riot of devil-worship, into which they seek to draw living victims, to damn them body and soul. One victim sees the devil thus:

At the end of the room where the windows seemed to have disappeared so that he could see the stars, there rose up into view, far against the sky, grand and terrible, the outline of a man. A kind of gray glory enveloped him so that it resembled a steel-cased statue, immense, imposing, horrific in its distant splendor. The gray radiance from its mightily broken visage, august and mournful, beat down upon his soul, pulsing like some dark star with the powers of spiritual evil.

Here, as in many instances elsewhere, the sadness of the diabolic character is emphasized, a definite human element. The Miltonic influence seems evident in such cases.

Kipling has a curious dæmonic study in *Bubble Well Road*, a story of a patch of ground filled with devils and ghosts controlled by an evil-minded native priest, while in *Haunted Subalterns* the imps terrorize young army officers by their malicious mischief.

The allegorical and symbolic studies of diabolism are among the more impressive creations in later fiction, as in Tolstoi's *Ivan, the Fool*, where the demons are responsible for the marshaling of armies, the tyranny of money, and the inverted ideas of the value of service. The appearance of the devil in later stories is more terrible and effective in its variance of type and its secret symbolism than the crude enginery of diabolism in Gothic fiction, as the muscular fiend[1] that athletically hurls the man and woman from the mountain top, or the invisible physical strength manifested in *Melmoth, the Wanderer*. The crude violence of these novels is in keeping with the fiction of the time, yet modern stories show a distinct advance, as such instances as J. H. Shorthouse's *Countess Eve*, where the devil appears differently to each tempted soul, embodying with hideous wisdom the form of the sin that that particular soul is most liable to commit. He bears the shape of committed sin, suggesting that evil is so powerful as to have an independent existence of its own, apart from the mind that gave it birth, as the devil appears as evil thought materialized in Fernac Molnar's drama, *The Devil*. Fiona McLeod's strange Gaelic tale, *The Sin-Eater* introduces demons symbolically. The sin-eater is a person that by an ancient formula can remove the sins from an unburied corpse and let them in turn be swept away from him by the action of the pure air. But if the sin-eater hates the dead man, he has the power to fling the transgressions into the sea, to turn them into demons that pursue and torment the flying soul till Judgment Day.

[1] In *The Monk* or *Zofloya*.

One aspect of the recent stories of diabolism is the subtleness by which the evil is suggested. The reader feels a miasmatic atmosphere of evil, a smear on the soul, and knows that certain incidents in the action can be accounted for on no other basis than that of dæmonic presence, as in Barry Pain's *Moon Madness*, where the princess is moved by a strange irresistible lure to dance alone night after night in the heart of the secret labyrinth to mystic music that the white moon makes. But one night, after she is dizzy and exhausted but impelled to keep on, she feels a hot hand grasp hers; someone whirls her madly round and she knows that *she is not dancing alone!* She is seen no more of men, and searchers find only the prints of her little dancing slippers in the sand, with the mark of a cloven hoof beside them. The most revolting instances of suggestive diabolism are found in Arthur Machen's stories, where supernatural science opens the way for the devil to enter the human soul, since the biologist by a cunning operation on the brain removes the moral sense, takes away the soul, and leaves a being absolutely diabolized. Worse still is the hideousness of *Seeing the Great God Pan*, where the dæmonic character is a composite of the loathsome aspects of Pan and the devil, from which horrible paternity is born a child that embodies all the unspeakable evil in the world.

In pleasant contrast to dreadful stories are the tales of the amusing devils that we find frequently. The comic devil is much older than the comic ghost, as authors showed a levity toward demons long before they treated the specter with disrespect,—one rather wonders why. Clownish devils that appeared in the miracle plays prepared the way for the humorous and satiric treatment of the Elizabethan drama and late fiction. The liturgical imps were usually funny whether their authors intended them as such or not, but the devils in fiction are quite conscious of their own wit, in fact, are rather conceited about it. Poe shows us several amusing demons who display his curious satiric humor,—for instance, the old gentleman in *Never Bet the Devil your Head*. When Toby Dammit makes his rash assertion, he beholds

the figure of a little lame old gentleman of venerable aspect. Nothing could be more reverend than his whole appearance; for he not only had on a full suit of black, but his shirt was perfectly clean and the collar turned down very neatly over a white cravat, while his hair was parted in front like a girl's. His hands were clasped pensively over his stomach, and his two eyes were carefully rolled up into the top of his head.

This clerical personage who reminds us of the devil in *Peer Gynt*, who also appears as a parson, claims the better's head and neatly carries it off. This is a modern version of an incident similar to Chaucer's *Friar's Tale*, where the devil claimed whatever was offered him in sincerity. The combination of humor and mystery in Washington Irving's *The Devil and Tom Walker* shows the black woodsman in an amusing though terrifying aspect, as he claims the keeping of the contracts made with him by Tom and his miserly wife. When Tom goes to search for his spouse in the woods, he fails to find her.

She had probably attempted to deal with the black man as she had been accustomed to deal with her husband; but though the female scold is generally considered a match for the devil, yet in this instance she appears to have had the worst of it. She must have died game, however, for it is said Tom noticed many prints of cloven feet deeply stamped about the tree, and found handsful of hair that looked as if they had been plucked from the coarse shock of the black woodsman. Tom knew his wife's prowess by experience. He shrugged his shoulders as he looked at the fierce signs of clapper-clawing. "Egad!" he said to himself, "Old Scratch must have had a tough time of it!"

The devil amuses himself in various ways, as is seen by the antics of the mysterious stranger in Poe's *The Devil in the Belfry*, who comes curvetting into the old Dutch village with his audacious and sinister face and curious costume, to upset the sacred time of the place. The visitant in *Bon Bon* is likewise queer as to dress and habits. He wears garments in the style of a century before, having a queue but no shirt, a cravat with an ecclesiastic suggestion, also a stylus and black book. His facial expression is such as would have struck Uriah Heap dumb with envy, and the hint of hoofs and a forked tail is cleverly given though not obtruded. The most remarkable feature of his appearance, however, is that he has no eyes, simply a dead level of flesh. He declares that he eats souls and prefers to buy them alive to insure freshness. He has a taste for philosophers, when they are not too tough.

The satiric devil, like the satiric ghost, is seen in modern fiction. Eugene Field has a story of a demon who seems sympathetic, weeping large, gummy tears at hearing a mortal's woes, and signing the conventional contract on a piece of asbestos paper. He agrees to do everything the man wishes, for a certain term of years, in return for which he is to get the soul. If the devil forfeits the contract, he loses not only that victim but the souls of two thousand already in his clutches. The man shrewdly demands trying things of him, but the demon is game, building and endowing churches, carrying on philanthropic and reform work without complaint, but balking when the man asks him to close the saloons on Sunday. Rather than do that, he releases the two thousand and one souls and flies away twitching his tail in wrath.[1]

[1] *Daniel and the Devil.*

The most recent, as perhaps the most striking, instance of the satiric devil is in Mark Twain's posthumous novel, *The Mysterious Stranger*. A youth, charming, courtly, and handsome appears in a medieval village, confessing to two boys that he is Satan, though not the original of that name, but his nephew and namesake. He insists that he is an unfallen angel, since his uncle is the only member of his family that has sinned. Satan reads the thoughts of mortals, kindles fire in his pipe by breathing on it, supplies money and other desirable things by mere suggestion, is invisible when he wills it so, and is generally a gifted being. This perennial boy—only sixteen thousand years old—makes a charming companion. He says to Marget that his papa is in shattered health and has no property to speak of,—in fact, none of any earthly value,—but he has an uncle in business down in the tropics, who is very well off, and has a monopoly, and it is from this uncle that he drew his support. Marget expresses the hope that her uncle and his would meet some day, and Satan says he hoped so, too. "May be they will," says Marget. "Does your uncle travel much?"

"Oh, yes, he goes all about,—he has business everywhere."

The book is full of this oblique humor, satirizing earth, heaven, and hell. The stranger by his comments on theological creeds satirizes religion, and Satan is an intended parody of God. He sneers at man's "mongrel moral sense," which tells him the distinction between good and evil, insisting that he should have no choice, that the right to choose makes him inevitably choose the wrong. He makes little figures out of clay and gives them life, only to destroy them with casual ruthlessness a little later and send them to hell. In answer to the old servant's faith in God, when she says that He will care for her and her mistress, since "not a sparrow falleth to the ground without His Knowledge," he sneers, "But it falls, just the same! What's the good of seeing it fall?" He is a new diabolic figure, yet showing the composite traits of the old, the dæmonic wisdom and sarcasm, the superhuman magnetism to draw men to him, and the human qualities of geniality, sympathy, and boyish charm.

One of the most significant and frequent motifs of the diabolic in literature is that of the barter of the human soul for the devil's gift of some earthly boon, long life or wealth or power, or wisdom, or gratification of the senses. It is a theme of unusual power,—what could be greater than the struggle over one's own immortal soul?—and well might the great minds of the world engage themselves with it. Yet that theme is but little apparent in later stories. We have no such character in recent literature that can compare with Marlowe's Dr. Faustus or Goethe's Mephistopheles or Calderon's wonder-working magician. Hawthorne's Septimius Felton makes a bargain with the devil to secure the elixir of life, there is a legend in Hardy's *Tess of the D'Urbervilles* of a man that sold himself to the minister of evil, and the incident occurs in various stories of witchcraft, yet with waning power and less frequence. The most significant recent use of it is in W. B. Yeats's drama.[1] This is a drama of Ireland, where the peasants have been driven by famine to barter their souls to the devil to buy their children food, but their Countess sells her own soul to the demon that they may save theirs. This vicarious sacrifice adds a new poignancy to the situation and Yeats has treated it with power. This is the only recent appearance of the devil on the stage for he has practically disappeared from English drama, where he was once so prominent. The demon was a familiar and leading figure on the miracle and Elizabethan stage, but, like the ghost, he shows more vitality now

[1] *Countess Cathleen.*

in fiction. The devil is an older figure in English drama than is the ghost, but he seems to have played out.

The analysis and representation of the devil as a character in literature have covered a great range, from the bestiality of Dante's Demon in the *Inferno* to Milton's mighty angel in ruins, with all sorts of variations between, from the sneering cynicism of Goethe's Mephisto to the pinchbeck diabolism of Marie Corelli's sorrowful Satan, and the merry humor and blasphemous satire of Mark Twain's mysterious stranger. We note an especial influence of Goethe's Mephistopheles in the satiric studies of the demon, an echo of his diabolic climax when in answer to Faust's outcry over Margaret's downfall and death, he says, "*She is not the first!*" One hears echoing through all literature Man Friday's unanswerable question, "Why not God kill debbil?" The uses of evil in God's eternal scheme, the soul's free choice yet pitiful weakness, are sounded again and again. The great diabolic figures, in their essential humanity, their intellectual dignity, their sad introspection, their pitiless testing of the human soul to its predestined fall, are terrible allegorical images of the evil in man himself, or concepts of social sins, as in *Ivan, the Fool*. The devils of the great writers, reflecting the time, the racial characteristics, the personal natures of their creators, are deeply symbolic. Each man creates the devil that he can understand, that represents him, for, as Amiel says, we can comprehend nothing of which we have not the beginnings in ourselves. As each man sees a different Hamlet, so each one has his own devil, or *is* his own devil. This is illustrated by the figure in Julian Hawthorne's *Lovers in Heaven*, where the dead man's spirit meets the devil in the after life,—who is his own image, his dæmonic double. Some have one great fiend, while others keep packs of little, snarling imps of darkness. A study of comparative diabolics is illuminating and might be useful to us all.

The Wizard and the Witch. The demon has his earthly partners in evil members of the firm of Devil and Company. Certain persons that have made a pact with him are given a share in his power, and a portion of his dark mantle falls upon them. The sorcerer and the witch are ancient figures in literature, and like others of the supernatural kingdom, notably the devil, they have their origin in the East, the cuneiform writings of the Chaldeans showing belief in witchcraft. And the Witch of Endor, summoning the spirit of Samuel to confront Saul, is a very real figure in the Old Testament. The Greeks believed in witches, as did the Romans. Meroe, a witch, is described in the *Metamorphoses* of Lucius Appuleius, from whom perhaps the witch Meroe in Peele's *Old Wives' Tale* gets her name and character. In classical times witches were thought to have power to turn men into beasts, tigers, monkeys, or asses—some persons still believe that women have that power and might give authenticated instances.

The sorcerer, or wizard, or warlock, or magician, as he is variously called, was a more common figure in early literature than in later, perhaps because, as in so many other cases, his profession has suffered a feminine invasion. The Anglo-Saxon word *wicca*, meaning " witch," is masculine, which may or may not mean that witchcraft was a manly art in those days, and the most famous medieval enchanter, Merlin, was a man, it should be noted. The sorcerer of primitive times has been gradually reduced in power, changing through the astrologer and alchemist of medieval and Gothic romance into the bacteriologist and biologist of recent fiction, where he works other wonders. In general, warlocks and wizards, while frequent enough in early literature and in modern folk-tales, have become less numerous in later fiction. Scott[1] has a medical magician with supernatural power of healing by means of an amulet, which, put to the nostrils of a person practically dead, revives him at once, but which loses its efficacy if given in exchange for money. Hawthorne has an old Indian sachem with wizard power,[2] who has concocted the elixir of life. We see the passing of the ancient sorcerer into the scientific wonder-worker in such fiction as Sax Rohmer's Fu-Manchu stories that depict a Chinese terror, or in H. G. Wells's supernatural investigators in his various stories of science. The magician is not really dead in fiction but has passed over into another form, for the most part.

We still have the hoodoo man of colored persuasion, and the redskin medicine-man, together with Oriental sorcerers from Kipling and others. Examples are: *In the House of Suddoo*, by Kipling, where the wonder-worker unites a canny knowledge of the telephone and telegraph along with his unholy art; *Red Debts*, by Lumley Deakin, where the Indian magician exacts a terrible penalty for the wrong done him, and where his diabolic appearance to claim his victim leaves one in doubt as to whether he has not sent his chief in his place; *The Monkey's Paw*, by W. W. Jacobs, a curdling story of a magic curse given by an Oriental sorcerer, by which the paw of a dead monkey grants three wishes that have a dreadful boomerang power; *Black Magic*, by Jessie Adelaide Weston,—who claims that all her supernatural stories are strictly true—the narrative of an old Indian sorcerer that changes himself into a hair mat and is shot for his pains. He has obtained power over the house by being given a hair from the mat by the uninitiated mistress. Hair, you must know, has great power of evil in the hands of witches and sorcerers, as in the case of the

[1] In *The Talisman*.　　　　[2] In his *Septimius Felton*.

evil ones in *The Talisman*, who received their thrall over the maidens by one hair from each head. F. Marion Crawford's *Khaled* is a story of magic art. Khaled is one of the genii converted by reading the Koran, who wishes to be a mortal man with a soul. He is given the right to do so if he can win the love of a certain woman. Hence he is born into the world, like Adam, a full-grown man, to be magically clothed and equipped, by the transformation of leaves and twigs into garments and armor, and the changing of a locust into an Arabian steed. After many supernatural adventures, he receives his soul from an angel. The soul, at first a crescent flame,

immediately took shape and became the brighter image of Khaled himself. And when he had looked at it fixedly for a few minutes—the vision of himself had disappeared and before he was aware it had entered his own body and taken up its life with him.

This is a parallel to the cases of ghostly doubles discussed in the previous chapter.

The magician shows a disposition to adapt himself to contemporary conditions and to change his personality with the times. Not so the witch. She is a permanent figure. She has appeared in the various forms of literature, in Elizabethan drama, in Gothic romance, in modern poetry, the novel and the short story, and is very much alive to-day. We have witches young and old. We have the fake witch, like the hoax ghost; the imputed witch and the genuine article. We have witch stories melodramatic, romantic, tragic, comic, and satiric, showing the influence of the great creations of past literature with modern adaptations and additions. English poetry is full of witchery, perhaps largely the result of the Celtic influence on our literature. The poetic type of witchcraft is brought out

in such poems as Coleridge's *Christabel*, where the beauty
and suggestiveness veil the sense of unearthly evil; or in
Shelley's *Witch of Atlas*, where the woman appears as
a symbol of alluring loveliness possessing none of the
hideous aspects seen in other weird women.   The water
enchantress in Shelley's fragment of an unfinished drama
might be mentioned as another example while Keats's *La
Belle Dame sans Merci* has a magical charm all her own.
Christina Rossetti's *Goblin Market* shows a peculiar aspect
of magic, as also Mrs. Browning's *The Lay of the Brown
Rosary*. On the contrary, Milton's *Comus*, Robert Herrick's
The Hag, and James Hogg's *The Witch of Fife* illustrate
the uglier aspects of enchantment.

There are two definite types of witches seen in English
fiction, the first being merely the reputed witch, the woman
who is falsely accused or suspected of black arts, and who
either is persecuted, or else gains what she wishes by hints
of her traffic in evil, like the Old Granny Young in *Mine
Host and the Witch*, by James Blythe, who chants as a
charm-rune,

> " A curse shall lay on water and land
>   For the thing denied the witch's hand,"

so that everybody is afraid to refuse her whatever she
demands.   This is a highly conventionalized type of the
motif and, though it is found in great numbers in modern
fiction, is not particularly important.   The principal complications of the plot are usually the same, the character
known as the witch being either an appealing figure win-
ning sympathy because of her beauty and youth, or else
touching to pity because of her age and infirmities.   No
person of average age or pulchritude is ever accused of
witchcraft in English fiction.   She is always very old and
poor or young and lovely.   Item also, she invariably has

two lovers, in the latter case. She is merely a romantic peg on which to hang a story, not always real as a human being and not a real witch. In these stories the only magic used is love, the fair maid having unintentionally charmed the heart of a villain, who, failing to win her, accuses her of witchcraft in order to frighten her into love. In some of the novels and stories the victim is actually executed, while in others she is rescued by her noble lover at the fifty-ninth second. We have the pursuing villain, the distressed innocence, the chivalric lover disporting themselves in late Gothic fashion over many romances. Even Mary Johnston with her knowledge of Colonial times and her power to give atmosphere to the past does not succeed in imparting the breath of life to her late novel of witchcraft, *The Witch*. These pink-and-white beauties who speak in Euphuistic sentences, who show a lamblike defiance toward the dark tempters, who breathe prayers to heaven for protection and forgiveness to their enemies in one breath, who die or are rescued with equal grace and propriety,—one is carried away from the scaffold by Kidd, the pirate, thus delaying for several chapters her rescue by her faithful lover—do not really touch the heart any more than they interest the intellect. Yet there are occasional instances of the imputed witch who seems real despite her handicap of beauty and youth, as Iseult le Desireuse, in Maurice Hewlett's *Forest Lovers*, whom Prosper le Gai weds to save from the hangman. The young woman in F. Marion Crawford's *Witch of Prague* might be called a problematic witch, for while she does undoubtedly work magic, it is for the most part attributed to her powers of hypnotism rather than to the black art itself. We find an excellent example of the reputed witch who is a woman of real charm and individuality, in D'Annunzio's *The Daughter of Jorio*, where the young girl is beset by cruel dangers because of her charm and her lonely condition, and who rises to tragic heights of sacrifice to save her lover from death, choosing to be burned to death as a witch to save him from paying the penalty of murder. She actually convinces him, as well as the others, that she has bewitched him by unholy powers, that she has slain his father and made him believe that he himself did it to save her honor, and she goes to her death with a white fervor of courage, with no word of complaint, save one gentle rebuke to him that *he* should not revile her.

The aged pseudo-witch is in the main more appealing than the young one, because more realistic. Yet there is no modern instance that is so touching as the poor old crone in *The Witch of Edmonton*, who is persecuted for being a witch and who turns upon her tormentors with a speech that reminds us of Shylock's famous outcry, showing clearly how their suspicion and accusation have made her what she is. We see here a witch in the making, an innocent old woman who is harried by human beings till she makes a compact with the devil. Meg Merrilies[1] is a problematic witch, a majestic, sibylline figure, very individual and human, yet with more than a suggestion of superhuman wisdom and power. Scott limned her with a loving hand, and Keats was so impressed with her personality that he wrote a poem concerning her. Elizabeth Enderfield, in Hardy's *Under the Greenwood Tree*, is a reputed witch and witch-pricking is also tried in his *Return of the Native*. Various experiments with magic are used in Hardy's work, as the instance of the woman's touching her withered arm to the neck of a man that had been hanged, consulting the conjurer concerning butter that won't come, and so forth. Old Aunt Keziah in Hawthorne's *Septimius Felton* might be called a problematic witch, as the woman in *The*

[1] Of Scott's *Guy Mannering*.

Witch by Eden Phillpotts. She has a great number of
cats, and something dreadful happens to anyone who
injures one of them; she calls the three black toads her
servants and goes through incantations over a snake
skeleton, the carcass of a toad, and the mummy of a cat.
Mother Tab may or may not be a *bona fide* witch, but
she causes much trouble to those associated with her.

The unquestioned witch, possessing indubitable powers
of enchantment, occurs frequently and conveys a genuine
thrill.   Her attributes have been less conventionalized
than those of her youthful companions who are merely
under the imputation of black art, and she possesses a
diabolic individuality. Though she may not remain
long in view, she is an impressive figure not soon forgotten. The old crone in Scott's *The Two Drovers* gives
warning to Robin Oig, "walking the deasil," as it is
called, around him, tracing the propitiation which some
think a reminiscence of Druidical mythology,—which is
performed by walking three times round the one in
danger, moving according to the course of the sun. In the
midst of her incantation the hag exclaims, "Blood on your
hand, and it is English blood!" True enough, before his
journey's end young Robin does murder his English companion. In the same story other evidences of witchcraft are shown, as the directions for keeping away the evil
influence from cattle by tying St. Mungo's knot on their
tails.

The subject of witchcraft greatly interested Hawthorne,
for he introduces it in a number of instances. *Young
Goodman Brown* shows the aspects of the diabolic union
between the devil and his earthly companions, their unholy
congregations in the forest, reports their sardonic conver-
sations and suggestions of evil in others, and pictures the
witches riding on broomsticks high in the heavens and
working their magic spells. The young husband sees in

that convocation all the persons whom he has most revered—his minister, his Sabbath-school teacher, and even his young wife, so that all his after-life is saddened by the thought of it. Witchcraft enters into *The Scarlet Letter*, *Main Street*, and *Feathertop*, and is mentioned in other stories.

Old Mother Sheehy in Kipling's *The Courting of Dinah Shadd* pronounces a malediction against Private Mulvany and the girl he loves, prophesying that he will be reduced in rank instead of being promoted, will be a slave to drink so that his young wife will take in washing for officers' wives instead of herself being the wife of an officer, and that their only child will die,—every bitter word of which comes true in after years. The old witch mother in Howard Pyle's *The Evil Eye* inspires her daughter to cast a spell over the man she loves but who does not think of her, causing him to leave his betrothed and wed the witch daughter. When understanding comes to him, and with it loathing, the girl seeks to regain his love by following the counsel of an old magician, who gives her an image to be burnt. But that burning of the image kills her and looses the man from her spell. That incident is similar to that in D'Annunzio's *Sogno d'un Tramonto d'Autunno* where the Dogaressa seeks to slay her rival, both probably being based on the unforgettable employment of the theme in Rossetti's *Sister Helen*, where the young girl causes the death of her betrayer by melting the image.

In Gordon Bottomley's play, *Riding to Lithend*, three old women enter, who seem to partake of the nature of the Parcæ as well as of Shakespeare's Weird Sisters. They have bat-webbed fingers, the hound bays uncannily at their approach, they show supernatural knowledge of events, and they chant a wild prophecy of doom, then mysteriously disappear. Fate marches swiftly on as they foretell.

The young and beautiful witch can work as much evil as the ancient crone, perhaps more, since her emotions are wilder and more unrestrained. She can project a curse that reaches its victim across the ocean, when the one who sent the curse is rotting in the tomb, as in *The Curse of the Cashmere Shawl*, where a betrayed and deserted woman in India sends a rare shawl to her rival, then drowns herself. Months after, when the husband, forgetful of the source, lays the shawl around his wife's shoulders, the dead woman takes her place. After this gruesome transfer of personality, the wife, impelled by a terrible urge she cannot understand, drowns herself as the other has done months before. Oscar Wilde[1] shows a young and lovely witch with a human longing for the love of the young man who throws away his soul for love of a mermaid. Through life's tragic satire, she is compelled, in spite of her entreaties, to show him how he may damn himself and win the other's affection. The jealousy shown here and in other instances is an illustration of the human nature of the witch, who, like the devil, makes a strong appeal to our sympathy in spite of the undoubted iniquity.

The element of symbolism enters largely into the witch-creations, even from the time of Shakespeare's Three in *Macbeth*, who are terrible symbolic figures of the evil in man's soul. They appear as the visible embodiment of Macbeth's thoughts, and by their mysterious suggestive utterances tempt him to put his unlawful dreams into action. They seem both cause and effect here, for though when they first appear to him his hands are innocent of blood, his heart is tainted with selfish ambition, and their whispers of promise hurry on the deed. In *Ancient Sorceries*, by Algernon Blackwood, the village is full of persons who at night by the

[1] In *The Fisherman and his Soul.*

power of an ancestral curse, a heritage of subliminal memory, become witches, horrible cat-creatures, unhuman, that dance the blasphemous dance of the Devil's Sabbath. The story symbolizes the eternal curse that rests upon evil, the undying quality of thought and action that cannot cease when the body of the sinner has become dust, but reaches out into endless generations.

In *Old Fires and Profitable Ghosts* by A. T. Quiller-Couch, we see a witch, a young woman whose soul is under a spell from the devil. She gives rich gifts to the church, but her offerings turn into toads and vipers, defiling the sanctuary, and as she sings her wild songs the bodies of drowned men come floating to the surface of the water and join in the words of her song. Her beauty is supernatural and accursed, yet her soul is innocent of wish to do evil, though it leaves her body and goes like a cresseted flame at night to follow the devil, while the body is powerless in sleep. Finally the devil comes in the form of a Moor, possibly a suggestion from *Zofloya*, and summons her, when she dies, with a crucifix clasped over her heart.

W. B. Yeats has pictured several witches for us, as the crone of the gray hawk, in *The Wisdom of the King*, a woman tall with more than mortal height, with feathers of the gray hawk growing in her hair, who stoops over the royal cradle and whispers a strange thing to the child, as a result of which he grows up in a solitude of his own mystic thoughts with dreams that are like the marching and counter-marching of armies. When he realizes that the simple joys of life and love are not for him, he disappears, some say to make his home with the immortal demons, some say with the shadowy goddesses that haunt the midnight pools in the forest. In *The Curse of the Fires and the Shadows*, Yeats pictures another witch, tall and in a gray gown, who is standing in the river and washing, washing the dead body of a man.

As the troopers who have murdered the friars and burned down the church ride past, each man recognizes in the dead face his own face,—just a moment before they all plunge over the abyss to death.

There are witches in most collections of English folk-tales, for the simpler people, the more elemental natures, have a strong feeling for the twilight of nature and of life. The weird woman has power over the forces of nature and can evoke the wrath of the elements as of unholy powers against her enemies. Stories of witches, as of sorcerers, occur in Indian folk-tales, as well as in those of the American Indian, differing in details in the tribal collections yet showing similar essential ideas. The Scotch show special predilection for the witch, since with their tense, stern natures, they stand in awe of the darker powers and of those that call them forth. They relate curious instances of the relations between the animal world and witchcraft, as in *The Dark Nameless One*, by Fiona McLeod, the story of a nun that falls in love with a seal and is forced to live forever in the sea, weaving her spells where the white foam froths, and knowing that her soul is lost. This is akin to the theme that Matthew Arnold uses,[1] though with a different treatment, showing similarity to Hans Christian Andersen's tale of *The Little Mermaid*. The cailleachuisge, or the water-witch, and the maighdeanmhara, the mermaid, and the kelpie, the sea-beast, are cursed with dæmonic spells and live forever in their witchery. When mortals forsake the earth and follow them their children are beings that have no souls. The Irish folk-tales, on the other hand, while having their quota of witches, do not think so much about them or take them quite so seriously, inclining more to the faëry forms of supernaturalism suited to their poetic natures. The

[1] In his *Forsaken Merman* and *The Neckan*.

sense of beauty of the Irish is so vivid and their innate poetry so intense that they glimpse the loveliness of magic, and their enchanted beings are of beauty rather than of horror.

We even have the humorous and satiric witch, to correspond to similar representations of the ghost and the devil in modern fiction. The instance in Burns's *Tam O'Shanter* needs only to be recalled, with the ludicrous description of the wild race at night to escape the dread powers. *Bones, Sanders, and Another*, by Edgar Wallace, introduces a witch with comic qualities, a woman whose husband has been a magician, and the reputed familiar of a devil. She cures people by laying her hands on them, once causing a bone that was choking a child to fly out with "a cry terrible to hear, such a cry as a leopard makes when pursued by ghosts." When this witch with a sense of humor is arrested as a trouble-maker by an army officer, she "eradicates" her clothes, causing very comic complications. The best example of the satiric witch is Hawthorne's Mother Rigby, in *Feathertop*, who constructs a man from a broomstick and other materials for a scarecrow. In this satiric sermon upon the shams and hypocrisies of life, Mother Rigby, with her sardonic humor, her cynical comments, parodies society, holds the mirror up to human life and shows more than one poor painted scarecrow, simulacrum of humanity, masquerading as a man. The figure that she creates, with his yearnings and his pride, his horror when he realizes his own falsity and emptiness, is more human, more a man, than many a being we meet in literature or in life.

Barry Pain has several witch stories that do not fall readily into any category, curious stories of scientific dream-supernaturalism, in the realm of the unreal. *Exchange* is the account of a supernatural woman, whether a witch or one of the Fates, one does not know, who

comes, clad in scarlet rags, to show human souls their destinies. She permits an exchange of fate, if one is willing
to pay her price, which is in each case terrible enough.
One young girl gives up her pictured future of life and
love, and surrenders her mind for the purpose of saving
her baby brother from his destined fate of suicide in
manhood. The crone appears to an old man that loves the
child, who takes upon himself her fate of being turned
into a bird to be tortured after human death, so that the
young girl may have his future, to be turned into a white
lamb that dies after an hour, then be a soul set free.
The Glass of Supreme Moments is another story of prophetic witchery, of revealed fate seen in supernatural
dreams. A young man in his college study sees the
fireplace turn into a silver. stairway down which a lovely
gray-robed woman comes to him. She shows him a
mirror, the glass of supreme moments, in which the
highest instants of each man's life are shown. She says
of it, "All the ecstasy of the world lies there. The
supreme moments of each man's life, the scene, the spoken
words—all lie there. Past and present and future—all
are there." She shows an emotion meter that measures
the thrill of joy. After he has seen the climactic instants
of his friends' lives he asks to see his own, when she tells
him his are here and now. She tells him that her name is
Death and that he will die if he kisses her, but he cries
out, "I will die kissing you!" And presently his mates
return to find his body fallen dead across his table.

There is something infinitely appealing about the character of the witch. She seems a creature of tragic loneliness, conscious of her own dark powers, yet conscious
also of her exile from the good, and knowing that all
the evil she evokes will somehow come back to her, that
her curses will come home, as in the case of *Witch Hazel*,
where the witch, by making a cake of hair to overcome her

rival in love, brings on a tempest that kills her lover and drives her mad. Each evil act, each dark imagining seems to create a demon and turn him loose to harry humanity with unceasing force, as Matthew Maule's curse in *The House of Seven Gables* casts a spiritual shadow on the home. Yet the witch is sometimes a minister of good, as Mephistopheles says of himself, achieving the good where he meant evil; sometimes typifying the mysterious mother nature, as the old Wittikin in Hauptmann's *Sunken Bell*, neither good nor evil, neither altogether human nor supernatural. Her strange symbolism is always impressive.

Dæmonic Spirits—Vampires. Closely related to the devil are certain diabolic spirits that are given supernatural power by him and acknowledge his suzerainty. These include ghouls, vampires, werewolves, and other demoniac animals, as well as the human beings that through a compact with the fiend share in his dark force. Since such creatures possess dramatic possibilities, they have given interest to fiction and other literature from early times. This idea of an unholy alliance between earth and hell, has fascinated the human mind and been reflected astonishingly in literature. In studying the appearance of these beings in English fiction, we note, as in the case of the ghost, the witch, and the devil, a certain leveling influence, a tendency to humanize them and give them characteristics that appeal to our sympathy.

The vampire and the ghoul are closely related and by some authorities are considered the same, yet there is a distinction. The ghoul is a being, to quote Poe, "neither man nor woman, neither brute nor human" that feeds upon corpses, stealing out at midnight for loathsome banquets in graveyards. He devours the flesh of the dead, while the vampire drains the blood of the living. The ghoul is an Asiatic creature and has left but slight impress upon English literature, while the vampire has been a definite motif. The vampire superstition goes back to ancient times, being referred to on Chaldean and Assyrian tablets. William of Newbury, of the twelfth century in England, relates several stories of them; one vampire was burned in Melrose Abbey, and tourists in Ireland are still shown the grave of a vampire. Perhaps the vampire superstition goes back to the savagery of remote times, and is an animistic survival of human sacrifices, of cannibalism and the like. The vampire is thought of as an evil spirit issuing forth at night to attack the living in their sleep and drain the blood which is necessary to prolong its own revolting existence. Certain persons were thought to be especially liable to become vampires at death, such as suicides, witches, wizards, persons who in life had been attacked by vampires, outcasts of various kinds, as well as certain animals, werewolves, dead lizards, and others.

The vampire superstition was general in the East and extended to Europe, it is thought, by way of Greece. The Greeks thought of the vampire as a beautiful young woman, a lamia, who lured young men to their death. The belief was particularly strong in central Europe, but never seemed to gain the same foothold in England that it did on the continent, though it is evident here and has influenced literature. The vampire has been the inspiration for several operas, and has figured in the drama, in poetry, in the novel and short story, as well as in folk-tales and medieval legends. The stories show the various aspects of the belief and its ancient hold on the popular mind. The vampire, as well as the ghost, the devil, and the witch, has appeared on the English stage. *The Vampire*, an anonymous melodrama in two acts, *The Vampire*, a tragedy by St. John Dorset (1821), *The Vampire Bride*, a play, *Le Vampire*, by Alexander Dumas père, and *The Vampire, or the Bride of the Isles*, by J. R.

Planche, were presented in the London theater. The latter which was published in 1820 is remarkably similar to *The Vampyre*, a novelette by Polidori, published in 1819,—the story written after the famous ghost session where Byron, the Shelleys, and Polidori agreed each to write a ghostly story, Mary Shelley writing *Frankenstein*.

Polidori's story, like the play referred to, has for its principal character an Englishman, Lord Ruthven, the Earl of Marsden, who is the vampire. In each case there is a supposed death, where the dying man asks that his body be placed where the last rays of the moon can fall upon it. The corpse then mysteriously vanishes. In each story there is a complication of a rash pledge of silence made by a man that discovers the diabolical nature of the earl, who, having risen from the dead, is ravaging society as a vampire. In each case a peculiar turn of the story is that the masculine vampire requires for his subsistence the blood of young women, to whom he must be married. He demands a new victim, hence a hurried wedding is planned. In the play the ceremony is interrupted by the bride's father, but in the novelette the plot is finished and the girl becomes the victim of the destroyer. It is a question which of these productions was written first, and which imitated the other, or if they had a common source. The author of the drama admits getting his material from a French play, but where did Polidori get his?

Byron seems to have been fascinated with the vampire theme, for in addition to his unsuccessful short story, he has used the theme in his poem, *The Giaour*. Here he brings in the idea that the vampire curse is a judgment from God for sin, and that the most terrible part of the punishment is the being forced to prey upon those who in life were dearest to him, which idea occurs in various stories.

"But first on earth as Vampyre sent
Thy corse shall from its tomb be rent;
Then ghastly haunt thy native place
And suck the blood of all thy race;
There from thy *daughter, sister, wife*,
At midnight drain the stream of life;
Yet loathe the banquet which perforce
Must feed thy livid, living corse.
Thy victims, ere they yet expire
Shall know the demon for their sire;
As, cursing thee, thou cursing them,
Thy flowers are withered on the stem.
But one, that for thy crime must fall,
The youngest, best-beloved of all,
Shall bless thee with a *father's* name—
That word shall wrap thy heart in flame!
Yet must thou end the task and mark
Her cheek's last tinge, her eye's last spark,
And the last glassy glance must view
Which freezes o'er its lifeless blue;
Then with unhallowed hand shall tear
The tresses of her yellow hair,
Of which, in life, a lock when shorn
Affection's fondest pledge was worn,—
But now is borne away by thee
Memorial of thine agony!
Yet with thine own best blood shall drip
Thy gnashing teeth and haggard lip;
Then stalking to thy sullen grave
Go—and with ghouls and Afrits rave,
Till these in horror shrink away
From specter more accursed than they!"

Southey in his *Thalaba* shows us a vampire, a young
girl in this case, who has been torn away from her husband
on their wedding day. The curse impels her to attack
him, to seek to drain his lifeblood. He becomes

aware of the truth and takes her father with him to the
tomb, to await her coming forth at midnight, which is
the striking hour for vampires. When she appears,
"in her eyes a brightness more terrible than all the
loathsomeness of death," her father has the courage to
strike a lance through her heart to dispel the demon and
let her soul be at peace.

> "Then howling with the wound
> The fiendish tenant fled. . . .
> And garmented with glory in their sight
> Oneiza's spirit stood."

Keats uses the Greek idea of the vampire as a lamia or
beautiful young woman luring young men to death,—
the same theme employed by Goethe in his *Die Braut
von Corinth*. In *Lamia*, when the evil spirit in the form
of a lovely, alluring woman, is accused by the old philosopher, she gives a terrible scream and vanishes. This
vanishing business is a favorite trick with vampires—
they leave suddenly when circumstances crowd them.

F. Marion Crawford, in *For the Blood Is the Life*, has
given us a terrible vampire story, in which the dream
element is present to a marked degree. The young man,
who has been vainly loved by a young girl, is after her
death vampirized by her, something after the fashion
of Turgeniev's Clara Militch, and when his friends get
an inkling of the truth, and go to rescue him, they find
him on her grave, a thin red line of blood trickling from
his throat.

And the flickering light of the lantern played upon another
face that looked up from the feast,—upon two deep, dead
eyes that saw in spite of death—upon parted lips redder than
life itself—upon gleaming teeth on which glistened a rosy
drop.

The hawthorne stake is driven through her heart and the vampire expires after a terrific struggle, uttering diabolic, human shrieks. There is a certain similarity between this and Gautier's *La Morte Amoreuse*, where the truth is concealed till the last of the story and only the initiated would perhaps know that the reincarnated woman was a vampire. It is also a bit like Turgeniev's *Phantoms*, where a subtle suggestion at the last gives the reader the clue to vampirism, though the author really asks the question at the close, Was she a vampire? The character of the woman is problematic here, as in Gautier's story, less pronounced than in Crawford's.

The idea of occult vampirism used by Turgeniev is also employed by Reginald Hodder in his work, *The Vampire*. Here peculiar power is possessed by a woman leader of an occult band, who vampirizes by means of a talisman. Her ravages are psychic rather than physical. Theosophists, according to the *Occult Magazine*, believe in vampires even in the present. According to their theory, one who has been very wicked in life is in death so inextricably entangled with his evil motives and acts that he is hopelessly lost and knows it, yet seeks to delay for a time his final damnation. He can ward off spiritual death so long as he can keep alive by means of blood his physical corpse. The *Occult Review* believes that probably only those acquainted with black magic in their lifetime can become vampires,—a thought comforting to some of us.

It is in Bram Stoker's *Dracula* that one finds the tensest, most dreadful modern story of vampirism. This novel seems to omit no detail of terror, for every aspect of vampire horror is touched upon with brutal and ghastly effect. The combination of ghouls, vampires, ghosts, werewolves, and other awful elements is almost unendurable, yet the book loses in effect toward the last, for the mind cannot endure four hundred pages of vampiric outrage and respond to fresh impressions of horror. The initial vampire here is a Hungarian count, who, after terrorizing his own country for years, transports himself to England to start his ravages there. Each victim in turn becomes a vampire. The combination of modern science with medieval superstition to fight the scourge, using garlic and sprigs of the wild rose together with blood transfusion, is interesting. All the resources of modern science are pitted against the infection and the complications are dramatically thrilling. The book is not advised as suitable reading for one sitting alone at night.

There are other types of vampirism in addition to the conventional theme and the occult vampirism. H. G. Wells gives his customary twist of novelty to supernaturalism by the introduction of a botanical vampire in his *The Flowering of the Strange Orchid*. An orchid collector is found unaccountably dead in a jungle in the Andaman Islands, with a strange bulb lying under him, which bulb is brought to England and watched carefully by a botanist there till it comes to flower. When at last its blossoms burst open, great tentacles reach out to grasp the man, sucking his blood and strangling him. The tentacles dripping blood have to be torn away and the man snatched violently from the plant just in time to save his life.

Algernon Blackwood, who has touched upon every terrible aspect of supernaturalism, gives us two types of vampires in his story, *The Transfer*. The one is a psychic vampire, stealing the vital power from others, a human sponge, absorbing the strength, the ideas, the soul, of others. The governess describes him: "I watched his hard, bleak face; I noticed how thin he was, and the curious, oily brightness of his steady eyes. And everything he said or did announced what I may dare to call the *suction* of his presence." This human vampire comes in contact with one of another sort, a soil vampire, the Forbidden Corner, a bald, sore place in the rose garden, like a dangerous bog. The woman and a little child know the truth of this spot so barren in the midst of luxurious growth, so sinister in its look and implication. The child says of it, "It's bad. It's hungry. It's dying because it can't get the food it wants. But I know what would make it feel right." The earth vampire stretches out silent feelers from its secret strength when the man comes near the evil spot; the empty, yawning spot gives out audible cries, then laughs hideously as the man falls forward into the middle of the patch. "His eyes, as he dropped, faded shockingly, and across the countenance was written plainly what I can only call an expression of destruction." The man lives on physically, yet without vitality, without real life. But it was otherwise with the Forbidden Corner, for soon "it lay untouched, full of great, luscious, driving weeds and creepers, very strong, full-fed and bursting thick with life."

And so the vampire stories vary in theme and in treatment. Indian folk-tales appearing in English show that the Jigar-Khor, or Liver-eater of India is a cousin to the vampire, for he can steal your liver by just looking at you. (It has long been known that hearts can be filched in this way, but the liver wrinkle is a new one.) There are several points to be noted in connection with these stories of the Un-dead, the incorruptible corpses, the loathsome spirits that haunt the living. Many of the stories have a setting in the countries where the vampire superstition has been most common, though there are English settings as well. Continental countries are richer in vampire lore than England, which explains the location of the incidents even in many English stories and poems.

Another point to be noted is the agreement of the stories in the essential features. While there are numerous variants, of course, there is less divergence than in the case of ghosts, for instance. The description of the dæmonic spirit tenanting the body of a dead person, driving him by a dreadful urge to attack the living, especially those dear to him in life, is much the same. The personality of the vampire may vary, in one line of stories being a young woman who lures men to death, in the other a man who must quench his thirst with the blood of brides. These are the usual types, though there are other variants.

The Werewolf and Others. Another dæmonic figure popular in fiction is the werewolf. The idea is a very old one, having been mentioned by various classical writers, it is said, including Pomponius Mela, Herodotus, and Ovid. The legend of the werewolf is found in practically all European countries, especially those where the wolf is common. In France many stories of the loup-garou are current. The werewolf is a human being cursed with the power or the obligation to be transformed into an animal who goes forth to slay and devour. Like a vampire, he might become such as a curse from God, or he might be an innocent victim, or might suffer from an atavistic tendency, a cannibalistic craving for blood. Distinction is to be made between the real werewolf and the lycanthrope,—the latter a human being who, on account of some peculiar twist of insanity, fancies himself a wolf and acts accordingly. There is such a character in *The Duchess of Malfi*, a maniac who thinks himself a mad wolf, and another in *The Albigenses*, a creature that crouches in a corner of its lair, gnawing at a skull snatched from the graveyard, uttering bestial growls. Algernon Blackwood has a curdling story of lycanthropy, where the insane man will eat nothing but raw meat and devours every-

thing living that he can get hold of. He confesses to a
visitor that he used to bite his old servant, but that he
gave it up, since the old Jew tasted bitter. The servant
also is mad, and "hides in a vacuum" when his master
goes on a rampage. Stories of lycanthropy illustrate an
interesting aspect of the association between insanity
and the supernatural in fiction.

The most revolting story of lycanthropy is in Frank
Norris's posthumous novel, *Vandover and the Brute*. This
is a study in soul degeneration, akin to the moral decay
that George Eliot has shown in the character of Tito
Melema, but grosser and utterly lacking in artistic restraint. We see a young man, at first sensitive, delicate,
and with high ideals, gradually through love of ease and
self-indulgence, through taking always the line of least
resistance, becoming a moral outcast. The brute that
ever strains at the leash in man gains the mastery and the
artist soul ends in a bestial creature. Dissipation brings
on madness, called by the doctors "lycanthropy-mathe-
sis." In his paroxysms of insanity the wretch thinks
that his body is turned into the beast that his soul symbolizes, and runs about his room, naked, four-footed,
growling like a jungle animal and uttering harsh, raucous
cries of *Wolf-wolf!*

Kipling's *The Mark of the Beast* is midway between a
lycanthrope and a werewolf story, for while the soul of the
beast—or whatever passes for the brutish soul—enters
into the man and drives out his spirit, and while
many bestial characteristics result, including the revolting odor, the man does not change his human
form.

While lycanthropy has never been a frequent theme in
fiction, the werewolf is a common figure, appearing in
various forms of literature, from medieval ballads and
legends to modern short stories. Marie de France, the

Anglo-Norman writer,[1] tells of a werewolf that is by day a gallant knight and kindly gentleman, yet goes on nocturnal marauding expeditions.   When his wife shows curiosity concerning his absences and presses him for an explanation, he reluctantly tells her that he is a werewolf, hiding his clothes in a hollow tree, and that if they were removed he would have to remain a wolf.   She has her lover steal his clothes, then marries the lover.   One day long afterward the king's attention is called to a wolf that runs up to him and acts strangely.   It is a tame and well-mannered beast till the false knight and his wife appear, when he tries to tear their throats.   Investigation reveals the truth, the clothes are fetched, and the curse removed. Arthur O'Shaughnessy's modern version of this, as of others of Marie's *lais*, is charming.

Like the vampire, the werewolf is under a curse that impels him to prey upon those dearest to him.   Controlled by a dæmonic spirit, the human being, that in his normal personality is kindly and gentle, becomes a jungle beast with ravening instincts.   The motif is obviously tangled up with the vampire superstition here, and it would be interesting, if possible, to trace out the two to a point of combination.   This irresistible impulse to slay his dear ones introduces a dramatic element into the plot, here as in the vampire stories.   The wolf is not the only animal around whom such plots center, but being most common he has given his name to the type.   *The Albigenses* tell of a young husband who, as a werewolf, slays his bride, then vanishes to be seen no more.

There are interesting variants of the werewolf story, introducing other elements of supernaturalism.   In *A Vendetta of the Jungle*,[2] we have the idea of successive infection of the moral curse, similar to the continuation of

[1] In her lay of *Bisclaverat*.
[2] By Arthur Applier and H. Sidney Warwick.

vampirism. Mrs. Crump, a lady in India, is eaten by a tiger, who has a good digestion for he assimilates not only her body but her soul. So that now it is Mrs. Crump-Tiger, we might say, that goes about the jungle eating persons. In time she devours her successor in her husband's affection. The man is aware that it is his first wife who has eaten his second, so he starts out to kill the animal to clear off the score. But by the time he reaches the jungle the beast has had time to digest his meal and when the husband levels his gun to fire, the eyes that look out at him from the brutish face are his beloved's eyes. What could he do?

Eugene Field gives a new turn to the idea by representing the werewolf curse as a definite atavistic throw-back. His wolf-man is an innocent marauder, the reincarnation of a wicked grandfather, yet a gentle, chivalrous soul very different from his grandparent. The old gentleman has left him heir to nothing but the curse and a magic spear given him by the witch Brunhilde. The werewolf bears a charmed life against which no weapon of man can avail, and the country is panic-stricken over his ravages. The legend is that the beast's fury cannot be stopped till some man offers himself as a voluntary sacrifice to the wolf. The youth does not know that he is the guilty one until his reprehensible grandfather appears to him in a vision, demanding his soul. He hears that there is to be a meeting in the sacred grove on a certain day and begs his beloved to remain away, lest the werewolf come. But when she insists that she will go, he gives her his magic spear, telling her to strike the wolf through the heart if he approaches her. True to his accursed destiny the wolf does come to the grove and lunges at the girl. All the men flee but one, and his weapons fail,—then the terrified girl hurls the spear, striking the beast to the heart. But when he falls, it is young Harold who is dying, who has given himself a voluntary sacrifice to save others. The curse is lifted but he is dead.

In *The Camp of the Dog*, by Algernon Blackwood, we have another unconscious werewolf, a gentle, modest, manly young fellow madly in love with a girl who doesn't care for him. In his sleep he goes questing for her. While his body lies shrunken on a cot in his tent, his soul takes the form of a wolf and goes to the hilltop, uttering unearthly howls. By an equally strong psychic disturbance the girl is impelled to go in a somnambulistic state to the hilltop. Each is in waking hours utterly unaware of their strange jaunts, till the father shoots the wolf. The young man in this case suffers only curious psychic wounds, from which he recovers when the girl promises to marry him, and the wolf is seen no more.

The panther plays his part in this were-menagerie. Ambrose Bierce, in *The Eyes of the Panther*, tells of a young girl who, because of a prenatal curse similar to that affecting Elsie Venner, is not wholly human. She is conscious of her dual nature and tells the man she loves that she cannot marry him since she is a panther by night. He thinks her mildly insane till one night a settler sees a beast's eyes glaring into his window and fires. When they follow the blood-tracks, they find the girl dying. This is one of the conventions of the werewolf story, the wounding of an animal that escapes and the blood-trail that leads to a human being wounded just as the beast was.

Elliott O'Donnell, in a volume called *Werewolves* published in London in 1912, gives serious credence to the existence of werewolves not only in the past but also in the present. He tells a number of stories of what he claims are authenticated instances of such beings in actual life. He relates the experience of a man who told him that he had himself seen a youth turn himself into a tiger after preparatory passes of enchantment. The watcher made haste to climb a sacred Vishnu tree when the transformation was complete. O'Donnell tells a tale of a widow with three children that married a Russian nobleman. She saw him and his servant change into werewolves, at least partially, remaining in a half state, devouring her children whom she left behind in her escape.

O'Donnell relates several stories of authentic (according to him) werewolf stories of England in recent times, giving the dates and places and names of the persons who saw the beasts. The incidents may be similar to those spoken of in Dicken's *Haunted House*, where the famous "'ooded woman with the howl" was seen,—or at least, many persons saw the owl and knew that the woman must be near by. These witnesses of werewolves may have seen animals, all right enough. Modernity is combined with medieval superstition here, and it seems uncanny, for instance, to identify a werewolf by means of an electric pocket flashlight.

In collections of folk-tales, the tribal legends of the American redmen as well as of Kipling's India and of England, there are various stories of werewolves. Among primitive peoples there is a close relation between the brute and the human and the attributing of human characteristics and powers to the beast and *vice versa* is common, so that this supernatural transfer of personality is natural enough. A madwolf might suggest the idea for a werewolf.

Algernon Blackwood advances the theory that the werewolf is a true psychical fact of profound importance, however it may have been garbled by superstition. He thinks that the werewolf is the projection of the untamed slumbering sanguinary instincts of man, "scouring the world in his fluidic body, the body of desire." As the mind wanders free from the conscious control of the will in sleep, so the body may free itself from the fetters of mind or of custom and go forth in elemental form to satisfy its craving to slay, to slake its wild thirst for blood. O'Donnell says that werewolves may be phantasms of the dead that cannot be at peace, or a certain kind of Elementals. He also thinks that they may be the projection of one phase of man's nature, of the cruelty latent in mankind that seeks expression in this way. According to that theory, a chap might have a whole menagerie inside him, to turn loose at intervals, which would be exciting but rather risky for society. It was doubtless a nature such as this that Maupassant attempts to describe in his story *The Wolf*, where the man has all the instincts of the wolf yet never changes his human form.

The werewolf in fiction has suffered the same leveling influence that we have observed in the case of the ghost, the devil, the witch, and the vampire. He is becoming a more psychical creature, a romantic figure to be sympathized with, rather than a beast to be utterly condemned. In recent fiction the werewolf is represented as an involuntary and even unconscious departure from the human, who is shocked when he learns the truth about himself. Whether he be the victim of a divine curse, an agent of atavistic tendencies, or a being who thus gives vent to his real and brutish instincts, we feel a sympathy with him. We analyze his motives—at a safe distance—seek to understand his vagaries and to estimate his kinship with us. We think of him now as a noble figure in fiction, a lupine Galahad like Blackwood's, a renunciatory hero like Eugene Field's or what not. Or we reflect that he may be a case of metempsychosis and treat him courteously, for who knows what we may be ourselves some day? The werewolf has not figured in poetry or in the drama as have other supernatural beings, as the ghost, the devil, the witch, the vampire,—one wonders why.   He is a dramatic figure and his character-analysis might well furnish themes for poetry though stage presentation would have its difficulties.

.Perhaps the revival of interest in Elizabethan literature has had a good deal to do with the use of supernatural beings in literature of recent times.   The devil and the dæmonic spirits he controls, the witches and wizards, the vampires, the enchanted animals, to whom he delegates a part of his infernal power, appear as impressive moral allegories, mystical stories of life, symbols of truths.   As literature is a reflection of life, the evil as well as the good enters in.   But since the things of the spirit are intangible they must be represented in concrete form, as definite beings whom our minds can apprehend.   Thus the poets and dramatists and story-makers must show us images to shadow forth spiritual things.   As with a shudder we close the books that tell us horrifying tales of satanic spirits, of accursed beings that are neither wholly animal nor human, of mortals with diabolic powers, we shrink from the evils of the soul that they represent, and recognize their essential truth in the guise of fiction.

V
Supernatural Life

THE fiction dealing with immortal life shows, more than any other aspect of the subject, humanity's deep hunger for the supernatural. Whether it be stories of continuance of earthly existence without death as in the legends of the undying persons like the Wandering Jew; or of supernaturally renewed or preserved youth as described in the tales of the elixir of life; or of the transference of the soul after death into another body; or of life continued in the spirit in other worlds than this after the body's death,—all show our craving for something above and beyond what we know here and now. Conscious of our own helplessness we long to feel ourselves leagued with immortal powers; shrinking affrighted from the grave's near brink we yearn for that which would spare us death's sting and victory. Sadly knowing with what swift, relentless pace old age is overtaking us we would fain find something to give us eternal youth. But since we cannot have these gifts in our own persons we seek them vicariously in fiction, and for a few hours' leisured forgetfulness we are endowed with immortal youth and joy. Or, looking past death, we can feel ourselves more than conquerors in a life beyond.

"Oh world unknowable, we touch thee!
Inapprehensible, we clutch thee!"

174

We somehow snatch a strange comfort from these stories of a life beyond our own. We are comforted for our mortality when we see the tragedy that dogs the steps of those who may not die, whether Swift's loathsome Struldbrugs or the Wandering Jew. Our own ignorance of the future makes us credulous of any man's dream of heaven and at the same time sceptical of anybody else's hell. We are such indestructible optimists that we can take any sort of raw material of fiction and transmute it into stuff that hope is made of.

The Wandering Jew. There is no legend more impressive than that of the Wandering Jew, and none save the Faust theme that has so influenced literature. The story is as deathless as the person it portrays and has wandered into as many lands, though it is impossible to trace with certainty its origin or first migrations. There is an Arabian legend of one Samiri who forever wanders, crying, "Touch me not!" as there is a Buddhist account of a man cursed for working miracles for show, to whom Buddha said, "Thou shalt not attain Nirvana while my religion lasts." There are similar Chinese and Indian versions and the idea occurs in English folk-tales, where the plovers are thought to be the souls of those that crucified Christ, condemned to fly forever over the world, uttering their plaintive cry.

The first appearance of the Wandering Jew in English literature is in the Chronicles of Roger of Wendover, who reports the legend as being told at the monastery of St. Albans by an Armenian bishop, in 1228, but to hearers already familiar with it. There are two distinct versions of the story appearing in English literature. One relates that the wanderer is a certain Cartapholus, a servant in Pilate's palace, who struck Jesus a brutal blow as He was led forth to death, and to whom He said, "Thou shalt wander till I come!" The other is of German origin giving the personality of Ahasuerus, a shoemaker of Jerusalem, who mocked the Savior as He passed to Golgotha.   Bowed under the weight of the cross, Christ leaned for a moment's rest against the door of the little shop, but Ahasuerus said scornfully, "Go faster, Jew!"   With one look of deep reproach, Christ answered, "I go, but tarry thou till I come!"

The Wandering Jew story is cosmopolitan, used in the literature of many lands.   In Germany it has engaged the attention of Berthold Auerbach, Kingemann, Schlegel, Julius Mosen, and Chamisso, in France that of Edgar Quinet and Eugene Sue.   Hans Christian Andersen has used it while Heijermans has written a Dutch play on it and Carmen Sylva, late Queen of Roumania, made it the basis for a long dramatic poem.

The theme has appeared in various forms in English literature, besides in fiction where it has been most prominent.   A comedy[1] was published in 1797, by Andrew Franklin, though the wanderer is here used only as a hoax. Wordsworth has a poem entitled *The Song of the Wandering Jew*, and Shelley was fascinated by the legend, as we see from the fact that he used it three times.   One of his first poems, a long dramatic attempt, written at eighteen, is *The Wandering Jew*, a fevered poem showing the same weaknesses that his Gothic romances reveal, yet with a hint of his later power.   The Wandering Jew appears as a definite character in both *Queen Mab* and *Hellas*, in the first Ahasuerus being summoned to testify concerning God, while he appears in the latter to give supernatural vision of events.   In both poems he is very old, for in the first it is said:

"His port and mien bore marks of many years. . . .

"Yet his cheek bore the mark of youth," while in the latter he is described as being "so old he seems to have

---

[1] *The Wandering Jew*, or *Love's Masquerade*.

outlived a world's decay." Shelley follows the German version, as used in a fragment he picked up torn and soiled in Lincoln's Inn Fields, whose author he did not know.

Mr. Eubule-Evans, in a long dramatic poem of considerable power,[1] tells the story of Theudas, who could be released from his doom of immortality if only he would repent, but he will not. He renews his youth every forty years, growing suddenly from a decrepit man to a handsome, gifted youth, which naturally suggests complications of human love-affairs. Other elements of supernaturalism are used, as angels, demons, and so forth while the Æons and the Intermedii (whoever they are!) appear as chorus.

The Wandering Jew, a Christmas Carol,[2] retells the story with variations and with some power. The Jew here is shown to be very old and feeble, clad in antique raiment, with stigmata of the wounds on hands and feet. He is symbolic of the Christ, of His failure to win men.

> "For lo, at last I knew
>   The lineaments of that diviner Jew,
>   That like a Phantom passeth everywhere,
>   The world's last hope and bitterest despair,
>   Deathless, yet dead!
>   And lo! while all men come and pass away
>   That phantom of the Christ, forlorn and gray,
>   Haunteth the earth, with desolate footfall."

The Wandering Jew is seen definitely once in Gothic fiction, in Lewis's *The Monk*, where a mysterious stranger, bearing on his forehead a burning cross imprinted, appears and is spoken of as the Wandering Jew. He is unable to stay more than fourteen days in any one place but must

---

[1] *The Curse of the Wandering Jew.*   [2] By Robert Buchanan.

forever hurry on. Rev. T. Clark[1] gives a bird's-eye
view of history such as a person of the long life and exten-
sive migrations of the wanderer would see it.

The idea of a deathless man appealed strongly to Hawthorne, who plays with the theme in various passages
in his works and notebooks. In *A Virtuoso's Collection*,
where Peter Rugg, the Missing Man, is door-keeper and
where the collection includes a letter from the Flying
Dutchman to his wife, together with a flask of the elixir
of life, the virtuoso himself is none other than the Wandering Jew. He speaks of his destiny and says that human
prayers will not avail to aid him. The touch of his hand
is like ice, conveying a sense of spiritual as well as physical
chill. The character appears also as one of the guests
in *A Select Party*, of whom the author remarks: "This
personage, however, had latterly grown so common by
mingling in all sorts of society and appearing at the beck
of every entertainer that he could hardly be deemed a
proper guest in an exclusive circle." This bit of satire
illustrates how common the theme had become at that
time in fiction.

There are various threads of narration tangled up with
the Wandering Jew motif. He is said by some writers
to have supernatural power to heal disease, while by others
he is thought to be the helpless bearer of evil and death.
Eugène Sue in his novel represents him as carrying the
plague, knowing his awful destiny, yet, while wildly
regretting it, powerless in the clutch of fate. Here he
appears as a voluntary agent of good toward the Rennepont family and an involuntary minister of evil in other
ways. An anonymous story[2] uses the same idea of the
plague association but carries it further, for here the

[1] In *The Wandering Jew*, or the *Travels and Observations of Bareach
the Prolonged*.

[2] *In the Track of the Wandering Jew*.

wanderer is not a personality but the plague itself, passing like a doom over the world, which shows how far that phase of the legend has gone.

The legend has been utilized variously to impress religious truths. Charles Granville[1] writes a symbolic story with a definite religious message. The idea of the immortal wanderer is represented as the concept of a part of humanity urged by an earnest longing which dominates their whole life and thought, the desire that a new kingdom of God might come. The book is a social satire, an appeal for the coming of a real democracy, real justice and genuine spirituality. George Croly[2] has for his purpose the proving that Christ's second coming is near at hand. Lew Wallace, who himself uses the theme of the Wanderer, thought this book one of the half dozen volumes which taken alone would constitute a British literature. We are likely to find ourselves questioning Wallace's judgment in the matter, for while the novel is interesting and has a sermon impressed with some interest, it is by no means a great piece of literature. Salathiel is pictured as a young, enthusiastic, passionate Jew striving to defend his country against the woes that threaten her. His life is given in detail immediately following his unpardonable sin, and his definite career ends with the destruction of Jerusalem, though his immortality is suggested at the close. The book describes many supernatural happenings, the miraculous phenomena accompanying the death of Christ and manifestations following the fate of the city.

In Lew Wallace's *The Prince of India* the deathless man appears again. In the beginning of the story he enters a vault from which he removes the treasure from mummy cases, remarking that the place has not been visited since he was there a thousand years before. He

[1] In *The Plaint of the Wandering Jew.*
[2] In *Salathiel the Immortal,* or *Tarry Thou Till I Come.*

has numerous impressive experiences, such as seeing a
monk that seems the reincarnation of Jesus, and hearing
again the centurion's call to him. Wallace pictures the
Jew as old, a philosopher, in contrast to Salathiel's impetu-
ous youth. He is striving to bring the sons of men into
closer spiritual truth with each other and with God, as
Salathiel tries to prevent the material destruction of the
city. The sense of responsibility, the feeling of a mission
toward others, expressed in this novel, may be compared
with that of Eugène Sue's Wandering Jew who acts as a
friend to the Rennepont family, protecting their interests
against the wily Jesuits.

The Wandering Jew has been represented in many
ways, with stress placed on various aspects of his life
and character. He has been depicted psychologically,
as a suffering human being, mythologically to illustrate
the growth and change in life, religiously to preach
certain tenets and beliefs, and symbolically to show
forth the soul of man. He appears symbolically as the
creature accursed of God, driven forever in the face of
doom. Shelley and others show him as vainly attempting
suicide, but living on, anguished yet deathless, in the face
of every effort to take his own life as in the teeth of torture
from others. He stands at once for the undying power
of God's plan, and, as in Robert Buchanan's version, for
the typified failure of Christ's mission. He is used to
prove that Christ's second coming is near, and to prove
also that He will never come. To the Christian he stands
for the evidence of Christ's power of divinity, while to
the Jew he is a symbol of that unhappy race that wanders
ever, with no home in any land.

Besides those mentioned, other English and American
writers who have made use of the legend are Kipling;
Bram Stoker, who discusses him in his assembly of Famous
Impostors; M. D. Conway, who gives various versions

of the story; David Hoffman, Henry Seton Merriman, S. Baring-Gould, W. H. Ainsworth, and others.

A legend closely associated with this and yet separate, is that of a woman who bore the curse of eternal wandering. One version brings in Herodias as the doomed woman, while the character of Kundry in *Parsifal* represents another feminine wanderer. William Sharp, in his *Gypsy Christ*, gives the story differently still, saying that it is not correctly told in *Parsifal*. As Sharp tells it, it is a piece of tragic symbolism. Kundry, a gypsy woman of evil life, mocks Christ on Golgotha and demands of Him a sign, to whom He says, "To thee and thine I bequeath the signs of my Passion to be a shame and horror among thy people forevermore!" Upon her hands and feet appear the stigmata of His wounds, never to fade away, and to be borne by her descendants in every third generation. Various ones of her descendants are crucified, and wherever the wanderers go on earth they bear the marks of horror. The curse would be lifted from them only when a Gypsy Christ should be born of a virgin; but then the Children of the Wind should be dispersed and vanish from among men. In the last chapter Naomi prophesies that she is to give birth to the Gypsy Christ.

The theme of the Wandering Jew, while rivalling the Faust legend in impressiveness and in the frequence with which it has been used in literature, yet is different in having had no adequate representation. No truly great poem or drama or novel has been written concerning this tragic, deathless character. Perhaps it may come yet. Only hints of his personality have appeared in very recent fiction, such as the reincarnation in the character of the young Jew in A. T. Quiller-Couch's story, *The Mystery of Joseph Laquedem,* or the humorous reference to him in Brander Matthews's *Primer of Imaginary Geography*, or *The Holy Cross* by Eugene Field, where the wanderer is pitied by a Spanish priest in Cortez's train in Mexico. His prayers win forgiveness and the tortured Jew dies. After his death an earthquake supernaturally splits a gulf on each side of the grave and a cross of snow appears there, to remain forever. Perhaps the theme is fading out now in fiction and drama, to disappear completely, or perhaps it is lying forgotten for a while, waiting the master hand that shall give it adequate treatment.

Elixir of Life. Immortality that proves such a curse in the case of the Wandering Jew forms the basis for various other stories. The elixir of life was a favorite theme with the Gothicists, being used by Maturin, Godwin, and Shelley, and has continued to furnish complication for fiction since that time. The theme has been popular on the continent as well as in England, Balzac and Hoffman being the most impressive users of it.

Bulwer-Lytton, in *A Strange Story*, introduces the elixir of life together with other forms of supernaturalism, such as mesmerism, magic, spectral apparitions, invisible manifestations, awful bodiless Eyes, a gigantic Foot, and so forth. Margrave attempts to concoct the potion that shall give him endless life, but after mysterious preparations, incantations, and supernatural manifestations, at the crucial moment a stampede of maddened beasts, urged forward by the dreadful Foot, dashes the beaker from his lips. The irreplaceable liquid wastes its force on the desert sands, where a magic richness of herbage instantly springs up in contrast to the barrenness around it. Flowers bloom, myriads of insects hover round them, and all is life, but the man who sought the elixir with such pains lies dead. The author suggests a symbolic meaning for his story, hinting that the scientist's laboratory holds many elixirs of life, that all growth and life are magical, that all being is miraculous.

Rider Haggard, in *She* and *Ayesha*, its sequel, describes a wonderful woman who possesses the secret of eternal life and has lived for thousands of years, ever young and beautiful, supernaturally enchanting. Her magic potion not only gives her length of days but protection against danger as well, for her rival's dagger glances harmlessly away from her, and she is proof against chance and fate. She gains her immortal life partly by bathing in a secret essence or vapor whose emanations give her mystic force and immortal beauty. There are many other elements of supernaturalism in association with the not impossible She,—magic vision, reincarnation, a mystic light that envelops her body, the power to call up the dead, to reanimate the skeletons in the desert and raise them to dreadful life. She is an interesting but fearsome personality.

In *Ahrinziman*, by Anita Silvani, we have magic chemistry yielding up the elixir of life. Jelul-uh-din has lived for five hundred years and looks forward to a still more protracted existence. His magic drug not only gives him prolonged life but will do anything he wishes besides, since he has hypnotized it. Yet he is found dead. "On his wrists were marks of giant fingers, scorched and burnt into the flesh like marks of hot iron. And on his throat were marks of a similar hand which had evidently strangled him." It is apparent that his master, the De'il, got impatient and cut short the leisurely existence that he felt belonged to him.

Hawthorne was greatly interested in the theme of the elixir of life. He gives us two brews of it in *Septimius Felton*, one an Indian potion concocted by an old sachem. The red man gets so old that his tribe find him a great nuisance and obstacle to progress so they gravely request permission to kill him. But his skull is so hard that the stone hammers are smashed when they try to brain him,

his skin so tough that no arrows will pierce it, and
nothing seems to avail. Finally they fill his mouth and
nostrils with clay and put him in the sun to bake, till
presently his heart bursts with a loud explosion, tearing
his body to fragments. This brew of his is matched by
one made by an European scientist after long endeavors.
Here the ultimate ingredient is supposed to be a strange
herb that grows from a mysterious grave. At last, just
when the youth thinks he has the right combination, the
woman who has lured him on to destruction dashes the
cup from his lips, saving him from the poison he would
have drunk. The flower has grown from the grave of
her lover, whom the young scientist has murdered.

In *The Dolliver Romance*, that pathetic fragment Hawthorne left unfinished at his death, we find another treatment of the theme. It seems symbolic that in his old
age and failing powers, he should have been thinking of
immortal youth, of deathless life. In this story various
magical elements are introduced. The herbs grown in
old Grandsir Dolliver's garden have a strange power,
for when a woman lays a flower from one on her breast,
it glows like a gem and lends a bloom of youth to her
cheeks. The old man seeks the one unknown essence,
the incalculable element necessary to make up the elixir
of life, as did the youth in *Septimius Felton*. He drinks
occasional mouthfuls of a strange cordial that he finds
in an old bottle on the shelf, and seems to grow younger
and stronger. He, too, like Septimius, has a visitor; a
man that demands the cordial as belonging to him by
ancestral right, snatches it from the aged hands, drinks
it down at a draught and grows violently young, but dies
in convulsions.

In *Dr. Heidigger's Experiment* Hawthorne gives us
another sad symbolic story of the quest of the elixir of
youth. The old physician invites four aged friends to

make an experiment, to drink of a cordial which shall restore youth, but which he himself is too wise to share. The strange potion proves its power by restoring to beauty and perfume a rose that has been dead for over fifty years. When the old persons drink they become young and happy and beautiful once more. Age drops from them like a mantle discarded and the world glows again with passion and color and joy. But alas! it is only ephemeral, for the effects soon pass away and senility is doubly tragic after one snatched hour of joy and youth. There is a sad philosophy of life expressed in these symbolic allegories such as Hawthorne alone knows how to tell.

Elsewhere Hawthorne shows his deep interest in the theme. In *The Birthmark* the scientist intimates that he could brew the life elixir if he would, but that it would produce a discord in nature such as all the world, and chiefly he that drank it, would curse at last. The subject is referred to in other places,[1] and a flask of the precious, dreadful elixir is one of the treasures in the Virtuoso's collection. In a note concerning his use of the theme in *The Dolliver Romance* Hawthorne states that he has been accused of plagiarizing from Dumas, but that in reality Dumas plagiarized from him, since his book was many years the earlier.

H. G. Wells[2] uses this theme combined with the transfer of personality. An aged man bargains with a youth to make him his heir on certain conditions. The purpose, unknown to the young fellow, is to rob him of his youth to reanimate the old man. A magic drink transfers the personality of the octogenarian to the body of youth and leaves the young man's soul cabined in the worn-out frame. But the drug is more powerful than Mr. Elvesham supposed, for it brings death to both who drink

[1] In *Dr. Bullivant.*
[2] In *The Story of the Late Mr. Elvesham.*

it and the bargain has a ghastly climax. Barry Pain has
a somewhat similar situation of the tragic miscalculation,
in *The Wrong Elixir*, the story of an alchemist who brews
the life-giving potion but means to keep it all to himself. On a certain night he will drink it and become im-
mortally young, in a world of dying men. While he waits,
a gypsy girl asks him to give her a poison to kill a man she
hates. He prepares the potion for her and sets it aside.
He drinks at the time he planned, but instead of eternal
life, the draught brings him swift-footed death. Does he
drink the wrong elixir, or have all his calculations been
wrong?

An example of the way in which the magic of the old
fiction of supernaturalism has been transferred into the
scientific in modern times, is seen in *The Elixir of Youth*,
by Albert Bigelow Paine. A man in an upper room
alone is wishing that he had the gift of immortal youth,
when a stranger in black enters and answers his thought.
He tells him that to read the mind is not black magic,
but science; that he is not a magician, but a scientist, and
as such he has compounded the elixir of youth, which he
will give to him. This drug will enable a man to halt his
age at any year he chooses and to make it permanent, as
Peter Ibbetson and the Duchess of Towers did in their
dream-life. The stranger leaves the flask with the man
and goes away. But the one who wished for immortal
life decides that after all God must know best, and,
though his decision not to drink has not crystalized, he
is not greatly sorry when the flask is shattered and the
liquid spilled. This is symbolic of the real wisdom of
life.

The frequent use of the theme of the elixir of life, of
deathless youth, illustrates how humanity clutches at
youth with pathos and shrinks from age. Red Ranrahan,
the loved singer of Ireland, whom W. B. Yeats creates

for us with unforgettable words, makes a curse against old age when he feels it creeping on him.

Various other stories of supernatural length of years appear in English fiction, besides those based on the definite use of the life elixir. *The Woman from Yonder*, by Stephen French Whitman, shows us the revived, re-animated body of a woman who has been buried in a glacier since Hannibal crossed the Alps, till she is dug out and miraculously restored, by blood-transfusion, by an interfering scientist. The writer queries, "If the soul exists, where had that soul been? What regions did it relinquish at the command of the reviving body?" A humorous application of the idea of the deathless man is seen in A. Conan Doyle's *The Los Amigos Fiasco*, where the citizens of a frontier town, wishing to kill a criminal by some other method than the trite rope, try to kill him by putting him in connection with a big dynamo. But their amateur efforts have a peculiar effect. They succeed only in so magnetizing his body that it is impossible for him to die. They try shooting, hanging, and so forth, but he has gained such an access of vitality from electricity that he comes out unscathed through everything, resembling the ancient sachem in Hawthorne's novel.

The Flying Dutchman forms the theme for stories in folklore, of a wanderer of the seas condemned to touch shore only once in seven years, because he swore he would round Cape Horn in spite of heaven and hell. Hawthorne has preserved a letter from the Dutchman to his wife, in the Virtuoso's collection, and John Kendrick Bangs has furnished the inevitable parody in his *Pursuit of the House-boat*. *The Dead Ship* of Harpwell is another story of a wandering, accursed ship. There is a similar legend told by C. M. Skinner,[1] of a man, who, for a cruel murder of a

[1] In *Myths and Legends of Our Land*.

servant, was condemned to wear always a halter round his neck and was unable to die.

Bram Stoker furnishes us with several interesting specimens of supernatural life, always tangled with other uncanny motives. The count, in *Dracula*, who has lived his vampire life for centuries, is said to be hale and fresh as if he were forty. Of course, all vampires live to a strange lease on life, but most of them are spirits rather than human beings as was Dracula. In *The Lair of the White Worm*, Stoker tells of a woman who was at once an alluring woman and a snake thousands of years old. The snake is so large that, when it goes out to walk, it looks like a high white tower, and can gaze over the tops of the trees.

Bulwer-Lytton's *The Haunters and the Haunted* tells the story of a mysterious being who passes through untold years with a strange power over life and the personality of others. He appears, no man knows whence nor why, and disappears as strangely, while about his whole career is a shroud of mystery. Thackeray, in his *Notch on the Axe*, burlesques this and similar stories in playful satire, yet seems to enjoy his theme. It is not wholly a burlesque, we may suppose. He adds a touch of realism to his humorous description by the fact that, throughout his hero's long-continued life, or series of lives—one doesn't know which—he retains always his German-Jewish accent. Andrew Lang describes[1] the person who may have been the original of these stories in real life. Horace Walpole has mentioned him in his letters and he seems to have a teasing mystery about his life and career that makes him much talked-of.

Edwin Lester Arnold[2] tells a story of continued life with an Oriental setting and mystery. Edward Bellamy's

[1] In *St. Germain the Deathless.*
[2] In *The Strange Adventures of Phra the Phœnician.*

Looking Backward, by the introduction of a magic sleep
makes a man live far beyond the natural span and be able
to see into the distant future, while the youth in Mark
Twain's *A Connecticut Yankee at King Arthur's Court* has
a magic length of life, living a dual existence, in Arthurian
England and in present-day America.   H. G. Wells[1] uses
something of the same idea, in that he makes his hero
live a very long time in a few hours, compressing time
into minute tabules, as it were, as he does in another story
of the magic accelerator that makes a man live fast and
furiously with tenfold powers at crucial moments.   The
story of Peter Rugg, the Missing Man, is that of another
immortal wanderer, whose story is told in *Myths and
Legends of Our Land,* and utilized by Alfred Austin.   He
goes out into a storm, saying, "I will see home to-night
or I will never see it!"   He flies forever pursued by the
storm, never resting, and never seeing his home.   This is
symbolic of the haunted soul pursued by its own destiny.

The theme of the elixir of life is one of the old motifs
of supernaturalism retained in modern fiction.   The conventional alchemist has given place to a more up-to-date
investigator in the chemical laboratory, yet the same thrill
of interest is imparted by the thought of a magic potion
prepared by man that shall endow him with earthly immortality.   The theme has changed less in its treatment
and symbolism than most of the supernatural elements in
fiction, for though we see the added elements of modern
satire and symbolism, its essential aspects remain the
same.

Metempsychosis. The idea of metempsychosis, the
thought that at death the soul of a human being may
pass into another mortal body or into a lower stage, into
an animal or even a plant, has been used considerably
in English fiction.   This Oriental belief has its basis in

[1] In his *Time Machine.*

antiquity, in animistic ideas in primitive culture. One of
the earliest appearances of the theme in English fiction is
that middle-eighteenth-century story of Dr. John Hawkesworth's,[1] an account of a soul that has not behaved itself
seemly, so descends in the spiritual scale till it ends by
being a flea. The German Hoffmann used the theme
repeatedly, and Poe, who was to a certain extent influenced
by his supernaturalism, employs it in several stories. In
A Tale of the Ragged Mountains, the young man named
Bedlo experiences, in dreams of extraordinary vividness,
the life of battle, of confusion, ending in death, in a tropi-
cal city. He sees himself die, struck on the temple by a
poisoned arrow. He is recognized by an elderly man as
the exact counterpart of a Mr. Oldeb who perished in the
manner dreamed of in a battle in Benares. Mr. Bedlo,
while wandering in the mountains of Virginia, contracts
a cold and fever, for the cure of which leeches are applied,
but by mistake a poisonous sangsue is substituted for the
leech, and the patient dies of a wound on the temple,
similar to that caused by a poisoned arrow. Poe's concept in other stories is not that of the conventionally
easy passage of the soul into the body of a new-born babe
that wouldn't be expected to put up much of a fight,
but he makes the psychic feature the central horror,
saying in that connection that man is on the brink of
tremendous psychical discoveries. In *Morella* the theme
is used with telling power, where the wife, once greatly
loved but now loathed, on her deathbed tells her husband
that her child will live after her. The daughter grows
up into supernatural likeness of her mother, but remains
nameless, since her father, for a reason he cannot analyze,
hesitates to give her any name. But at last, as she stands
before the altar to be christened, some force outside the
father causes him to call her Morella.

[1] *The Transmigration of a Soul.*

What more than fiend convulsed the features of my child, and overspread them with the hues of death, as, starting at that scarcely audible sound, she turned her glassy eyes from earth to heaven, and falling prostrate on the black slabs of our ancestral vault, responded, "I am here"!

The young girl is found to be dead and the father says: "With my own hands I bore her to the tomb; and I laughed, with a long and bitter laugh, as I found no traces of the first in the charnel where I laid the second Morella."

An obvious imitation of Poe's story is found in Bram Stoker's novel, *The Jewel of Seven Stars*, where the soul of an Egyptian princess enters into the body of a baby born to one of the explorers who rifle her tomb. The child grows into the perfect duplicate of the princess, even showing on her wrists the marks of violence that cut off the mummy's hand. The Egyptian's familiar, a mummified cat, comes to life to revenge itself upon the archæologists who have disturbed the tomb. When by magic incantations and scientific experiments combined, the collectors try to revivify the mummy, the body mysteriously disappears, and the young girl is found dead, leading us to suppose that the reanimated princess has stolen the girl's life for her own.

In *Ligeia*, another of Poe's morbid studies of metempsychosis, the theme is clearly announced, as quoted from Joseph Glanville: "Man doth not yield himself to the angels nor unto death utterly save only through the weakness of his own feeble will." The worshipped Ligeia dies, and in an hour of madness her husband marries the Lady Rowena. The bride soon sickens and as the husband watches alone by her bed at midnight, he sees drops of ruby liquid fall from some mysterious source, into the wine he is offering her. When the Lady Rowena presently dies, the husband, again alone with her, sees the corpse undergo an awful transformation. It is reanimated, but the body that lives is not that of Rowena, but of Ligeia, who has come back to life again by exerting her deathless will over the physical being of her rival. The climax with which the story closes has perhaps no parallel in fiction. As for the ruby drops, are we to think of them as an elixir of life for the dead Ligeia struggling back to being, or as poison to slay the living Rowena?

Ligeia's story is reflected, or at least shows an evident influence, in *The Second Wife*, by Mary Heaton Vorse. Here again the dead wife comes to oust her supplanter, but in this instance the interloper does not die, but without dying merely *becomes* the person and the personality of the first wife. The change is gradual but incontrovertible, felt by the woman herself before it is complete, and noticed by the husband and the mother-in-law. Here the human will, indestructible by death, asserts itself over mortal flesh and effects a transfer of personality. But where did the second wife's soul go, pray,—the "she o' the she" as Patience Worth would say?

A similar transfer of soul, effected while both persons are living but caused by the malignance of an evil dead spirit, is found in Blackwood's *The Terror of the Twins*. A father, who resents the fact that instead of a single heir twins are born to him, swears in his madness before he dies, that before their majority he will bring it to pass that there shall be only *one*. By the help of powers from the Pit he filches from the younger his vitality, his strength of mind and soul and body, his personality, and gives this access of power to the elder. The younger dies a hopeless idiot and the elder lives on with a double dower of being. Ambrose Bierce carries this idea to a climax of horror,[1] when he makes an evil spirit take possession of a dead mother's body and slay her son, who

---

[1] In *The Death of Halpin Frazer*.

recognizes his loved mother's face, knows that it is her eyes that glare fiend-like at him, her hands that are strangling him,—yet cannot know that it is a hideous fiend in her corpse.

The theme of metempsychosis is found tangled up with various other motives in fiction, the use of the elixir of life, hypnotism, dream-supernaturalism, witchcraft and so forth. Rider Haggard has given a curious combination of metempsychosis, and the supernatural continuance of life by means of the elixir, in *She* and its sequel, *Ayesha*. The wonderful woman, the dread She-who-must-be-obeyed who keeps her youth and beauty by means of bathing in the magic fluid, recognizes in various stages of her existence the lover whom she has known thousands of years before. Not having the advantage of the Turkish bath or patent medicine, he dies periodically and has to be born all over again in some other century. This is agitating to the lady, so she determines to inoculate him with immortality so that they can reign together without those troublesome interruptions of mortality. But the impatient lover insists on kissing her, which proves too much for him, since her divinity is fatal to mere mankind, so he dies again.

The close relation between metempsychosis and hypnotism is shown in various stories. Several cases of troublesome atavistic personality or reincarnation are cured by psychotherapy. Theodora, a young woman in a novel by Frances Fenwick Williams, bearing that title-name, realizes herself to be the reincarnation of a remote ancestress, an Orientalist, a witch, who has terrorized the country with her sorceries. She is cured of her mental hauntings by means of hypnotism. Another novel by the same author,[1] gives also the reincarnation of a witch character in modern life, with a cure effected by psycho-analysis.

[1] *A Soul on Fire.*

The young woman discovers herself to be the heiress of a curse, which is removed only after study of pre-natal influences and investigations concerning the subconscious self.

As is seen by these examples, the relation between witch-craft and metempsychosis is very close, since in recent fiction the witch characters have unusual powers of returning to life in some other form. In Algernon Black-wood's *Ancient Sorceries*, we have witch-metempsychosis on a large scale, the population of a whole village being but the reanimations of long-dead witches and wizards who once lived there. I know of no other case of mob-metempsychosis in English fiction, but the instances where several are reincarnated at once are numerous. Algernon Blackwood's recent novel, *Jules Le Vallon*, is based on a story of collective reincarnation, the chief characters in the dramatic action realizing that they have lived and been associated with each other before, and feeling that they must expiate a sin of a previous existence. Another recent novel by Blackwood, *The Wave*, has for its theme the reincarnation of the prin-cipal characters, realized by them. Blackwood has been much drawn to psychic subjects in general and metem-psychosis in particular, for it enters into many of his stories. In *Old Clothes* he gives us an instance of a child who knows herself to be the reborn personality of some one else and suffers poignantly in reliving the experiences of that long-dead ancestress, while those around her are recognized as the companions of her life of the far past, though they are unaware of it. The fatuous remark of lovers in fiction, that they feel that they have lived and loved each other in a previous exist-ence, is a literary bromide now, but has its basis in a recurrence in fiction. Antonio Fogazzaro's novel, *The Woman*, is a good example in Italian,—for the woman feels that she and her lover are reincarnations of long-dead selves who have suffered tragic experiences together, which morbid idea culminates in tragic madness.

The Mystery of Joseph Laquedem, by A. T. Quiller-Couch, is a striking story of dual reincarnation. A young Jew in England and a half-witted girl, a farmer's daughter, recognize in each other and in themselves, the personalities of a young Jew led to the lions for becoming a Christian, and a Roman princess who loved him. They recall their successive lives wherein they have known and loved each other, to be separated by cruel destiny each time, but at last they die a tragic death together. The character of the man here is given additional interest for us in that he is said to be a reincarnation of Cartapholus, Pilate's porter, who struck Jesus, bidding Him go faster, and who is immortalized as the Wandering Jew. Here he lives successive lives rather than a continuous existence. Somewhat similar to this is another combination of hypnotism and metempsychosis in *The Witch of Prague*, by F. Marion Crawford, where Uorna makes Israel Kafka go through the physical and psychical tortures of Simon Abeles, a young Jew killed by his people for becoming a Christian. By hypnotism the young man is made to pass through the experiences of a dead youth of whom he has never heard, and to die his death anew.

There is a close relation between dreams and metempsychosis, as is seen in certain stories. Kipling's charming prose idyll, *The Brushwood Boy*, may be called a piece of dream-metempsychosis, for the youth and girl when they first meet in real life recognize in each other the companions of their childhood and adolescent dream-life, and complete their dual memories. They have dreamed the same dreams even to minute details of conversation, and familiar names. Du Maurier combines the two motives very skillfully in his novels, for it is in successive dreams that the Martian reveals herself to Barty Joscelyn telling him of her life on another planet, and inspiring him to write—or writing for him—books of genius, before she takes up earthly life in one of his children.   She tells him that she will come to him no more in dreams, but that she will live in the child that is to be born.   And in dual dreams Peter Ibbetson and the Duchess of Towers live over again their childhood life together, are able to find at will their golden yesterdays, and know in happy reality the joys of the past, while the present keeps them cruelly apart.   They are able to call back to shadowy life their common ancestors, to see and hear the joys, the work, the griefs they knew so long ago.   They plumb their sub-consciousness, dream over again their sub-dreams, until they at last not only see these long-dead men and women, but *become* them.

We could each be Gatienne for a space (though not both of us together) and when we resumed our own personality again we carried back with it a portion of hers, never to be lost again—strange phenomenon if the reader will but think of it, and constituting the germ of a comparative personal immortality on earth.

Not only does Peter live in the past, but he has the power to transport these dead ancestors of his to his present and let them share in his life, so that Gatienne, a French woman dead for generations, lives over again in an English prison as Peter Ibbetson, or travels as Mary Towers, seeing things she never had dreamed of in her own life.

H. G. Wells in *A Dream of Armageddon* gives a curious story of the dream-future.   A man in consecutive visions sees himself killed.   He then dreams that he is another man, living in a different part of the world, far in the future, till he sees himself die in his second personality. He describes his experiences as given in "a dream so accurate that afterwards you remember little details you had forgotten." He suffers tortures of love and grief, so that his dream-life of the future is infinitely more real to him than his actual existence of his own time. What was the real "him o' him," to quote Patience Worth, the man of the dream-future, or the business man of the present telling the story to his friend?

A different version of metempsychosis is shown in *The Immortal Gymnasts*, by Marie Cher, for here the beloved trio, Pantaloon, Harlequin and Columbine are embodied as human beings and come to live among men. Harlequin has the power of magic vision which enables him to see into the minds and hearts of mortals by means of "cloud-currents." This question of—shall we say transmigration?—of fictive characters into actual life is found in various stories, such as Kipling's *The Last of the Stories*, John Kendrick Bangs' *The Rebellious Heroine*, and others. It illustrates the fantastic use to which every serious theme is sooner or later put. There is no motif in supernatural literature that is not parodied in some form or other, if only by suggestion.

The symbolic treatment of metempsychosis is strongly evident in recent fiction, as the theme lends itself particularly well to the allegoric and symbolic style. Barry Pain's *Exchange* shows aspects of transmigration different from the conventional treatment, for he describes the soul of the old man as giving up its right to peace that it might purchase ease for a soul he loved. He passes into the body of a captive bird beating its hopeless wings against the bars and tortured with pain and thirst, as a mark of the witch woman's wrath, while the soul of the young girl goes into the body of a snow-white lamb that lives a day then is set free. As she passes by, in the state of a freed soul, she sees the piteous bird, and says to herself, "I am glad I was never a bird."

Algernon Blackwood, in *The Return*, gives a peculiar story of metempsychosis, where the selfish materialist finds himself suddenly reinforced with a new personality from without. His eyes are opened miraculously to the magic and beauty of the world, and he knows beyond doubt that his friend, the artist, who promised to come to him when he died, has died and that his soul has become a part of his own being. The most impressive example of this sudden merging of two natures, two souls into one, is found in Granville Barker's *Souls on Fifth*. Here a man suddenly acquires, or recognizes, the power to see the souls that linger earth-bound around him, and comes to have a strange sympathy with that of a woman, whom he calls the "Little Soul." When he speaks of going away, after a time, she begs him not to leave her since she is very lonely in this wilderness of unbodied souls. She asks that if he will not take her into his soul, he carry her to some wide prairie, and there in the unspaced expanse leave her,—but instead he gives a reluctant consent for her to enter into his life. He presses the little symbolic figure to his heart, then feels a new sense of being, of personality, and knows that her soul has become forever a part of his.

Lord Dunsany, who lends a strange, new beauty to every supernatural theme he touches, has a little prose-poem of symbolic metempsychosis, called *Usury*, where Yohu, one of the evil spirits, lures the shadows to work for him by giving them gleaming lives to polish.

And ever Yohu lures more shadows and sends them to brighten his Lives, sending the old Lives out again to make them brighter still; and sometimes he gives to a shadow a Life that was once a king's and sendeth him with it down to the earth to play the part of a beggar, or sometimes he sendeth a beggar's Life to play the part of a king. What careth Yohu?

Spiritualism and Psychical Research. The influence of modern Spiritualism and Psychical Research on the literature of supernaturalism has been marked, especially of late years. It would be inevitable that movements which interest so many persons, among them many of more than ordinary intelligence, should be reflected in fiction. These two aspects of the subject will be treated together since they are closely allied. For though Spiritualism is a form of religion and Psychical Research a new science,—and so-called religion and so-called science are not always parallel—the lines of investigation here are similar. While Spiritualism endeavors to get in touch with the spirits of the dead that the living may be comforted and enlightened, and Psychical Research attempts to classify the supposedly authentic cases of such communication, and in so much their methods of approach are different,—yet the results may be discussed together.

Hawthorne was interested in Spiritualism as literary material, since a discussion of it is introduced in *Blithedale Romance* and various passages in his notebooks treat of the matter showing the fascination it had for him. Mrs. Elizabeth Stuart Phelps Ward, in addition to her fictional treatises of heaven, takes up Spiritualism as well. In *The Day of My Death* she gives a satiric account of the return of a spirit who says he is a lost soul tortured in hell. He doubtless deserves it, for he sticks the baby full of pins and ties it to a tree, and folds the clothes from the wash in the shape of corpses. He is still interested in this life, however, since he requests a piece of squash pie. In *Kentucky's Ghost* she depicts a spirit actuated by definite malice. In the previous story seven mediums tell a man that he will die at a certain day and hour, but he lives cheerfully on.

William Dean Howells has given a study in his usual

kindly satire and sympathetic seriousness, of the phenomena of Spiritualism and mesmerism, in *The Undiscovered
Country*. Dr. Boynton, a mistaken zealot, holds seances
assisted by his daughter, a delicate, sensitive girl who is
physically prostrated after each performance and begs
her father to spare her. She acts as medium where the
usual effects of rapping, table levitation, and so forth take
place, where spirit hands wave in the air and messages,
grave and jocular, are delivered. The characterization
is handled with skill to bring out the sincerity of each
person involved in the web of superstition and false belief,
and Howells shows real sympathy with each, the scoffers
as well as the misguided fanatics. It is only when the
doctor looks death in the face that he realizes his error
and seeks to know by faith in the Bible the truths of the
far country of the soul.

Hamlin Garland has shown considerable interest in
Spiritualism in his fiction. He refuses to commit himself
as to his own opinion of the question, but he has written
two novels dealing with it, *The Tyranny of the Dark* and
The Shadow World. The former is considerably like
Howells's novel, for here also a young girl is made the
innocent victim of fanatics, her mother and a preacher
who has fallen in love with her. She is made to take part
in spiritualistic manifestations, whether as a victim of
fraud or as a genuine medium the author leaves in doubt.
When the girl casts him off the preacher kills himself that
he may come into closer communication with her after
death than he has been able to do in life. Richard Harding
Davis has contributed a volume with a similar plot, the
exploitation of an innocent and, of course, beautiful girl
by fanatics, in *Vera the Medium*. Here the girl is more
than half aware that she is a fraud and in her last seance,
at the conclusion of which she is to be carried trium-
phantly away by her lover, the New York district attorney,

she dramatically confesses her deception.   As a sympathy-
getter, she pleads that she was very lonely, that because
her grandmother and mother were mediums, she had been
cut off from society.   "I used to play round the kitchen
stove with Pocahontas and Alexander the Great, and
Martin Luther lived in our china closet."

David Belasco's *The Return of Peter Grimm*, drama and
novel, is based upon spiritualistic manifestations.   We
are told that the "envelope" or shadow-self of a sleeper
has been photographed by means of radio-photography.
When a certain part of the shadow body is pricked with a
pin, as the cheek, the corresponding portion of the sleeper's
body is seen to bleed.   Peter Grimm comes back from the
other world to direct the actions of the living, and though
at first only a child sees him,—for children are the best
sensitives save animals,—eventually the adults recognize
him also and yield to his guidance.   Spiritualism enters
directly or indirectly into many works of fiction of late
years.   Whether people believe in it or not, they are
thinking and writing about it.   The subject receives its
usual humorous turn in various stories, as Nelson Lloyd's
The Last Ghost in Harmony, the story of a specter who
complains of the scientific unimaginativeness of his village, saying that though he had entreated the spooks
to hold out for a little while as he had heard Spiritualism
was headed that way and would bring about a revival of
interest in ghosts, the spirits all got discouraged and quit
the place.   And we recall Sandy's mournful comment to
Mark Twain's Captain Stormfield, that he wished there
was something *in* that miserable Spiritualism, so he could
send word back to the folks.

The Proceedings of the Psychical Research Society have
a twofold association with literature, for not only have
various modern novels and stories been inspired by such
material, but the instances recorded are similar in many

cases to the classical ghost stories.   Lacy Collison-Morley
in his *Greek and Roman Ghost Stories* says, "There are a
number of stories of the passing of souls which are curiously like some of those collected by the Psychical Research Society, in the Fourth Book of Gregory the Great's
Dialogues."   The double source of many modern stories
may be found by a comparative study of Collison-Morley's
book and Myers's *Human Personality*, while G. H. Gerould's volume, *The Grateful Dead*, introduces recent
instances that are like classical stories.   The inability of
the soul to have rest in the other world if its body was
unburied, as held by the ancients, is reflected in Gothic
romance, Elizabethan drama as well as in the classics.
The ghost of Jack, whom Peele tells us about, is a case of
a ghost coming back to befriend his undertaker.   From
these comparisons it would appear that there is something
inherently true to humanity in these beliefs, for the
revenge ghost and the grateful dead have appeared all
along the line.   Perhaps human personality is largely the
same in all lands and all times, and ghosts have the same
elemental emotions however much they may have acquired a veneer of modernity.

There are many instances of the compact-ghost, the
spirit who returns just after death in accordance with a
promise made in life, to manifest himself to some friend
or to some skeptic.   Algernon Blackwood gives several
stories based on that theme, one a curious case where the
ghost is so lifelike his friend does not dream he is not the
living man, and assigns him to a bedroom.   Later he is
invisible, yet undoubtedly present, for his heavy breathing,
movements of the covers, and impress on the bed are
beyond dispute.   *Afterwards*, by Fred C. Smale, shows a
ghost returning to attend a neighborhood club.   When his
name is called by mistake, he takes part on the program,
speaking through the lips of a young man present, who

goes off in a cataleptic trance. During this coma the youth, who is ignorant of music, gives a technical discussion of notation, analyzing diatonic semi-tones and discussing the note a nightingale trills on. When he wakes he says he has felt a chill and a touch. Alice Brown relates a story of a lover who promised to come to his sweetheart at the moment of death, but who, like Ahimeas in the Bible, runs before he is ready, and keeps his ghostly tryst while the rescuers bring him back to life. He hasn't really been drowned at all.

A recent novelette by Frances Hodgson Burnett, called *The White People*, has psychical phenomena for its central interest. A little child, born after her father's tragic death and when her dying mother is conscious of his spiritual presence, grows up with a strange sensitiveness to manifestations from the other world. Her home is on a lonely estate in Scotland, so that her chief companionship is with the "white people," the spirits of the dead, though she does not so recognize them. Her playmate is Wee Brown Elsbeth, who has been murdered hundreds of years before, and she is able to see the dead hover near their loved ones wherever she goes. So when she comes to realize what a strange vision is hers, she has no horror of death, and when her lover dies she does not grieve, but waits to see him stand smiling beside her as in life. The theme of the story is the nearness of the dead to the living, the thin texture of the veil that separates the two worlds.

Basil King tells a poignant story of a soul trying vainly to return in body to right a wrong done in life but unable to accomplish her purpose by physical means. At last she effects it by impressing the mind of a living woman who carries out the suggestion psychically given. One of the most effective recent accounts of a spirit's return to earth to influence the life of the living, to give messages or to control destiny, is in Ellen Glasgow's *The Shadowy*

Third.   Here the ghost of a child, a little girl whom her stepfather has done to death for her money, returns to cause his death in an unusual way.   She throws her little skipping-rope carelessly on the stairway where he must trip up in it when he sees her phantom figure in front of him in the gloom, so to fall headlong to his death.   This is an impressive revenge ghost.

Henry James based his ghost story, *The Turn of the Screw*, on an incident reported to the Psychical Society, of a spectral old woman corrupting the mind of a child. The central character in Arnold Bennett's novel, *The Ghost*, is a specter, one of the most rabid revenge ghosts in literature, who is eaten up with jealousy lest the woman he loved in life shall care for some one else.   Algernon Blackwood uses much psychical material in his numberless stories of the supernatural, often mentioning the work of the Society, and Andrew Lang has contributed much to the subject.   Arthur Machen has just published a collection of stories of war-apparitions that are interesting psychical specimens, called *The Bowmen*.   In one story in the volume he shows us how a contemporary legend may be built up, since from a short piece of fiction written by him has evolved the mass of material relating to the angels at Mons.   One tale is a story of the supernatural intervention of Saint George and his army to drive back the Germans and save the hour for the Allies, while another describes the vision of a soldier wounded in battle defending his comrades, who sees the long-dead heroes of England file past him to praise him for his valor. The minister gives him wine to drink and

His voice was hushed.   For as he looked at the minister the fashion of his vesture was changed.   He was all in armor, if armor be made of starlight, of the rose of dawn, and of sunset fires; and he lifted up a great sword of flame.

"Full in the midst, his Cross of Red
Triumphant Michael brandished
And trampled the Apostate's pride."

Another case of collective apparitions is the experience
of a soldier, wounded in battle, who tells of strange
fighters who have come in to aid the English. He thinks
they are some of the tribesmen that Britain employs,
but from his descriptions the minister knows that they
are the long-dead Greeks who have arisen to take part in
the struggle which their modern descendants are reluctant
to share. These stories are only a few among the many
instances of supernaturalism in fiction traceable to the
influence of the war.

Certain volumes of ghost stories have appeared, claiming to be not fiction but fact, accounts of actual apparitions seen and snap-shotted. This sort of problematic fiction is not new, however, since Defoe long ago published
one of the best of the kind, the story of Mrs. Veal, who
appeared to her friend Mrs. Bargrave, and conversed with
her, gravely telling her that heaven is much like the descriptions in a certain religious book written shortly before
that. She seems very realistic, with her dress of newly
scoured silk, which her friend rubs between her fingers,
and her lifelike conversation. This story has usually been
regarded as one of Defoe's "lies like truth," but recent
evidence leads one to believe that it is a reportorial account
of a ghost story current at the time, which missed being
reported to the Society for Psychical Research merely
because the organization did not exist then. The modern
stories that stridently claim to be real lack the interest
in many instances that Mrs. Veal is able to impart, and
in most cases the reader loses his taste for that sort of
fiction because it is rammed down his throat for fact.
They don't impress one, either as fact or as fiction.

One of the most interesting aspects of the literature relating to psychic matters in recent years is the number of books that claim to be spirit-inspired. These instances of psychography are not what we might expect immortals to indite, but it appears that there must be a marked decrease of intelligence when one reaches the other world. The messages sent back by dead genius lack the master style, even lacking that control over spelling and grammar which low, earth-bound editors consider necessary. But perhaps the spirits of the great grow tired of being made messenger boys, and show their resentment by literary strikes. Anita Silvani has published several volumes that she claims were written while she was in a semi-trance,— which statement no reader will doubt. Her accommodating dictator furnishes illustrations for her stuff, as well, for she says she would have inner visions of the scenes described, "as if a dioram passed" before her. These romances of three worlds are quite peculiar productions. The inner voices asked her in advance not to read any literature on theosophy or Spiritualism or the supernatural since they wished her mind to be free from any previous bias. Mrs. Elsa Barker is another of these literary mediums, for she has put out two volumes of letters in narrative form, which she makes affidavit were dictated to her by a disembodied spirit, the ghost of the late Judge Hatch, of California. She states that while she was sitting in her room in Paris one day, her hand was violently seized, a pencil thrust into it, and the automatic writing began. Mrs. Campbell-Praed is another of these feminine stenographers for spooks, but like the rest she has left nothing that could well be included in a literary anthology. These spirit-writers tell us of life after death, but nothing that is a contribution to existing ignorance on the subject. According to Judge Hatch, whose post-mortem pen-name is X, the present war has its parallel in a conflict of spirits, and the astral world is in dire confusion because of overcrowding, so that the souls of the slain must go through torments and struggle with demons.

The most recent instance of psychography comes to us by way of the ouija-board from St. Louis, the authenticity of which is vouched for by Mr. Casper Yost, of the editorial staff of the *Globe-Democrat*. But if the ouija-board dictated the stories and plays, giving the name of Patience Worth as the spirit author, and if Mrs. Curran took them down, why does Mr. Yost appear as the author? Patience Worth says that she lived a long time ago. Mr. Yost insists that her language is Elizabethan, but it seems rather a curious conglomeration, unlike any Elizabethan style I am familiar with. She has written stories, lyrics, a long drama, and other informal compositions, a marvelous output when one considers the slow movements of the ouija-board. The communications seem to have human interest and a certain literary value, though they bring us no messages from the Elizabethan section of eternity.[1]

Automatic writing appears in *The Martian* by Du Maurier, where the spirit from Mars causes Barty Joscelyn in his sleep to write books impossible to him in his waking hours. The type has been parodied by John Kendrick Bangs in his *Enchanted Typewriter*, which machine worked industriously recording telegraphic despatches from across

[1] Other examples of the books that claim to be inspired by spirits are: *An Angel Message*, Being a Series of Angelic and Holy Communications Received by a Lady; *Nyria*, by Mrs. Campbell-Praed; *Letters from a Living Dead Man*, by Elsa Barker, and *War Letters from a Living Dead Man*; *Stranger than Fiction*, by Mary L. Lewis; *The Soul of the Moor*, by Straford Jolly, *Ida Lymond and Her Hour of Vision*, by Hope Crawford; *The Life Elysian; The Car of Phoebus; The Heretic; An Astral Bridegroom; Through the Mists, The Vagrom Spirit*, and *Leaves from the Autobiography of a Soul in Paradise*, by Robert James Lee. This last-named gentleman seems to be in touch with spirits as rapid in composition as Robert W. Chambers.

the Styx. The invisible operator gives his name as Jim Boswell. The writer states:

The substance of the following pages has evolved itself between the hours of midnight and four o'clock, during a period of six months, from a type-writing machine standing in a corner of my library, manipulated by unseen hands.

It is astonishing how many ghosts are trying to break into print these days. And.after all, what do the poor things get out of it? No royalties, scant praise, and much ridicule when their style fails to come up to specifications.

Interesting psychical material is found in a new volume of plays by Theodore Dreiser.[1] He gives curious twists to the unearthly, as in *The Blue Sphere*, where a shadow and a fast mail are among the *dramatis personæ*, typifying the fate idea of the old drama. The shadow lures a child monstrosity out on to the railway track, after he has caused the elders to leave the gate open, and the train, made very human, kills the child. The psychic effects in *In the Dark* are even more peculiar, the characters including various spirits, a wraith, and a ghost with red eyes, who circle round the human beings and force them to discover a murder that has been committed. The effect of supernatural manifestation on animals is brought out here, in the bellowing of the bull and the howling of the dogs as the ghosts pass by. In *A Spring Recital* troops of nymphs and hamadryads, fauns, clouds of loathsome spirits of hags and wastrels, "persistences" of fish, birds, and animals, "various living and newly dead spirits wandering in from the street," the ghost of an English minister of St. Giles, who died in 1631, a monk of the Thebaid, of date 300 and three priests of Isis of 2840 B.C. enter to hear the organist play. He is unaware that anybody is hearing his music save the four human beings

---

[1] *Plays of the Natural and the Supernatural.*

who have happened in. These dramas of course are purely literary plays, impossible of presentation on the stage, and in their curious character show a likeness to some of the late German supernaturalism, such as the plays of August Stramm. They show in an extreme form the tendency toward psychic material that the American and English drama has evidenced lately.

Life after Death. Mankind is immensely interested in heaven and hell, though he knows but little concerning these places. But man is a born traveler and gives much thought to distant countries, whether he definitely expects to go there or not. This interest is no new thing, for classical mythology is full of doleful accounts of the after life. The early English stage represented heaven and hell in addition to the earth, and Elizabethan drama shows many references to the underworld, with a strong Senecan influence. There are especially frequent allusions to certain famous sufferers in Hades, as Ixion, Tantalus, Sisyphus, and Tityus. Modern English fiction has likewise been influenced by the epic supernaturalism, reflecting the heaven and hell of Dante and Milton. Yet as in his own thinking each person lays out a Celestial City for himself and pictures his own inferno to fit his ideas of mercy and justice, peopling them with appropriate beings, changing and coloring the conceptions of Bunyan, for instance, to suit his own desires, so it is in fiction. Some think of heaven and hell as definite places, while to others they are states of mind. To some the devil is as real as in the darkey folk-song, where,

> "Up stepped de debbil
> Wid his iron wooden shubbil,
> Tearin' up de yearth wid his big-toe nail!"

while to others he is an iconoclastic new thought. Heaven and hell have been treated in every conceivable way in

English fiction—conventionally, symbolically, humorously, and satirically, so that one may choose the type he prefers. There are enough kinds to go around.

Among the portrayers of the traditional heaven and hell Mrs. Elizabeth Stuart Phelps Ward is prominent. Her works on contemporary immortality are said to have had a tremendous vogue in the period following the Civil War, when death had claimed so many that the living were thinking of the other world more than of this. Her pictures of heaven in *Gates Ajar* are comforting, for she assures to each person his own dearest wish in fulfillment, to the ambitious youth his books, to the young girl her piano, and to the small child her ginger-snaps instead of earthly bread and butter. In *The Gates Between* the physician, suddenly killed, finds himself embarrassed by immortality. He doesn't know how to adjust himself to eternity and at first brings many of earth's problems with him. In the third of the series, *The Gates Beyond*, she describes a very material yet spiritual heaven. Bodies are much like those on earth, not vaporous projections; there are museums, hospitals, universities, telephones, concerts and all up-to-date improvements and conveniences. The dead woman discovers that she remembers what she read on earth, takes pleasure in simple things such as the smell of mignonette, hears the birds sing a Te Deum, while a brook and a bird sing a duet, and the leaves are also vocal. There is a Universal Language which must be learned by each soul, and heaven holds all sorts of occupations, material, mental, and spiritual. She says that near earth are many earth-bound spirits occupied in low and coarse and selfish ways, who lack "spiritual momentum to get away." "They loved nothing, lived for nothing, believed in nothing, they cultivated themselves for nothing but the earth,"—which may be compared with the state of the souls on Fifth Avenue, described by Granville Barker.

Mrs. Ward's pictures of heaven may seem sentimental and conventional to us to-day, yet to be appreciated they must be considered in relation to the religious thought of her time. She represented a reaction against the rigid theology, the stern concepts of an older generation than her own, and she wished to make heaven more homelike. She did have an influence in her day, as may be illustrated by a remark from a sermon recently delivered by a New York pastor, that the reading of her books had exerted a great influence over him, that they made heaven over for him.

Mrs. Oliphant is another of the conductors of fictive Cook's tours through heaven and hell, after the fashion started by Dante and Milton, and modernized by Mrs. Ward. She devotes volumes to describing the future worlds in their relation to mortal destiny. One story[1] tells of a soul that comes back from purgatory to be comforted by the old minister and sent away happy; another[2] is the account of a spirit returning from heaven to right a wrong that her husband is doing another. Still another[3] gives the experiences of a woman who is distressed when she finds herself in heaven, because she has hidden her will and her young niece is thereby left penniless, but she asks advice of various celestial authorities and finally succeeds in returning to earth and righting matters. *A Beleaguered City* is a peculiar story of a French town besieged by the dead, who drive out the inhabitants because of their cruelty toward some nuns. A strange gloom pervades the place, the cathedral bells ring of themselves, and flaming signs appear on the church doors, till after much penance the citizens are allowed to return and the invading hosts from eternity withdraw.

[1] *The Open Door.*   [2] *The Portrait.*   [3] *Old Lady Mary.*

In one story,[1] Mrs. Oliphant gives her ideas of heaven, as a place of light, of rest, of joy, of service, where the great angel Pain helps the souls to wisdom. In a counter-picture,[2] she shows hell, the world of the unhappy dead, where are cruelty, selfishness, suffering, a world filled with tears that drip from earth. Yet it is a hell as well-regulated, as thoroughly disciplined as a German municipality, with various punishments,—the most terrible being a lecture platform from which are delivered eternal addresses.

These would-be-realistic stories of heaven and hell somehow leave the reader cold, after Dante and Milton, however much one may feel the sincerity of the authors. Heaven and hell are such vast provinces that one cannot chart them in imagination sufficiently to grasp somebody else's concept in story.

Other stories of life after death, given from the spirit-angle rather than from the mortal point of view as in most ghost stories, are among the recent types of supernaturalism. Alice Brown has several stories of the kind, in one showing a woman who comes to tell her friend not to be afraid of dying, because There is much like Here, and another symbolic of the power of love to come back even from the pit of blackness after death. Olivia Howard Dunbar's *The Shell of Sense* gives the psychosis of a woman who cannot go to heaven because she is jealous of her husband. She *sees* the form of the wind, *hears* the roses open in the garden, and senses many things unknown to human beings, yet is actuated by very human motives. Katherine Butler[3] suggests that death must be a painless process and the after life much like mortality, since the man doesn't realize that he is dead but attempts to go about his affairs as usual.

[1] *The Little Pilgrim in the Unseen.*   [2] *The Land of Darkness.*
[3] In *In No Strange Land.*

The symbolic treatment of the theme of life after death is more effective and shows more literary art than the conventional pictures of Mrs. Ward's and Mrs. Oliphant's. No human vocabulary is able to describe immortality of glory or despair, hence it is more effective merely to suggest the thought by allegory or symbolism. Hawthorne gives us a symbolic morality in *The Celestial Railroad*, where he pictures the road between heaven and hell, drawing on Bunyan's imagery to describe the landscape and characters. Apollyon is engineer and emits realistic blasts of smoke. Eugene Field[1] tells of a mother just entering heaven who asks an angel where she may find her little baby, dead long ago, to whom the angel whispers that she is the babe, grown to maturity in Paradise. Julian Hawthorne's *Lovers in Heaven* is a symbolic picture of the after life, where a man just dead goes in search of the beloved he lost long before. He sees her on the far slope of a heavenly hill, but before he can reach her the devil appears to him in his own double, "the Satan of mine own self, the part of me wherein God had no share." This is a quite modern concept of diabolism. But love struggles to save him, and he resists his evil self.

Ahrinziman, by Anita Silvani, shows lurid pictures of the world to come. In the Inferno of the Dark Star the soul sees the attendant genii of his life, each symbolizing some passion of his nature. There are horrible astral birds and beasts and combinations unknown to mortal biology, while vultures hover overhead and a foul astral odor fills the air. The spirits are of peculiar substance, for they fight and slay each other, some being torn to pieces. The soul is supposed to progress toward the Silver and later the Golden Star. Marie Corelli's *Romance of Two Worlds* is a queer production, preaching the doctrine

[1] In *The Mother in Paradise*.

of psychical electricity, which is to be a sort of wonder-working magician, and in other novels she gives theories of radio-activity, a theosophical cure-all for this world and the next.

A Vision of Judgment, by H. G. Wells, is a satire on man's judgment of sin and character and of destiny after death, showing the pettiness and folly of Ahab, proud of his sins, and the hyprocrisy of a so-called saint, conceited over his self-torture. "At last the two sat side by side, stark of all illusions, in the shadow of the robe of God's charity, like brothers." The picture of God and the throne vanish and they behold a land austere and beautiful, with the enlightened souls of men in clean bodies all about him. This symbolic allegory setting forth the shallowness of human judgment as set against God's clarity of vision and charity of wisdom is like Oscar Wilde's *The House of Judgment*, a terrible piece of symbolism expressed in a few words. A soul who has been altogether evil comes at last before God to be judged. God speaks to him of his vileness, his cruelty, his selfishness, to all of which the soul makes confession of guilt.

And God, closing the book of the man's Life, said, "Surely I will send thee into Hell. Even unto Hell will I send thee."

And the man cried out, "Thou canst not!"

And God said to the man, "Wherefore can I not send thee to Hell, and for what reason?"

"Because in Hell I have always lived," answered the man.

And there was silence in the house of judgment.

And after a space God spake and said to the man, "Seeing that I may not send thee into Hell, I will send thee into Heaven. Surely unto Heaven I will send thee."

And the man cried out, "Thou canst not!"

And God said to the man, "Wherefore can I not send thee unto Heaven, and for what reason?"

"Because, never, and in no place, have I been able to imagine it!" answered the man.

And there was silence in the house of judgment.

The fact that a man's thoughts make his heaven or his hell is brought out in a recent book, *The Case of John Smith*, by Elizabeth Bisland, where the central character receives a revelation while working at his typewriter one day. The message says, "Oh, Peevish and Perverse! How know you that you have not died elsewhere and that this is not the Heaven which there you dreamed? How know you that your Hell may not lie only in not recognizing this as Heaven?"

In many recent examples of allegory and symbolism we get suggestive impressions of the other life, of the soul's realities. Some of these have the inevitable words, the fatal phrases that seem to penetrate into the real heaven and hell for us. The most remarkable instance of symbolic treatment of the after-life is in *Souls on Fifth*, by Granville Barker, where the spirits of the dead are represented as unable to rise above the level of the ideals they had held in life, and drift endlessly up and down the Avenue, some in the form of tarnished gilt, some with white plague spots of cowardice, or blisters of slanderous thoughts, some horny with selfishness, some with lines of secret cruelty. There are few squares but mostly irregular shapes of sin.

The purely humorous treatment of life after death, the comic pictures of heaven and hell, are of a piece with the humorous treatment of other phases of supernaturalism, and are distinctly modern. The flippant way in which sacred subjects are handled is a far cry from the heaven and hell of Dante and Milton. Modern writers slap the devil on the back, make fun of the archangels and appeal to the ridiculous in one-time sacred situations, with a

freedom that would have made the Puritans gasp.   For
instance, St. Peter has been the butt of so many jokes
that he is really hackneyed.

The Flying Dutchman, whom Brander Matthews
introduces in his *Primer of Imaginary Geography*, and
who says that the Wandering Jew is the only person he
can have any satisfactory chats with now, speaks of
knowing Charon, "who keeps the ferry across the Styx.
I met him last month and he was very proud of his new
electric launch with its storage battery." He says that
hell is now lighted by electricity and that Pluto has put
in all the modern improvements.   John Kendrick Bangs,
in his *House-boat on the Styx*, brings together the shades
of many illustrious persons; Queen Elizabeth, Walter
Raleigh, Socrates, Xantippe, Captain Kidd, and many
others. From them we get pictures of the life after death
and of their characteristic attitudes toward it and each
other. He continues the situation in *The Pursuit of the
House-boat*, as the redoubtable Captain Kidd makes off
with the ship and the ladies, leaving all the men behind.
But they follow the bold buccaneer and after exciting
adventures reaching from the Styx to Paris, they recap-
ture the fair. Carolyn Wells has recently given us a
Styx River Anthology. In modern stories we visit the
comic devil on his native heath, see him in his own home
town, as in previous chapters we discussed him in his
appearances on earth.   Kipling's *The Last of the Stories*
shows us the Hades of literary endeavor, the limbo of lost
characters, presided over by a large and luminous devil
of fluent tongue. Kipling recognizes many persons from
fiction, and sees various tortures in process. All do
obeisance to the shade of Rabelais, the Master. Kipling
is terrified by the characters he himself has brought into
being and begs to hide his face from them. F. Marion
Crawford gives us another glimpse of literary eter-

nity,[1] where the spirits of learned personages meet and discuss life. A recent poem describes a meeting and dialogue in Hades between Chaucer and Cressida.

It is possibly Bernard Shaw who would be most liable to prosecution by the devil for lèse-majesté, for in *Man and Superman*, Mine Host of the Pit is represented as an affable gentleman who tries to make hell attractive to his guests, and exercises not the least constraint on their movements. They are free to leave him and go to heaven if they like,—he only warns them that they will find it tiresome. He converses with Don Juan and a couple of other blasé mortals, uttering Shavian iconoclasms with an air of courteous boredom. He is very different from the sinister personage of conventional fiction.

Mark Twain has given humorous views of heaven in his *Extract from Captain Stormfield's Visit to Heaven*. A bluff, hearty old salt finds the celestial regions very different from the traditional descriptions of them. The heavenly citizens are a polite set, wishful for him to do what he likes, yet he tires of the things he thought paradise consisted of, lays aside his harp and crown, and takes his wings off for greater ease. He finds his pleasures in the meeting of an occasional patriarch, or prophet, and the excitement of the entry of a converted bartender from Jersey City. He changes his views on many points, saying for instance, "I begin to see a man's got to be in his own heaven to be happy," and again, "Happiness ain't a thing in itself,— it's only a contrast with something that ain't pleasant." Again Sandy, his friend, says, "I wish there was something *in* that miserable Spiritualism so we could send the folks word about it."

Something of the same combination of humor and earnestness is found in Nicholas Vachell Lindsay's poem, *General William Booth Enters into Heaven*.

[1] In *Among the Immortals*.

"Booth led boldly with his big bass drum,
Are you washed in the blood of the Lamb?
The saints smiled gravely as they said, 'He's come.'
Are you washed in the blood of the Lamb?
    (Bass drums)
Walking lepers followed, rank on rank,
Lurching bravos from the ditches dank,
Drabs from the alley-ways and drug-fiends pale
Minds still passion-ridden, soul-power frail!
Vermin-eaten saints with mouldy breath,
Unwashed legions with the ways of death,—
Are you washed in the blood of the Lamb?

    (Reverently sung—no instruments)
And while Booth halted by the curb for prayer
He saw his Master through the flag-filled air.
Christ came gently with a robe and crown
For Booth the soldier, while the crowd knelt down.
He saw King Jesus—they were face to face—
And he knelt a-weeping in that holy place.
Are you washed in the blood of the Lamb?"

This combination of realism with idealism, of homely
details with celestial symbolism, is also seen in another
recent poem, *The Man with the Pigeons*, by William Rose
Benet, who shows us two pictures, the first of a tramp in
Madison Square Garden, who loves the pigeons and has
them ever clustering around him in devotion. The next
is of heaven, with the celestial gardens, where among the
goldhaired angels the old tramp stands at home, still
wearing his rusty shoes and battered derby hat. The
quaint commingling of fancy and fact reminds us of
Hannele's dreams of heaven, in Hauptmann's *Hannele*,
where the schoolmaster is confused with the angels, and
heaven and the sordid little room are somehow united.

H. G. Wells, in *A Wonderful Visit* shows us another
side of the picture, for he draws an angel down and lets

him tell the citizens of the earth of the land he comes from. I make no attempt in this discussion to decide concerning the personality of angels, whether they are the spirits of the just made perfect or pre-Adamite creatures that never were and never could be man. For the present purpose, they are simply angels. This book of Wells's is an example of the satiric treatment of heaven and earth that constitutes a special point of importance in the modern supernaturalism. It is a social satire, and a burlesque on the formal and insincere manifestations of religion. A vicar takes a pot shot at what he supposes is a rare bird, seeing a rainbow flash in the sky,—but instead, an angel comes tumbling down with a broken wing. This thrusts him upon the vicar as a guest for some time, and introduces complications in the village life. The parishioners do not believe in angels save in stained glass windows or in church on Sunday, and they make life difficult for the vicar and his guest. The angel shows a human sense of humor, that quaint philosophy of the incongruous which is the basis of all true humor, and his naïve comments on earthly conventions, his smiling wonder at the popular misconceptions in regard to his heaven—to which he is surprised to learn that mortals are thought to go, since he says he has never seen any there—make him a lovable character. But village custom compels him to fold his shining wings under a coat till he looks like a hunch-back, put boots on so that he "has hoofs like a hippogrif," as he plaintively says to the vicar, and he finds conformity to convention a painful process. The novel ends sadly, symbolizing the world's stupid harshness, for the angel is sent away from the village as unworthy to live among the people, and his heart is almost broken.

The same type of humor and satire may be found in James Stephens's *The Demi-Gods*, and in Anatole France's, *The Revolt of the Angels*. Stephens's novel

contains an insert of a short story of heaven previously published, which depicts a preliminary skir-
mish in heaven over a coin a corpse has had left in his
hand and has taken to eternity with him. In each novel
several angels come tumbling down from heaven and take
up earthly life as they find it, engaging in affairs not
considered angelic. Stephens, in addition to the two
fighting celestials, gives us an archangel, a seraph, and a
cherub. There is in both stories a certain embarrassment
over clothes, the fallen ones arriving in a state of nudity.
The necessity for donning earthly garments, the removal
of the wings, and the adaptation to human life furnish
complication and interest, with the added feminine
element, though Stephens's novel is not marred by the
unclean imaginings of Anatole France.

The revolters in the French novel take up Parisian life,
while Stephens's angelic trio join an itinerant tinker and
his daughter who are journeying aimlessly about, accompanied by a cart and a sad-eyed philosopher, an ass.
They engage in activities and joys not conventionally
archangelic, such as smoking corn-cob pipes, eating cold
potatoes, and, when necessary, stealing the potatoes. The
contrasts between heavenly ideas and Irish tramp life are
inimitable. At last when the three, having decided to go
back to heaven, don their wings and crowns and say
good-bye, the cherub turns back for one more word of
farewell with Mary. Seeing her tears over his going, he
tears his shining wings to shreds and casts them from him,
electing to stay on earth with the tinker's cart, for the
sake of love. It is really quite a demi-god-like thing to do.

Unlike France's book, which is a blasting satire on
religion, these two English novels are amusing, with a
certain measure of satire, yet with a whimsicality that
does not antagonize. France's angels remain on earth
and become more corrupt than men, and Wells's wonderful

visitor is banished from the village as an undesirable alien.   Stephens's archangel and seraph go back to heaven after their vacation, while the cherub turns his back on mmortal glory rather than break a woman's heart.   In all three of these books we notice the same leveling tendency shown in characterization of the angels that we have observed heretofore in the case of ghosts and devils, werewolves, and witches.   The angels are human, with charming personality and a piquant sense of humor, whose attempts to understand mortal conventions reveal the essential absurdity of earthly ideas in many instances. The three taken together constitute an interesting case of literary parallelism and it would be gratifying to discover whether France was influenced by Wells and Stephens, or Stephens by Wells and France,—but in any event Wells can prove a clear alibi as to imitation, since his novel appeared a number of years before the others.   The possible inspiration for all of these in Byron's *Heaven and Earth* suggests an interesting investigation.   A more recent story, *The Ticket-of-Leave Angel*, brings an angel down to a New York apartment, where he has peculiar experiences and illustrates a new type of angelic psychology.   The tendency to satirize immortality has crept even into poetry, for in a recent volume by Rupert Brooke there are several satiric studies.   One, entitled *On Certain Proceedings of the Psychical Research Society*, ridicules the idea that spirits would return to earth to deliver the trivial messages attributed to them, and another, *Heaven*, is a vitriolic thrust at the hope of a better life after death, sneering at it with unpleasant imagery.

One of the recent instances of satiric pictures of the hereafter is Lord Dunsany's *The Glittering Gate*, a one-act drama, where Bill and Jim, two burglars, crack the gate of heaven to get in.   Sardonic laughter sounds while they are engaged in the effort to effect an entrance, and wondering what heaven will be like. Bill thinks that his mother will be there.

"I don't know if they want a good mother in there who would be kind to the angels and sit and smile at them when they sing, and soothe them if they were cross. (Suddenly) Jim, they won't have brought me up against her, will they?"

Jim: "It would be just like them to. Very like them."

When the glittering gate of heaven swings open and the two toughs enter eagerly, they find nothing—absolutely nothing but empty space, and the sardonic laughter sounds in their ears. Bill cries out, "It is just like them! Very like them"!

Was not this suggested by Rupert Brooke's poem, *Failure?*

In the stories treating satirically or humorously of the future life we find the purpose in reality to be to image this life by illustration of the other. Eternity is described in order that we may understand time a little better. Angels and devils are made like men, to show mortal potentialities either way. The absurdities of mankind are illustrated as seen by angel eyes, the follies as satirized by devils. The tendency now is to treat supernatural life humorously, satirically or symbolically, rather than with the conventional methods of the past. Commonplace treatment of great subjects is liable to be unsatisfactory, and any serious treatment, other than symbolically simple, of heaven or hell seems flat after Dante and Milton.

In considering these various types of stories dealing with supernatural life, whether continued beyond the mortal span on earth, renewed by reincarnation, or taken up in another world after death, we find that several facts seem to appear with reference to the type chosen for treatment by men as distinct from women, and *vice versa*. So far as my search has gone, I have found no instance in English literature where a woman has used either the motif of the Wandering Jew or the Elixir of Life. I do not say that no such instances exist, but I have not found them. Carmen Sylva is the only woman I know of at all who has taken up the characterization of the Wandering Jew. On the other hand, women write often of heaven, most of the stories of conventional ideas of heaven being by women. Where men have pictured heaven or hell they have done it for the most part humorously, satirically or symbolically. They seem to curve round the subject rather than to approach it directly. Yet where it is a question of continuing life here in this world, by means of an elixir or other method, or as an ever-living being like the Jew, men have used the theme frequently. Since fiction does reflect our thought-life and our individual as well as racial preferences, the conclusions that might be drawn, if one were sure of their basis, would be interesting. Can it be that men are more deeply interested in this life on earth and cling to it in thought more tenaciously than women, and that women are more truly citizens of the other world? Are men skeptical of the existence of any but a satiric or symbolic heaven, or merely doubtful of reaching there?

CHAPTER VI

The Supernatural in Folk-Tales

THE folk-tale is one of the new fashions in fiction. True, folk-lore has long constituted an important element of literature, constantly recurring in poetry, particularly in the ballad, in the drama, the novel, and short story. Yet it has been in solution. It has not been thought important enough to merit consideration for its own sake, but has been rather apologized for, covered up with other materials, so that its presence is scarcely recognized. Now, however, as Professor Kittredge says, folk-lore is no longer on the defensive, which fact is evident in fiction as elsewhere. Scholars of our day are eagerly hunting down the various forms of folk-lore to preserve them in literature before they vanish completely, and learned societies are recording with care the myths and legends and superstitions of peasants. Many volumes have appeared giving in literary form the fictions of various races and tribes, and comparative folk-lore is found to be an engrossing science.

The supernatural forms a large element of folk-literature. The traditions and stories that come down to us from the childhood of any race are like the stories that children delight in, tales of the marvelous, of the impossible, of magic and wonder. Folk-literature recks little of realism. It revels in the romantic, the mystic. Tales of gods and demi-gods, of giants and demons, of fairy-folk, of animals endowed with human powers of speech and cunning, of supernatural flora as well as fauna, of ghosts, devils, of saints, and miracles, are the frame-work of such fiction. English literature is especially rich in these collections, for not only are the sections of English-speaking countries themselves fortunate fields for supernatural folk-tales, but the English, being a race of colonizers, have gone far in many lands and from the distant corners of the earth have written down the legends of many tribes and nations. This discussion does not take into consideration primarily folk-tales translated from other languages, but deals only with those appearing in English, though, of course, in many cases, they are transcripts from the spoken dialects of other people. But it is for their appearance as English fiction, not for their value as folk-lore, that they are taken up here.

Wherever in fiction the life of the peasant class is definitely treated, there is likely to be found a good deal of folk-lore in the form of superstitions, taboos, racial traditions of the supernatural. This is present to a marked degree in the stories of Sir Walter Scott, and in fact one might write a volume on the supernatural in Scott's work alone. For example, we have Oriental magic and wonder,[1] supernatural vision,[2] superhuman foreknowledge,[3] unearthly "stirs,"[4] the White Lady of Avenel,[5] the bahrgeist,[6] besides his use of diabolism, witch-craft, and so forth already discussed. Thomas Hardy's work, relating as it does almost wholly to rustic life, is rich in superstitions and traditions of the peasants. *The Withered Arm* gives a gruesome account of a woman's attempt to cure her affliction by touching her arm to the corpse of a man who has been hanged, the complicating

---

[1] In *The Talisman*.
[2] In *My Aunt Margaret's Mirror*.
[3] In *The Two Drovers*.
[4] In *Woodstock*.
[5] In *The Monastery*.
[6] In *The Betrothed*.

horror being furnished by the fact that the youth is her husband's secret son. He gives a story[1] of a supernatural coach that heralds certain events in the family life, charms for securing love as for making refractory butter come when the churn is bewitched, and so forth. Similar elements occur in others of his novels and stories. Eden Phillpotts' fiction[2] shows a large admixture of the folk-supernaturalism of the Dartmoor peasants, as do *Lorna Doone*, *Wuthering Heights* and numberless other novels and stories of other sections. There are guild superstitions reflected in the work of various writers of the sea, as in W. W. Jacobs' stories, for instance, tales of mining life, and so on.

American fiction is equally rich in such material. Stories of the South, showing life in contact with the negroes, reveal it to a marked degree, as in the work of Thomas Nelson Page, Joel Chandler Harris, Ruth McEnery Stuart, Will Allen Dromgoole, and others. The Creole sense of the supernatural appears in George W. Cable's novels and stories, the mountain superstitions in those of John Fox, Jr., and Charles Egbert Craddock, those of New England in Mary Wilkins Freeman, Alice Brown, and their followers, the Indian traditions in Helen Hunt Jackson, J. Fenimore Cooper, the Dutch supernaturalism in Washington Irving, who also gives us the legendry of Spain in his tales of the Alhambra. Thomas A. Janvier has recreated antique Mexico for us in his stories of ghosts and saints, of devils and miracles.

In most fiction that represents truly the life of simple people there will be found a certain amount of superstition which is inherent in practically every soul. There is no one of us but has his ideas of fate, of luck, of taboo. We are so used to these elements in life that we scarcely pay heed to them in fiction, yet a brief glance at books will

[1] In *Tess*.　　　　[2] *Children of the Mist*, *The Witch*, and others.

recall their frequent appearance. They color poetry to a marked degree. In fact, without the sense of the marvelous, the unreal, the wonderful, the magical, what would poetry mean to us? So we should feel a keen loss in our fiction if all the vague elements of the supernatural were effaced. Absolute realism is the last thing we desire.

Now the folk-tale, told frankly as such, with no apology for its unreality, no attempt to make of it merely an allegory or vehicle for teaching moral truth, has taken its place in our literature. The science of ethnology has brought a wider interest in the oral heritage of the past, linking it to our life of the present. And the multiplication of volumes recording stories of symbolic phenomena of nature, of gods, demi-gods, and heroes, of supernormal animals and plants, of fairies, banshees, bogles, giants, saints, miracles, and what-not make it possible to compare the widely disseminated stories, the variants and contrasting types of folk-supernaturalism. But my purpose in this discussion is to show the presence of the folk-supernaturalism in literature, in prose fiction particularly. There is no science more fascinating than comparative folk-lore and no language affords so many original examples of oral literature as the English. As we study its influence on fiction and poetry, we feel the truth of what Tylor says[1]:

Little by little, in what seems the most spontaneous fiction, a more comprehensive study of the sources of poetry and romance begins to disclose a cause for each fancy, a story of inherited materials from which each province of the poet's land has been shaped and built over and peopled.

The Celtic Revival, the renascence of wonder in Ireland, has done more than anything else to awaken modern

[1] In *Primitive Culture*, vol. i., page 273.

love for antiquity, to bring over into literature the legends
of gods and men

> "Beyond the misty space
> Of twice a thousand years."

While the movement concerns itself more with poetry
and the drama than with prose,—Ireland has been likened
to "a nest of singing birds," though the voices of some
have been sadly silenced of late—yet fiction has felt its
influence as well. The land of the immortals glooms and
gleams again for us in storied vision, and the ancient past
yields up to us its magic, its laughter, its tears. These
romances are written, not in pedestrian prose as ordinary
folk-tales, but with a bardic beauty that gives to style the
lifting wings of verse. Each fact and figure is expressed
in poetic symbols, which Yeats calls "streams of passion
poured about concrete forms." A sense of ancient, divine
powers is in every bush and bog, every lake and valley.
Ireland has enriched universal fancy and the effect on
literature will perhaps never be lost.

One of the most interesting aspects of folk-loristic
supernaturalism is that concerned with nature. The
primitive mind needs no scientific proof for theories of
causation, since, given a belief in gods, it can manage the
rest for itself. With the Celts there is ever a feeling of
nature as a mighty personality. Every aspect, every
phase of her power is endowed with life and temperament.
Celtic pantheism saw in every form a spirit, in every spring
or cloud or hill-top, in every bird or blossom some unearthly divinity of being. A primrose is vastly more than
a yellow primrose, but one of "the dear golden folk";
the hawthorn is the barking of hounds, leek is the tear
of a fair woman, and so on, which poetic speech bears a
likeness to the Icelandic court poetry. This figurative

sense suggests "an *after-thought* of the old nature-worship lingering yet about the fjords and glens where Druidism never was quite overcome by Christianity." It lends to the Celtic folk-tales their wild, unearthly beauty, their passionate poetry and mystic symbolism akin to the classic mythology and such as we find in no other folk-literature of the present time.

In the stories of Lady Gregory, John Synge, Yeats, Lady Wilde, and various other chroniclers of Celtic legendry, we find explanations of many phenomena, accounts of diverse occurrences. Lady Wilde[1] (Speranza) tells of natural appearances, such as a great chasm which was opened to swallow a man who incurred the anger of God by challenging Him to combat for destroying his crops. A supernatural whirlwind caught up the blasphemer and hurled him into the chasm that yawned to receive him. Many of the aspects of nature are attributed to the activities of giants, and later of demons; as the piling up of cyclopean walls, massive breast-works of earth, or gigantic masses of rocks said to be the work of playful or irate giants. The titans were frolicsome and delighted in feats to show off. There is a large body of legends of diabolized nature, as the changing of the landscape by demons, the sulphurizing of springs, and the cursing of localities.

Many other aspects of nature are made the basis for supernatural folk-tales too numerous to mention. Stories of the enchanted bird, music, and water appear in various forms, and the droll-tellers of the Cornish country tell many stories of the weird associated with out-of-doors. The Celtic superstitions and tales have lived on through successive invasions and through many centuries have been told beside the peat fire. They have been preserved as an oral heritage or else in almost illegible manuscripts

---

[1] In *Ancient Legends and Superstitions of Ireland.*

in antique libraries, from which they are taken to be put into literature by the Celtic patriots of letters. The sense of terror and of awe, a belief in the darker powers, as well as an all-enveloping feeling of beauty is a heritage of the Celtic mind. It is interesting to note the obstinacy of these pantheistic, druidic stories in the face of Irish Catholicism. In many other bodies of folk-supernaturalism in English we have similar legends of nature, as in the Hawaiian, the Indian, African, Canadian, Mexican stories, and elsewhere. But the material is so voluminous that one can do no more than suggest the field.

Certain forces of nature are given supernatural power in drama and fiction, as the sea that is an awful, brooding Fate, in Synge's drama, or the wind and the flame in Algernon Blackwood's story, *The Regeneration of Lord Ernie*, or the goblin trees in another of his tales, that signify diabolic spirits, or the trees[1] that have a strange, compelling power over men, drawing them, going out bodily to meet them, luring them to destruction. Blackwood has stressed this form of supernaturalism to a marked degree. In *Sand* he shows desert incantations that embody majestic forces, evocations of ancient deities that bring the Sphynx to life, and other sinister powers. He takes the folk-loristic aspects of nature and makes them live, personifying the forces of out-door life as mythology did. The trees, the sand, the fire, the snow, the wind, the stream, the sea are all alive, with personality, with emotion, and definite being. His trees are more awesome than the woods of Dunsinane, for they actually do move upon their foe. In *The Sea Fit* he contends that the gods are not dead, but merely withdrawn, that one true worshiper can call them back to earth, especially the sea-gods. The sea comes in power for the man with the Viking soul and takes him to itself. His going is symbolic.

[1] In *The Man Whom the Trees Loved*.

Uttering the singing sound of falling waters, he bent forward, turned. The next instant, curving over like a falling wave he swept along the glistening surface of the sands and was gone. In fluid form, wave-like, his being slipped away into the Being of the Sea.

The uncanny potentialities of fire are revealed[1] where the internal flame breaks out of itself, the inner fire that burns in the heart of the earth and in men's hearts. The artist trying to paint a great picture of the Fire-worshiper is consumed by an intense, rapturous fever, and as he dies his face is like a white flame. The snow appears embodied as a luring woman.[2] She tries to draw a man to his death, with dæmonic charm, seen as a lovely woman, but a snow demon. Blackwood shows the curious combination of the soul of a dead woman with the spirit of a place,[3] where a man is ejected by his own estate, turned out bodily as well as psychically, because he has become out of harmony with the locale. Nature here is sentient, emotional, possessing a child, expressing through her lips and hands a message of menace and warning. The moon is given diabolic power in one of Barry Pain's stories, and the maelstrom described by Poe has a sinister, more than human, power. August Stramm, the German dramatist, has given an uncanny force to the moor in one of his plays, making it the principal character as well as the setting for the action. This embodiment of nature's phases and phenomena as terrible powers goes back to ancient mythology with a revivifying influence.

The supernatural beast-tale has always been a beloved form. Æsop's fables, the beast-cycles of medievalism, Reynard the Fox, the German Reineche Fuchs, all show how fond humanity is of the story that endows animals with human powers. Naturally one thinks of Kipling's

---

[1] In *The Heath Fire*.   [2] In *The Glamor of the Snow*.
[3] In *The Temptation of the Clay*.

Jungle Tales and Joel Chandler Harris' *Uncle Remus* stories as the best modern examples, and these are so well known as to need but mention. Similar beast-cycles are found in the folk-fiction of other countries. Of course, it is understood that the *Uncle Remus* stories are not native to America, but were brought from Africa by the slaves and handed down through generations in the form in which Harris heard them by the cabin firesides in his boyhood. They are not "cooked" or edited any more than he could help, he tells us, but given in the dialectic form in which they came to him. There are various tales similar to this series, as Kaffir tales, collected by Theal, Amazonian tortoise myths brought together by Charles F. Hart, and *Reynard, the Fox in South Africa*, by W. H. I. Bleek. J. W. Powell in his investigations for the Smithsonian Institute found legends among the Indians that led him to believe the *Uncle Remus* stories were originally learned from the red men, but Harris thought there was no basis for such theory. *Anansi Stories*, by Mary Pamela Milne-Horne, includes animal tales of the African type. Anansi is a mysterious being, a supernatural old man like a Scandinavian troll or English lubber-fiend, who plays tricks like those of the fox and like the jackal in Hindu stories. He is a spider as well as a man and can assume either shape at will.

In primitive races and in the childhood of peoples there is the same element of close association between man and the animals that one finds in child-life. An animal is often nearer and dearer to a child than is a human being, as in crude races man is more like the animals, candid, careless, unreflecting. His sensations and emotions are simple, hunger, love, hate, fear. Animals, in turn, are lifted nearer the human in man's thinking, and are given human attributes in folk-lore which bridges the gulf that civilization has tended to fix between man and animals, and gives one more of a sense of the social union that Burns longed for. There is in these stories of whatever country a naïveté reflecting the childhood of the race and of the world, a primitive simplicity in dealing with the supernatural.

The folk-fiction of each country gives stories of the animals common to that section. In tropic countries we have stories of supernatural snakes, who appear in various forms, as were-snakes, shall we say? by turns reptiles and men, who marry mortal women, or as diabolic creatures that, like the devil, lose their divinity and become evil powers. We also see in the tropics elephants, lions, tigers, baboons, gorillas, and so forth, as well as certain insects, while in colder climes we have the fox, the wolf, the bear, and their confrères. In island countries we find a large element of the supernatural associated with fishes and sea-animals. Hawaiian stories recount adventures of magic beings born of sharks and women, who are themselves, by turns, human beings living a normal human life, and sharks, devouring men and women. Several of Eugene Field's stories are drawn from Hawaiian folk-supernaturalism, as *The Eel-king*, and *The Moon Lady*.

The Gaelic stories of Fiona McLeod show the supernatural relation existing between mortals and seals. The seals may wed human beings and their children are beings without souls, who may be either mortal or animal. The power of enchantment exercised by the creatures of the sea may turn men and women into sea-beasts, forever to lose their souls. This may be compared with *The Pagan Seal-Wife*, by Eugene Field, Hans Christian Andersen's sad story of the little mermaid, and *The Forsaken Merman*, by Matthew Arnold. Fiona McLeod tells the story of the Dark Nameless One, a nun who became the prey of a seal and was cursed with the penalty of living under the sea to weave fatal enchantments. The mermaids, the kelpies, the sea-beasts are all half-human, half sea-beast, and have a fatal power over human souls, drawing them with a strange lure to give up their immortality.   The kelpie appears in several of Fiona McLeod's stories and in *The Judgment of God* the maighdeanhmara, a sea-maid, bewitches Murdoch, coming up out of the water as a seal and turning him into a beast, to live with her forever, a black seal that laughs hideously with the laughter of Murdoch.   Edward Sheldon has recently written a play[1] using the mermaid motif, and H. G. Wells employs it as a vehicle for social satire[2] where a mermaid comes ashore from The Great Beyond and contrasts mortal life with hers.   *The Merman and the Seraph*, by William Benjamin Smith, is an unusual combination of unearthly creatures.

In *The Old Men of the Twilight*, W. B. Yeats describes the enchantment inflicted on the old men of learning, the ancient Druids, who were cursed by being turned into gray herons that must stand in useless meditation in pools or flit in solitary flight cross the world, like passing sighs.   Lady Gregory tells of magic by which Lugh of the Long Hand puts his soul into the body of a mayfly that drops into the cup that Dechtire drinks from, so that she drinks his soul and must follow him to the dwelling-place of the Sidhe, or fairy people.   Her fifty maidens must go with her under a like spell that turns them into birds, that fly in nine flocks, linked together two by two with silver chains, save those that lead who have golden chains.   These beautiful birds live in the enchanted land far away from their loved ones.   J. H. Pearce tells a touching story of the Little Crow of Paradise, of the bird that was cursed and sent to hell because it mocked Christ on the cross, but because it had pity on a mortal sufferer in hell and brought some cooling drops of water in its bill to cool his parching tongue, it was allowed to fly up and light on the

[1] *The Mermaid.*   [2] In *The Sea Lady.*

walls of Paradise where it remains forever. Oscar Wilde's
story *The Nightingale and the Rose* is symbolic of tragic
genius, of vain sacrifice, where the tender-hearted bird
gives his life-blood to stain a white rose red because a
careless girl has told the poet who loves her that she must
wear a red rose to the ball. But at the last she casts the
rose aside and wears the jewels that a richer lover has sent,
while the nightingale lies dead under the rose-tree.

So we see everywhere in folk-fiction the supernatural
power given to animals, which acts as an aid to man, as
a shield and protection for him, or for his undoing. We
see human beings turned into beasts as a curse from the
gods for sin or as expressing the kinship between man and
nature. In the different cycles of beast-tales we find a
large element of humor, the keener-witted animals
possessing a rare sense óf the comical and relishing a joke
on each other as on man. The *Uncle Remus* stories are
often laughable in the extreme, and Bre'er Rabbit,
who, we might at first thought decide, would be stupid,
is no mean wit. We see a tragic symbolism in the stories
of unhappy beasts who must lure mortals to their damnation, yet feel a sense of human sorrow and remorse. In
these animal stories we find most of the significant qualities of literature, humor, romance, tragedy, mysticism,
and symbolic poetry, with a deep underlying philosophy
of life pervading them all.

Lord Dunsany in his modern aspects of mythology,
perhaps drawn in part from classic mythology though
perhaps altogether Celtic in its material, brings together
animals to which we are not accustomed. He has a story
of a centaur, a frolicsome creature two hundred and fifty
years young, who goes caracoling off the end of the world
to find his bride. Algernon Blackwood tells of a man who
remembers having been a centaur and lives in memory-
metempsychosis his experiences of that far-off time.

Dunsany introduces other curious, unfamiliar beasts to us, as the bride whom the man-horse seeks in her temple beside her sad lake-sepulchre, Sombelene, of immortal beauty, whose father was half centaur and half god, whose mother the child of a desert lion and the sphinx. There is the high-priest of Maharrion, who is neither bird nor cat, but a weird gray beast like both. There is the loathsome dragon with glittering golden scales that rattles up the London streets and seizes Miss Cubbige from her balcony and carries her off to the eternal lands of romance lying far away by the ancient, soundless sea. We must not forget the Gladsome Beast, he who dwells underneath fairyland, at the edge of the world, the beast that eats men and destroys the cabbages of the Old Man Who Looks after Fairyland, but is the synonym for joy. His joyous chuckles never cease till Ackronnion sings of the malignity of time, when the Gladsome Beast weeps great tears into an agate bowl. There are the hippogriffs, dancing and whirling in the far sunlight, coming to earth with whirring flight, bathing in the pure dawn, one to be caught with a magic halter, to carry its rider past the Under Pits to the City of Never. There are the gnoles in their high house, whose silence is unearthly "like the touch of a ghoul," over which is "a look in the sky that is worse than a spoken doom," that watch the mortals through holes in the trunks of trees and bear them away to their fate. Lord Dunsany looses the reins of his fancy to carry him into far, ancient lands, to show us the wonders that never were.

Magic forms an alluring element of the supernatural romance, and we find it manifesting itself in many ways. In the romances of William Morris, prose as well as poetry, we find enchantment recurring again and again, as in *The Water of the Wondrous Isles, The Wood beyond the World, The Well at the World's End*, and others. Yeats

said that Morris's style in these old stories was the most
beautiful prose he had ever read, and that it influenced
his own work greatly. He has unearthly characters,
such as the Witch-wife, the Wood-wife, the Stony
People, and so forth. He shows us the enchanted boat,
the Sending Boat, the cage with the golden bars which
prison the three maidens, magic runes with mighty
power, the Water of Might which gives to the one drinking it supernatural vision and magic power, the changing
skin, the Wailing Tower, the Black Valley of the Grey-
weathers, and so forth. Birdalone's swoon-dream in the
White Palace is unearthly, as the witches' wordless howls.
Part of the weirdness of Morris's prose is due to the
antique tone, the forgotten words, the rune-like quality
of the rhythm.

Yeats tells of magic whereby a woman is gifted with
immortal youth and beauty, so that she may wed the
prince of the fairies; of the glamour that falls on a mortal
so that he loses his wits and remains "with his head on his
knees by the fire to the day of his death"; of shadow
hares, of fire-tongued hounds that follow the lost soul
across the world, of whistling seals that sink great ships,
of bat-like darker powers, of the little gray doves of the
good.

Dr. Hyde, in his *Paudeen O'Kelly and the Weasel*, speaks
of a sun-myth, of a haunted forest, of a princess supernaturally beautiful, of the witch who complains to the
robber, "Why did you bring away my gold that I was for
five hundred years gathering through the hills and hollows
of the world?"

Lady Gregory tells of Diarmuid's love-spot, where
Youth touched him on the forehead, so that no woman
could look upon him without giving him her love; of
Miach who put the eye of a cat in a man's head, with
inconvenient results, for

when he wanted to sleep and take his rest, it is then the eye would start at the squeaking of the mice, or the flight of birds, or the movement of the rushes; and when he was wanting to watch an army or a gathering, it is then it was sure to be in a sound sleep.

She shows us Druid rods that change mortals into birds; of Druid mists that envelop armies and let the ancient heroes win; of Druid sleep that lasts sometimes for years; of the screaming stone; of kisses that turn into birds, some of them saying, "Come! Come!" and others "I go! I go!"; of invisible walls that shield one from sight; of magic that makes armies from stalks of grass; of wells of healing that cure every wound.

Oscar Wilde, in his fairy stories and symbolic allegories, tells of magic, whereby the Happy Prince, high on the pedestal on the square, has a heart of lead because he sees the misery of the people, and sends a swallow as his messenger to pick out his jeweled eyes and take them to the suffering ones. He speaks of the wonder by which the bodies of the mermaid and the fisherman who lost his soul for love of her, when they are buried in unconsecrated ground, send forth strange flowers that are placed on the sacred altar.

The dark enchantment appears in the poetry as often as in the prose, from Coleridge's *Christabel* to the present. Gordon Bottomley's *The Crier by Night* is a story of an evil presence that lurks in a pool, coming out to steal the souls of those it can lure into its waters. The woman, desperate from jealousy, who invokes its aid, says:

"For I can use this body worn to a soul
To barter with the Crier of hidden things
That if he tangle him in his chill hair
Then I will follow and follow and follow and follow

Past where the ringed stars ebb past the light
And turn to water under the dark world!"

The fairy has always been a favorite being with poets, dramatists, and romancers, from Shakespeare, Spenser, and Milton to the present time. There is no figure more firmly established in folk-literature, none more difficult to dislodge despite their delicacy and ethereal qualities than the Little People. The belief in fairies is firmly established in Gaelic-speaking sections and the Celtic peasant would as soon give up his religion as his belief in the Sidhe. W. B. Yeats, in *Celtic Twilight*, tells of an Irish woman of daring unbelief in hell, or in ghosts who, she held, would not be permitted to go trapsin' about the earth at their own free will, but who asserted, "There are fairies, and little leprechauns, and water-horses, and fallen angels." Everybody among the peasantry believes in fairies, "for they stand to reason." And there are not wanting others more learned that believe in the small folk, as W. Y. E. Wentz, who in his volume *Fairy Faith in Celtic Countries* puts up a loyal argument for the existence of the Sidhe. He says:

Fairies exist, because in all essentials they appear to be the same as the intelligent forces now recognized by psychological researchers, be they thus collective units of consciousness like what William James calls soul-stuff or more individual units like veridical apparitions.

If it were left to me, I'd as soon not believe in fairies as have to think of them as veridical units! Mr. Wentz has never seen any fairies himself, but he tells a number of stories to substantiate his faith in them.

The volumes of fairy stories are by no means all for juvenile consumption, since the modern adult dearly loves the type himself. Many, or most, of the stories of fairies told frankly for children are adaptations or variants of continental folk-legends. The more literary side of fairy-literature has come from the Celtic lore, for the Dim People are dearest of all supernatural beings to the Celtic soul. The Irish, more innately poetic than most races, cling more fondly to the beings of beauty and gather round them delicate, undying stories. W. B. Yeats, Lady Gregory, Lady Wilde, Oscar Wilde, John Singe, and Fiona McLeod have given in poetry and lyric prose the Celtic fairy-lore, and have made us know the same wild, sweet thrill that the peasants feel. The poetic thought of the primitive races peoples everything in nature, every bird and blossom and tree, with its own fairy personality.

Thackeray has written a fairy pantomime for great and small children, as he says, in which the adventures of Prince Giglio and Prince Bulbo are recounted. Eugene Field has a charming story of the *Fairies of Pesth*, and Charles Kingsley's *Water Babies* enriched the imagination of most of us in youthful or adult years with its charming nonsense of beings possible and impossible. J. M. Barrie in *Peter Pan* won the doubtful world over to a confessed faith in the fairy-folk, for did we not see the marvels before our eyes? In *The Little White Bird* Barrie tells us how fairies came to be,—that they have their origin in the first laugh of the first baby that broke into a million bits and went skipping about, each one a fairy. He shows us the wee folk in Kensington Gardens, where by the ignorant they are mistaken for flowers, but children and those with the poet heart can see the flashing faces and green garments of the fairies among the pansy beds.

W. B. Yeats is a favorite with the fairies, for they have given him the dower of magic vision, to glimpse the unseen things, to hear the faint, musical voices of fairy pipes and song. He tells us many stories of the Dim People, in his tales and dramas. *The Land of Heart's*

Desire, the story of the struggle between the divine and mortal forces and the powers of the Sidhe to claim the soul of the young wife and of the triumph of the fairies, by which the girl's body falls lifeless by the hearth while her spirit speeds away to live forever in the land "where nobody gets old or sorry or poor," has a poignant pathos, a wild, dreamy beauty that touches the heart. Yeats tells of the Imperishable Rose of Beauty, of fantastic doings of the fairy-folk who steal mortals away, especially new-born babies or new-wed brides, of evil fairies who slay men in malice, and of the dances by moonlit hillside when mortals are asleep.

James Stephens in *The Crock of Gold* mingles delightfully fairy-lore with other elements of the supernatural, as talking beasts, and insects, the gods, a leprechaun, and Pan, combining with the droll philosophy of the bachelor man to make a charming social satire. The union of the world of reality with that of the wee people is seen in the sad little story of H. G. Wells, *The Man Who Had Been in Fairyland*. A crude, materialistic middle-class Englishman, in love with an ordinary young woman, falls asleep on a fairy knoll one night and is kidnapped by the Dim People who take him to their country, where their queen falls in love with him. She vainly woos him, but he is stolidly true to the thick-ankled girl of the town, until the fairies send him back in sleep to mortal life. But when he wakes on the knoll he is home-sick for fairyland, he cares no more for the village girl who seems coarse and repulsive compared with the elfin creature whose love he might have kept in the land of wonder, so he is wretched, unable to fit again into mortal life and unable to reopen the doors that closed inexorably upon him by his wish. This is a modern version of the motif of the mortal lover and the fairy bride that we find so often in mediæval ballads and romances, a survival of the Celtic wonder-lore.

Arthur Lewis in *London Fairy Tales* writes philosophic human stories in the guise of fairy tales, attempting frankly to bring the impossible into contact with daily life.   They are weird little symbolic stories with an earthly wisdom associated with unearthly beings.   *The Passionate Crime*, by E. Temple Thurston, is a symbolic fairy novel, the fairies being figures of the man's besetting sins, bodiless presences blown on the winds of feeling, as the woman he loves is lured by the fairy of her own beauty.

Whether fairyland be an actual place or a state of mind, it is a province still open to romancers, and folk-lorists have aroused a new interest in the Little People who may come nearer to us than before.   The flood of volumes recounting Celtic folk-tales with their fairy-lore alone would make a long catalogue, and one can do no more than suggest the presence of the fairy in English fiction.   Andrew Lang was a faithful lover of the Sidhe and made many collections of fairy stories, Eden Phillpotts has written much of them, and various writers have opened their magic to us.   Some place the land of faerie under the ground, some in secret caves, some in the mind, and Lord Dunsany says that the Old Man Who Looks after Fairyland lives in a house whose parlor windows look away from the world, and "empties his slops sheer on to the Southern Cross."

We find many stories of gods, demigods, and heroes tangled up together in folk-tales and in the literature they have influenced.   It is sometimes difficult to distinguish between them, and again it is interesting to note how the hero-myth has been converted into the tale of a god. Celtic romances and folk-supernaturalism give many stories of gods, demigods, and heroes of superhuman force.   It would be interesting if one could trace them to their ultimate sources and discover how much they have been suggested or influenced by classical mythology.

In *Fiction of the Irish Celts*, by Patrick Kennedy, are numberless stories of the Fianna Eironn, or Heroes of Ireland, some of whom really flourished in the third century and whose adventures were the favorite stories of the kings and chiefs as sung by the ancient bards. Kennedy also retells many of the Ossianic legends. In *Bardic Stories of Ireland* he relates the exploits of personages dating back to druidic times and earlier, who reflect the remote stages of the legendary history of the people, such as the antique King Fergus, who was given supernatural power by the fairies and slew the sea-monster; Cormac, who did many doughty deeds assisted by the powers of the Immortals, and many others. W. B. Yeats, in his *Stories of Red Ranrahan*, gives us glimpses of an Irish François Villon, a man of wandering nature, of human frailties, yet with a divine gift of song.

Lady Gregory tells the wonderful saga of Cuchulain, the hero-god of Ireland, in *Cuchulain of Muirthemne*, which W. B. Yeats calls "perhaps the best book that has ever come out of Ireland." It was his mother Dechtire that drank the soul of Lugh of the Strong Hand, as he flew into her wine-cup in the form of a Mayfly, so that she was bound by enchantment and carried away with her fifty maidens as a flock of lovely birds. When anger came upon him the hero light would shine about his head, he understood all the arts of the druids and had supernatural beauty and strength in battle. Cuchulain, the Hound of Ulster, and his Red Branch have filled the legendry of Ireland with wonder.

Lady Gregory tells of the high king of Ireland who married Etain of the Sidhe; of the nine pipers that came out of the hill of the Sidhe, whom to fight with was to fight with a shadow, for they could not be killed; of Conchobar, the king, that loved Deirdre of the burning beauty for whom many candles of the Gael were blown out; of Cruachan, who knew druid enchantments greater than the magic of the fairies so that he was able to fight with the Dim People and overcome them, and to cover the whole province with a deep snow so that they could not follow him.　In *Gods and Fighting Men* Lady Gregory tells of ancient divinities that met men as equals.　We come to know Oisin, son of Finn, who is king over a divine country; of the Men of Dea who fought against the mis-shapen Fomer.　Men are called to the country of Under-Wave where the gods promise them all their desires, as the god Medhir tells Queen Etain that in his country one never grows old, that there is no sorrow, no care among invisible gods.　She tells us of Finn, who fought with monsters, who killed many great serpents in Loch Cuilinn, and Shadow-shapes at Loch Lein, and fought with the three-headed hag, and nine headless bodies that raised harsh screeches.　We meet Diarmuid, who married a daughter of King Under-Wave, who raised a house by en-chantment, and whom Grania, of the fatal beauty, loved.

Jeremiah Curtin, Aldis Dunbar, and many another writer have told us of the wonderful legends of the Celtic gods and heroes, who somehow seem more human than Arthur and his Table Round or any of the English mythi-cal heroes.

It is Lord Dunsany, however, who specializes in gods in recent times.　He fairly revels in divinities and demons, in idols and out-of-the-world creatures.　His dramas of this nature are mentioned in another connection, as *A Night at an Inn*, where a jade idol slays with silent horror the men who have stolen his emerald eye; *The Gods of the Mountains*, where seven beggars masquerade as the mountain gods come to life, and some of the people believe but some doubt.　But at last the seven gods from the mountain come down, terrible figures of green stone, and with sinister menace point terrible fingers at the beggars, who stiffen as on pedestals, draw their feet under them like the cross-legged posture of the images, and turn to stone, so that the people coming say: "They were the true gods. They have turned to stone because we doubted them." In *The Gods of Pegana* are many fantastic tales of divinities never heard of before, whom Dunsany calls to life with the lavish ease of genius and makes immortal. In *Time and the Gods* we see many gods, with their servant the swart, sinister Time who serves them, but maliciously. The gods dream marble dreams that have magic power, for "with domes and pinnacles the dreams arose and stood up proudly between the river and the sky, all shimmering white to the morning." But Sardathrion, this city of visions, is overthrown by hateful Time, whereat the mighty gods weep grievous tears. He tells us of Slid, a new god that comes striding through the stars, past where the ancient divinities are seated on their thrones, as a million waves march behind him; of Inzana, the daughter of all the gods who plays with the sun as her golden ball and weeps when it falls into the sea, so that Umborodom with his thunder hound must seek it again and again for her. He whispers to us of the prophet who saw the gods one night as they strode knee-deep in stars, and above them a mighty hand, showing a higher power. The gods are jealous of him that he has seen, so they rob him of knowledge of the gods, of moon and sky, of butter-flies and flowers, and all lovely things. And last they steal his soul away from him, from which they make the South Wind, forever to roam the waste spaces of the world, mournful, unremembering.

In *The Book of Wonder* are still other gods, as Hlo-Hlo, who wears the haloes of other gods on golden hooks along his hunting-belt; the Sphinx, who "remembers in her smitten mind at which little boys now leer, that she once knew well those things at which man stands aghast";

the certain disreputable god who knows nothing of etiquette and will grant prayers that no respectable god would ever consent to hear; Chu-chu and Sheemish, who become angry with each other and raise rival earthquakes that destroy their temple and them. We are told of the Gibbelins that eat men, whose home is beyond the known regions, and whose treasures many burglars try in vain to steal only to meet death instead. Alderic tries a crafty way to evade them but they are waiting for him. "And without saying a word *or even smiling* they neatly hang him on the outer wall,—and the tale is one of those that have not a happy ending." But enough of gods!—though we should not forget the Aztec legend on which Lew Wallace's novel, *The Fair God*, was founded, of the white divinity who was to come and rule the people.

There are many other elements of folkloristic supernaturalism that cannot be mentioned, as the banshee, the wailful creature that is a presager of death and the loss of the soul; the fetches, ghosts of the living, whom John and Michael Banim write much about; the pixies, as appearing in such works as S. Baring-Gould's *Eve*, and Stephens's *The Crock of Gold;* the mountain trolls that play pranks on Ibsen's Peer Gynt and Irving's Rip van Winkle; the "worrie-cow" that Scott tells about; the saints and miracles that abound in Celtic literature as in that of any Catholic country, and such as Thomas A. Janvier has told of so delightfully in his legends of the City of Mexico. The giant has almost faded from fiction, since, poor thing, he doesn't fit in well with the modern scheme of housing. He came into the Gothic novel from the Oriental tale where he had his origin, but now he appears in our fiction only sporadically, as in Oscar Wilde's *The Selfish Giant*, in a couple of stories by Blackwood, and a few others. We are glad to meet him occasionally in frank folk-tales since literature at large repudiates this favorite of our youth. He would not suit well on the stage, for obvious reasons, and realism rejects him.

Lord Dunsany tells of elves and gnomes, of the Moomoo, of the magic sword called Mouse, of the gnoles that caught Tonker, of the ancient Thuls, of the window that opened to the magic of the world, and of many other things which only the very young or the very wise care for.

Arthur Machen deals with strange, sinister aspects of supernaturalism unlike the wholesome folklore that other writers reveal to us. He seems to take his material chiefly from the Pit, to let loose upon the world a slimy horde of unnamable spirits of ageless evil. One reads of the White People, who are most loathsome fairies under whose influence the rocks dance obscene dances in the Witches' Sabbath, and the great white moon seems an unclean thing. Images of clay made by human hands come to diabolic life, and at mystic incantations the nymph Alanna turns the pool in the woodland to a pool of fire. In *The Great God Pan* the timeless menace comes to earth again, corrupting the souls of men and women, rendering them unbelievably vile. In *The Red Hand* he brings together ancient runes with magic power, black stones that tell secrets of buried treasure, flinty stone like obsidian ten thousand years old that murders a man on a London street, a whorl of figures that tell of the black heaven, giving an impression of vast ages of enigmatic power. One feels one should rinse his mind out after reading Arthur Machen's stories, particularly the collection called *The Three Impostors*.

This discussion has taken more note of the Celtic folk-fiction than of any other group influence, because more than any other it has left its imprint on modern literature. There are hundreds of volumes of folk-tales of the supernatural in English, but the Celtic Revival has molded its legends into literature that is its own excuse for being. In the work of this school we get a passionate mysticism, a poetic symbolism that we find scarcely anywhere else in English prose, save in such rhapsodic passages as some of De Quincey's impassioned prose. Melody, which forms so large a part of the effect of supernaturalism in poetry, is here employed to heighten lyric prose. Some of the wild stories are like the croon of the peasant mother by her cradle beside the peat-fire, some like wild barbaric runes of terrible unguessed import, some like the battle-cry of hero-gods, some like the keening of women beside their dead. The essential poetry of the Celtic soul pours itself forth in rapturous, wistful music, now like a chant, a hymn, a wedding-song, a lament for the lost soul.

In the Celtic folk-tales we get a mixture of romances, of the survivals of barbaric days, the ancient druid myths, the pagan legends, savage beliefs overlaid and interwoven with the later Christian traditions. Sometimes the old pagan myths themselves become moral allegories, the legend being used to tell a late-learned moral truth. But, for the most part, there is no attempt at teaching save that which comes spontaneously, the outburst of passionate, poetic romance, the heritage of a people that love wonder and beauty.

The pagan poetry of the Gaelic race lives on and throbs over again in Fiona McLeod's symbolic moralities. The mystical figures of awe and woe appear from the dim past, a rapturous paganism showing through the medieval religious brooding. Yet they are so symbolic of the spirit that they are timeless. Coming as they do out of the dim legendary past, they may reflect the veiled years of the future. They are mystic chronicles of the soul, as in *The Divine Adventure*, where the Body and Will alike shrink back from that "silent, sad-eyed foreigner, the Soul."

In the stories of Yeats we get similar effects, the weird

power of the old curse-making bards, the gift of second-sight, a spiritual vision, the spiritual sense that hears past the broken discordant sounds the music of the world, the power to catch the moment "that trembles with the Song of Immortal Powers." We hear faint whispers, catch fleeting glimpses of the Dim People, see again the druids, the culdees, the ancient bards and heroes. We discern in the Celtic literature a sadness, dim, unreasoning yet deep, such as we see in the faces of animals and little children. We see such symbolism as that of the self-centered lovers who have heart-shaped mirrors instead of hearts, seeing only their own images throughout eternity. We feel the poetic thoughts drifting past us like sweet falling rose-leaves, bright with the colors of bygone years, like fluttering bird-wings, like happy sighs. Yet again they are terrible trumpets blown in the day of doom. We have the modern mysticism and symbolism side by side with the old druidic mysticism, which seems like dream-stuff with deep spiritual import. Yeats makes us feel that the old divinities are not dead, but have taken up their abode in the hearts of poets and writers of romance, and that the land of faery is all about us if we would only see. But we lack the poetic vision. He makes us see the actuality of thought, that thinking has its own vital being and goes out into the world like a living thing, possessed by some wandering soul. He shows us that thought can create black hounds or silver doves to follow the soul, bring to life at will a divinity or a demon.

A certain supernatural element of style seems to lend itself to some of the writers of strange fiction. Some of Oscar Wilde's sentences unfold like wild, exotic flowers, in a perfumed beauty that suggests a subtle poison at the heart. Lord Dunsany writes joyously of fantastic creatures with a happy grace, sometimes like a lilting laugh, sometimes a lyric rhapsody. His evoked beings are sportive or awesome but never unclean.   Arthur Machen's stories have an effect like a slimy trail of some loathly beast or serpent.   William Morris's style is like an old Norse rune, while Algernon Blackwood makes us think of awakened, elemental forces hostile to man.   We feel bodiless emotions, feelings unclothed with flesh, sad formless spirits blown on the winds of the world.   These folk-tales reflect the sweet carelessness of the Irish soul, the stern sadness of the Scotch, the psychic subtlety of the modern English.   And as the study of folk-lore has influenced the fiction of the supernatural, so these published romances have aroused a wondering interest in the legendry of the past and made of folk-lore a science.

CHAPTER VII

Supernatural Science

THE application of modern science to supernaturalism, or of the supernatural to modern science, is one of the distinctive features of recent literature. Ghostly fiction took a new and definite turn with the rapid advance in scientific knowledge and investigation in the latter part of the nineteenth century, for the work of Darwin, Spencer, Huxley, and their co-laborers did as much to quicken thought in romance as in other lines. Previous literature had made but scant effort to reflect even the crude science of the times, and what was written was so unconvincing that it made comparatively little impress. Almost the only science that Gothic fiction dealt with, to any noticeable extent, was associated with alchemy and astrology. The alchemist sought the philosopher's stone and the elixir of life while the astrologer tried to divine human destiny by the stars. Zofloya dabbled in diabolic chemistry, and Frankenstein created a man-monster that was noteworthy as an incursion into supernatural biology, yet they are almost isolated instances. Now each advance in science has had its reflection in supernatural fiction and each phase of research contributes plot material, while some of the elements once considered wholly of the devil are now scientific. The sorcerer has given place to the bacteriologist and the botanist, the marvels of discovery have displaced miracles as basis for unearthly plot material, and it is from the laboratory that the ghostly stories are now evolved, rather than from the vault and charnel-room as in the past. Science not only furnishes extraordinary situations for curdling tales, but it is an excellent hook to hang supernatural tales upon, for it gives an excuse for believing anything, however incredible. Man is willing to accept the impossible, if he be but given a modern excuse for it. He will swallow the wildest improbability if the bait be labeled science or psychical research. No supernaturalism is incredible if it is expressed in technical terminology, and no miracle will be rejected if its setting be in a laboratory. One peculiar thing about modern scientific thought in its reaction upon fiction is that it is equally effective in realism, such as shown in the naturalistic novels of Zola, the plays of Brieux and others, and in supernaturalism, as in the work of H. G. Wells, for instance, where the ghostly is grafted on to cold realism.

The transition from the sorcerer, the wizard, the warlock of older fiction to the scientist in the present has been gradual. The sorcerer relied wholly upon supernatural, chiefly diabolic, agencies for his power, while the wizard of the modern laboratory applies his knowledge of molecules and gases to aid his supermortal forces. Modern science itself seems miraculous, so its employment in ghostly stories is but natural. The *Arabian Nights' Tales* seem not more marvelous than the stories of modern investigations. Hawthorne's narratives stand between the old and the new types of science, his Rappaccini, Dr. Heidigger, Gaffer Dolliver, Septimius Felton and his rivals in search for the elixir of youth, as well as the husband who sought to efface the birthmark from his young wife's cheek, being related in theme to the older conventional type and in treatment to the new. Poe's scientific stories are more modern in method and material,

Another aspect of the transfer of magic in modern fiction to a scientific basis is that of second sight or supernatural vision. This motif still retains all its former effect of the unearthly, perhaps gaining more, since the scientific twist seems to give the idea that the ghostly power resides in the atoms and molecules and gases and machines themselves, rather than in the person who manipulates them, which is more subtly haunting in its impression. Second sight has been used as a means for producing uncanny effects all along the line of fiction. Defoe even used it in a number of his hoax pamphlets, as well as in his *History of Duncan Campbell*, and folk-lore is full of such stories, especially in the Highlands.

The modern use of supernatural vision is based apparently on natural science, which makes the weird power more striking. *The Black Patch*, by Randolph Hartley, tells of an experiment in optics that produces a strange result. Two students exchange left eyeballs for the purpose of studying the effects of the operation, leaving the right eye in each case unimpaired. When the young men recover from the operation and the bandages are removed, they discover that an extraordinary thing has taken place. The first, while seeing with his right eye his own surroundings as usual, sees also with his left—which is his friend's left, that is—what that friend is looking at with his right eye, thousands of miles away. The severing of the optic nerve has not disturbed the sympathetic vision between the companion eyes, so this curious double sight results. In a quarrel arising from this peculiar situation, the first man kills the second, and sees on his left eye the hideous image of his own face distorted with murderous rage, as his friend saw it, which is never to be effaced, because the companion eye is dead and will see no more.

Another instance of farsightedness is told in John Kendrick Bangs's *The Speck on the Lens*, where a man has

such an extraordinary left eye that when he looks through
a lens he sees round the world, and gets a glimpse of the
back of his own head which he thinks is a speck on the
lens. Only two men in the world are supposed to have
that power.

The Remarkable Case of Davidson's Eyes, by H. G. Wells,
is an interesting example of this new scientific transference
of magic vision. Davidson is working in a laboratory
which is struck by lightning, and after the shock he finds
himself unable to visualize his surroundings, but instead
sees the other side of the world, ships, a sea, sands. The
explanation given by a professor turns on learned theories
of space and the Fourth Dimension. He thinks that
Davidson, in stooping between the poles of the electro-
magnet, experienced a queer twist in his mental retinal
elements through the sudden force of the lightning. As
the author says: "It sets one dreaming of the oddest
possibilities of intercommunication in the future, of
spending an intercalary five minutes on the other side of
the world, of being watched in our most secret operations
by unexpected eyes." Davidson's vision comes back
queerly, for he begins to see the things around him by
piecemeal, as apparently the two fields of vision overlap
for a time.

Brander Matthews in *The Kinetoscope of Time* introduces an instrument with eyepieces that show magic
vision. The beholder sees scenes from the past, from
literature as well as from life, has glimpses of Salome
dancing, of Esmerelda, witnesses the combat between
Achilles and Hector, the tourney between Saladin and
the Knight of the Leopard. The magician offers to show
him his future—for a price—but he is wise enough to
refuse.

Magic views of the future constitute an interesting
aspect of the supernatural vision in modern stories.

The Lifted Veil, by George Eliot, is an account of a man who has prophetic glimpses of his fate, which seem powerless to warn him, since he marries the woman who he knows will be his doom, and he is aware that he will die alone, deserted even by his servants, yet cannot help it. He sees himself dying, with the attendants off on their own concerns, knows every detail beforehand, but unavailingly. This suggests *Amos Judd*, by J. A. Mitchell, which is a curious instance of the transition stage of second sight, related both to the old sorcerer type and to the new scientific ideas. Amos Judd, so called, is the son of an Indian rajah, sent out of his country because of a revolution, and brought up in ignorance of his birth in a New England farmhouse. Vishnu, in the far past, has laid his finger on the brow of one of the rajah's ancestors, thereby endowing him with the gift of magic vision, which descends once in a hundred years to some one of his line. Amos Judd therefore, can see the future by pictures, beholding clearly everything that will happen to him. He sees himself lying dead at a desk, on which stands a calendar marking the date, November 4th. His friends persuade him to live past the date, and they think all is well, till one day while he is on a visit to a strange house he is killed by an assassin. They find him lying at a desk, with an out-of-date calendar beside him, marking November 4th.

Barry Pain endows a bulldog with the power to foretell the future, to reveal disaster and oppose it. Zero, in the story by that name, is a common bulldog greatly valued because he has a supernatural knowledge of any evil that threatens those he loves, and by his canine sagacity he forestalls fate. In the end, in protecting his master's little child, he is bitten by a mad dog, whose coming he has supernaturally foreseen, and he commits suicide as the only way out of the difficulty. Arthur Machen, in *The*

Bowmen and Others, tells varied stories of supernatural vision associated with the war.

The Door in the Wall, by H. G. Wells, depicts a man who in his dreamy childhood wanders into a secret garden where he is shown the book of his past and future, but who afterwards is unable to find the door by which he enters, though he seeks it often. Later in life, at several times when he is in a special haste to reach some place for an important appointment, he sees the door, but does not enter. Finally he goes in to his death. This is an instance of the suggestive supernaturalism associated with dreams and visions.

The use of mirrors in supernatural vision is significant and appears in a number of ways in modern fiction. Scott's *My Aunt Margaret's Mirror* is an early instance, where the magician shows the seeker a glass wherein she sees what is taking place in another country, sees her husband on his way to the altar with another woman, sees a stranger stop the marriage, and witnesses the fatal duel. Hawthorne has used mirrors extensively as symbolic of an inner vision, of a look into the realities of the soul. For instance, when poor Feathertop, the make-believe man, the animated scarecrow, looks into the mirror he sees not the brave figure the world beholds in him, but the thing of sticks and straw, the sham that he is, as the minister shrinks from the mirrored reflection of the black veil, symbol of mystery that he wears. Hawthorne elsewhere speaks of Echo as the voice of the reflection in a mirror, and says that our reflections are ghosts of ourselves. Mr. Titbottom, in George William Curtis's *Prue and I*, who has the power of seeing into the souls of human beings by means of his magic spectacles and catching symbolic glimpses of what they are instead of what they appear to be, beholds himself in a mirror and shrinks back aghast from the revelation of his own nature. Barry

Pain's story, referred to in another connection, shows a mirror wherein a supernatural visitant reveals to a young man the supreme moments of life, his own and those of others, pictures of the highest moments of ecstasy or despair, of fulfillment of dear dreams.

The Silver Mirror, by A. Conan Doyle, represents a man alone night after night, working with overstrained nerves on a set of books, who sees in an antique mirror a strange scene re-enacted and finds later that the glass has once belonged to Mary, Queen of Scots, and that he has seen the murder of Rizzio. Brander Matthews also has a story concerned with re-created images in an old mirror. The looking-glass in fiction seems to be not only a sort of hand conscience, as Markheim calls it, but a betrayer of secrets, a revealer of the forgotten past, a prophet of the future as well. It is also a strange symbol to show hearts as they are in reality, reflecting the soul rather than the body. It is employed in diverse ways and is an effective means of supernatural suggestion, of ghostly power.

The Fourth Dimension is another motif that seems to interest the writers of recent ghostly tales. They make use of it in various ways and seem to have different ideas concerning it, but they like to play with the thought and twist it to their whim. Ambrose Bierce has a collection of stories dealing with mysterious disappearances, in which he tells of persons who are transferred from the known, calculable space to some "non-Euclidean space" where they are lost. In some strange pockets of nowhere they fall, unable to see or to be seen, to hear or to be heard, neither living nor dying, since "in that space is no power of life or of death." It is all very mysterious and uncanny. He uses the theme as the basis for a number of short stories of ghostly power, which offer no solution but leave the mystery in the air. In some of these stories Bierce represents the person as crying out, and being heard, but no help can go, because he is invisible and intangible, not knowing where he is nor what has happened to him. H. G. Wells, in *The Plattner Case*, which shows an obvious influence of Bierce, gives a similar case. He explains the extraordinary happenings by advancing the theory that Plattner has changed sides. According to mathematics, he says, we are told that the only way in which the right and left sides of a solid body can be changed is by taking that body clean out of space as we know it, out of ordinary existence, that is, and turning it somewhere outside space. Plattner has been moved out into the Fourth Dimension and been returned to the world with a curious inversion of body. He is absent from the world for nine days and has extraordinary experiences in the Other-World. This happens through an explosion in the laboratory where he is working, similarly to Wells's story of Davidson, where the infringement on the Fourth Dimension is the result of a lightning stroke.

Mary Wilkins Freeman deals with the Fourth Dimension in *The Hall Bedroom*, where the boarder drifts off into unknown space, never to return, from gazing at a picture on the wall, as has happened in the case of previous occupants of the room. Richard Middleton employs the same idea in a story of a conjurer who nightly plays a trick in public, causing his wife to seem to disappear into space. One night she actually does so vanish, never to be seen again. Other instances of the form may be found in recent fiction. H. G. Wells uses the theme with a different twist in his *Time Machine*. Here the scientist insists that time is the Fourth Dimension, that persons who talk of the matter ordinarily have no idea of what it is, but that he has solved it. He constructs a machine which enables him to project himself into the future or into the past, and sees what will happen or what has happened in other centuries. He lives years in the space of a few moments and has amazing adventures on his temporal expeditions. But finally the Fourth Dimension, which may be thought of as a terrible Fate or inescapable destiny awaiting all who dally with it, gets him too, for he fails to return from one of his trips. Another story tells of a man who by drinking quantities of green tea could project himself into the Fourth Dimension.

A number of stories of scientific supernaturalism are concerned with glimpses into the future. *The Time Machine*, just mentioned, with its invasions of the unknown space and time, its trips into eternity by the agency of a miraculous vehicle, illustrates the method. The scientist finds that he can travel backwards or forwards, accelerating or retarding his speed as he will, and get a section of life in any age he wishes. He discovers that in the future which he visits many reforms have been inaugurated, preventive medicine established, noxious weeds eradicated, and yet strange conditions exist. Mankind has undergone a two-fold involution, the soft conditions of life having caused the higher classes to degenerate into flabby beings of no strength, while an underground race has grown up of horrible depraved nature, blind from living in subterranean passages, cannibalistic while the others are vegetarian. The lower classes are like hideous apes, while the higher are effeminate, relaxed. The traveler escapes a dire fate only by rushing to his machine and returning to his own time. Samuel Butler suggests that machines will be the real rulers in the coming ages, that man will be preserved only to feed and care for the machines which will have attained supernatural sensibility and power. He says that mechanisms will acquire feelings and tastes and culture, and that man will be the servant of steel and steam in the future, instead of master as now; that engines will wed and rear families which men, as slaves, must wait upon.

Frank R. Stockton[1] gives another supernatural scientific glimpse into the future, showing as impossibilities certain things that have since come to pass, while some of the changes prophesied as imminent are yet unrealized and apparently far from actualities. Jack London's *Scarlet Plague* pictures the earth returned to barbarism, since most of the inhabitants have been swept away by a scourge and the others have failed to carry on the torch of civilization. H. G. Wells[2] gives account of a tour into futurity, wherein the miracles of modern science work revolutions in human life, and[3] he satirizes society, showing a topsy-turvy state of affairs in A.D. 2100. His *Dream of Armageddon* is a story of futurity wherein a man has continuous visions of what his experiences will be in another life far in the future. That life becomes more real to him than his actual existence, and he grows indifferent to events taking place around him while rent with emotion over the griefs to come in another age. Of course, Edward Bellamy's *Looking Backward*, with its social and mechanistic miracles that now seem flat and tame to us, might be said to be the father of most of these modern prophecies of scientific futurity. Samuel Butler's *Erewhon* contains many elements of impossibility in relation to life, and is a satire on society, though perhaps not, strictly speaking, supernatural. These prophecies of the time to come are in the main intended as social satires, as symbolic analyses of the weaknesses of present life. They evince vivid imagination and much ingenuity in contriving the mechanisms that are to transform life, yet they are not examples of great fiction. Mark Twain reverses the type in his *Connecticut Yankee at King Arthur's Court*, for he shows a man of the present taking part in the life of the far past, managing to parody

[1] In *The Great Stone of Sardis.*
[2] In *A Story of Days to Come.*   [3] In *When the Sleeper Wakes.*

both mediævalism and the Yankee character at once.
H. G. Wells is particularly interested in studying the
unused forces of the world and fancying what would
happen under other conditions. His play of scientific
speculation has produced many stories that he does not
greatly value now himself, but which are of interest as
showing certain tendencies of fiction.

Views of other planets form a feature of modern supernaturalism, for the writer now sets his stories not only on
earth, in heaven, and in hell but on other worlds besides.
The astrologer of ancient fiction, with his eye fixed ever
on the stars, seeking to discern their influence on human
destiny, appears no more among us. He has been re-
placed by the astronomer who scans the stars yet with a
different purpose in fiction. He wishes to find out the
life of citizens of other planets rather than to figure out
the fate of mortals on the earth. Many stories of modern
times cause new planets to swim into our literary ken and
describe their citizens with ease. H. G. Wells stars here as
elsewhere. In his *War of the Worlds* he depicts a struggle
between the earth people and the Martians, in which
many supernatural elements enter. The people of Mars
are a repulsive horde of creatures, yet they have wonderful
organization and command of resources, and they conquer
the earth to prey upon it. This book has suffered the
inevitable parody.[1] In *The Crystal Egg*, Wells describes
a curious globe in which the gazer can see scenes reflected
from Mars. The author suggests two theories as to the
possibility of this,—either that the crystal is in both
worlds at once, remaining stationary in one and moving
in the other, and that it reflects scenes in Mars so that
they are visible on earth, or else that by a peculiar sympathy with a companion globe on the other planet it shows

[1] In *The War of the Wenuses*, by C. L. Graves and E. V. Lucas.

on its surface what happens in the other world. It is hinted that the Martians have sent the crystal to the earth in order that they might catch glimpses of our life.

In *The Star*, Wells gives yet another story of the future, of other planetary influences. By the passing of a strange star, life on earth is convulsed and conditions radically changed. These conditions are observed by the astronomers on Mars, who are beings different from men, yet very intelligent. They draw conclusions as to the amount of damage done to the earth, satirizing human theories as to Mars. *The Days of the Comet* shows earthly life changed by the passing of a comet, but instead of the destruction described in the other story, the social conditions are vastly improved and a millennium is ushered in. Wells[1] makes a voyage to the moon possible by the discovery of a substance which resists gravity. Other instances might be given, for there has been no lack of lunar literature, but they are not usually worth much.

Du Maurier's *The Martian*, which combines the elements of metempsychosis, automatic writing, and dream-supernaturalism, with the idea of ghostly astronomy, tells of a supernatural visitant from Mars. The Martian is a young woman whose spirit comes to inhabit a young man to whom she dictates wonderful books in his dreams. She writes letters to him in a sort of private code, in which she tells of her previous incarnations on Mars, of the Martians who are extraordinary amphibious beings, descended from a small sea animal. They have unusual acuteness of senses with an added sixth sense, a sort of orientation, a feeling of a magnetic current, which she imparts to her protégé, Barty Joscelyn. Jack London[2] tells a story of interplanetary metempsychosis, where the central character, a prisoner in San Quentin, finds himself able to will his body to die at times, thus

[1] In *The First Men in the Moon*.   [2] In *The Star Rover*.

releasing his spirit to fly through space and relive its experiences in previous incarnations.

Barry Pain's *The Celestial Grocery* is a phantasy of insanity and the supernatural, with its setting on two planets. It contains a cab horse that talks and laughs, and other inversions of the natural. A man is taken on a journey to another world, sees the stars and the earth in space beneath him, and finds everything different from what he has known before. People there have two bodies and send them alternately to the wash, though they seldom wear them. The celestial shop sells nothing concrete, only abstractions, emotions, experiences. One may buy measures of love, requited or unselfishly hopeless, of political success, of literary fame, or of power or what-not. Happiness is a blend, however, for which one must mix the ingredients for himself. The story is symbolic of the ideals of earth, with a sad, effective satire. The end is insanity, leaving one wondering how much of it is pure phantasy of a mad man's brain or how much actuality. It is reminiscent of Hawthorne's Intelligence Office with its symbolic supernaturalism.

Hypnotism enters largely into the fiction of modern times. Hypnotism may or may not be considered as supernatural, yet it borders so closely on to the realm of the uncanny, and is so related to science of to-day as well as to the sorcery of the past, that it should be considered in this connection for it carries on the traditions of the supernatural. In its earlier stages hypnotism was considered as distinctly diabolic, used only for unlawful purposes, being associated with witchcraft. It is only in more recent times that it has been rehabilitated in the public mind and thought of as a science which may be used for helpful ends. It is so mysterious in its power that it affords complications in plenty for the novelist and has been utilized in various ways. In some cases, as F. Marion Crawford's *The Witch of Prague*, it is associated still with evil power and held as a black art. Unorna has an unearthly power gained through hypnotism which is more than hypnotic, and which she uses to further her own ends. Strange scientific ideas of life and of death are seen here, and someone says of her: "You would make a living mummy of a man. I should expect to find him with his head cut off and living by means of a glass heart and thinking through a rabbit's brain." She embalms an old man in a continuous hypnotic lethargy, recalling him only at intervals to do mechanically the things necessary to prolong life. She is trying to see if she can cause human tissue to live forever in this embalmed state, hoping to learn through it the secret of eternal life. This, of course, suggests Poe's stories of the subject, *Mesmeric Revelations* and *The Facts in the Case of M. Waldemar*. The latter is one of the most revolting instances of scientific supernaturalism, for the dying man is mesmerized in the moment of death and remains in that condition, dead, yet undecaying, and speaking, repeating with his horrible tongue the statement, "I am dead." After seven months, further experiments break the spell, and he, pleading to be allowed to be at peace in death, falls suddenly away into a loathsome, liquid putrescence before the eyes of the experimenters.

The Portent, by George MacDonald, is a curious study of hypnotic influence, of a woman who is her true self only when in a somnambulistic state. A supernatural connection of soul exists between her and a youth born on the same day, and it is only through his hypnotic aid that she gains her personality and sanity. James L. Ford plays with the subject by having a group of persons in an evening party submit themselves to be hypnotized in turn, each telling a true story of his life while in that condition. W. D. Howells combines mesmerism with spiritualism in his novel,[1] where the séances are really the result of hypnotism rather than supernatural revelation as the medium thinks. H. G. Wells has used this theme, as almost every other form of scientific ghostliness, though without marked success. The prize story of hypnotism, however, still remains Du Maurier's *Trilby*, for no mesmerist in this fiction has been able to outdo Svengali.

Uncanny chemistry forms the ingredient for many a modern story. The alchemist was the favored feature of the older supernatural fiction of science, and his efforts to discover the philosopher's stone and to brew the magic elixir have furnished plots for divers stories. He does not often waste his time in these vain endeavors in recent stories, though his efforts have not altogether ceased, as we have seen in a previous chapter. A. Conan Doyle[2] is among the last to treat the theme, and makes the scientist find his efforts worse than useless, for the research student finds that his discovery of the art of making gold is disturbing the nice balance of nature and bringing injury to those he meant to help, so he destroys his secret formula and dies. *The Elixir of Youth* illustrates the transference of power from the sorcerer to the scientist, for the magician that gives the stranger a potion to restore his youth tells him that he is not a sorcerer, not a diabolic agent, but a scientist learning to utilize the forces that are at the command of any intelligence.

Barry Pain's *The Love Philter* is related both to the old and the new types of supernatural chemistry. A man loves a woman who doesn't care, so he asks aid of a wise woman, who gives him a potion that will surely win the stubborn heart. As he lies asleep in the desert, on his way back, he dreams that his love says to him that love gained

[1] *The Undiscovered Country.*
[2] In *The Doings of Raffles Haw.*

by such means is not love, so he pours the liquid on the sand. When he returns, the woman tells him that she has been with him in his dreams and loves him because he would not claim her wrongly. *Blue Roses* is another of his stories of magic that bring love to the indifferent. *Twilight*, by Frank Danby, is a novel based on the relation between morphia and the supernatural. A woman ill of nervous trouble, under the influence of opiates, continually sees the spirit of a woman dead for years, who relives her story before her eyes, so that the personalities are curiously merged. This inevitably suggests De Quincey's *Confessions of an English Opium-Eater* with its dream-wonders, yet it has a power of its own and the skillful blending of reality with dream-supernaturalism and insanity has an uncanny distinction.

Fu-Manchu, the Chinese wonder-worker in Sax Rohmer's series of stories bearing that name, is a representative example of the modern use of chemistry for supernormal effect. He employs all the forces of up-to-the-minute science to compass his diabolic ends and works miracles of chemistry by seemingly natural methods. By a hypodermic injection he can instantly drive a man to acute insanity incurable save by a counter-injection which only Fu-Manchu can give, but which as instantly restores the reason. By another needle he can cause a person to die—to all intents and purposes, at least,— and after the body has been buried for days he can restore it to life by another prick of the needle. He terrorizes England by his infernal powers, killing off or converting to slavery the leading intelligences that oppose him.

Stevenson's *Dr. Jekyll and Mr. Hyde* is perhaps the best-known instance of chemical supernaturalism. Here the magic drug not only changes the body, evolving from the respectable Dr. Jekyll his baser self in the form of Mr. Hyde, enabling him to give rein to his criminal instincts without bringing reproach on his reputation, but has the subtle power to fix the personality of evil, so that each time the drug is used Hyde is given a stronger force and Jekyll is weakened. This fictive sermon on dual nature, the ascendence ot evil over the nobler soul if it be indulged, seems yet an appallingly real story of human life. In a similar fashion Arthur Machen uses supernatural chemistry most hideously in *The Three Impostors*, where a certain powder perverts the soul, making man a sharer in the unspeakable orgies of ancient evil forces.

The Invisible Man, by H. G. Wells, shows an unusual application of chemistry to ghostly fiction that gives a peculiar effect of reality because its style is that of scientific realism. By experimentation with drugs a man finds a combination that will render living tissue absolutely invisible. When he swallows a portion of it, he cannot be seen. His clothes appear to be walking around by themselves and the complications are uncanny. As one may see, the comic possibilities are prominent and for a time we laugh over the mystification of the persons with whom he comes in contact, but soon stark tragedy results. During the man-chase, as the hunted creature seeks to escape, the people hear the thud-thud of running steps, watch bloody footprints form before their eyes, yet see nothing else. Here is a genuine thrill that is new in fiction. The man gradually becomes visible, but only in death is his dreadful figure seen completely again. This modern method of transferring to science the idea of invisibility so prominent in connection with ghosts, showing the invisibility as the result of a chemical compound, not of supernatural intervention, affecting a living man not a spirit, makes the effect of supernaturalism more vivid even than in the case of ghosts.

These are only suggestions of the varied uses to which chemistry has been put in producing ghostly plots and utilizing in novel ways the conventional motifs of older stories. These themes are more popular now than they would have been half a century ago because now the average reader knows more about scientific facts and is better prepared to appreciate them. A man ignorant of chemistry would care nothing for the throes of Dr. Jekyll or the complicating experiences of the invisible man, because he would have slight basis for his imagination to build upon. Each widening of the popular intelligence and each branch of science added to the mental store of the ordinary reader is a distinct gain to fiction.

Supernatural biology looms large in modern fiction, though it is not always easy to differentiate between the predominance of chemical and biological motifs. In many cases the two are tangled up together, and as, in the stories of dual personality and invisibility just mentioned, one may not readily say which is uppermost, the biological or the chemical side, for the experiments are of the effects of certain drugs upon living human tissue. There are various similar instances in the fiction of scientific supernaturalism. Hawthorne's *The Birthmark* is a case of chemical biology, where the husband seeking to remove by powerful drugs the mark from his wife's cheek succeeds in doing so but causes her death. Here the supernaturalism is symbolic, suggested rather than boldly stated, as is usually the case with Hawthorne's work.

A. Conan Doyle in *The Los Amigos Fiasco* shows supernaturalism based on the effect of electricity on the body, for the lynchers in trying to kill a man by connecting him with a dynamo succeed in so magnetizing him that he can't be killed in any way. Sax Rohmer tells one Fu-Manchu story of a mysterious murder committed by means of an imprisoned gas that escapes from a mummy case and poisons those exposed to it, and, in another, he introduces a diabolic red insect attracted by the scent of a poisonous orchid, that bites the marked victim.

Wells's *The Island of Dr. Moreau* is a ghastly study in vivisection. Two scientists on a remote island with no other human inhabitants try unspeakable experiments on animals, trying by pruning and grafting and training the living tissue to make them human. They do succeed in a measure, for they teach the beasts to talk and to observe a sort of jungle law laid down by man, yet the effect is sickening. The animals are not human and never can be, and these revolting experiments deprive them of all animal dignity without adding any of the human. In the end they revert to savagery, becoming even more bestial than before. The most dreadful biological experiments in recent fiction are described in Arthur Machen's volume of short stories, *The House of Souls*. In one story an operation on the brain enables a victim to "see the great god Pan," to have revelations of ancient supernaturalism wherein Pan and the devil are united in one character. In another, a delicate cutting of the brain removes the soul,—which takes the form of a wonderful jewel,—and utterly diabolizes the character. These curious and revolting stories are advanced instances of scientific diabolism and leave a smear on the mind. They are more horrible than the creation of Frankenstein's man-monster, for here moral monsters are evolved.

Medicated supernaturalism associated with prenatal influence occurs in various stories where a supernormal twist is given because of some event out of the ordinary. Ambrose Bierce's *The Eyes of the Panther*, a story of a young woman who is a panther for part of the time as a result of a shock, is associated with the snake nature of Elsie Venner. Barry Pain's *The Undying Thing* is one of the most horrible of such complications, for because of a mother's fright over a pack of wolves a monster is born, neither wolf nor human, neither animal nor man, neither mortal nor immortal. It is hidden in a secret cave to die, yet lives on, though not living, to fulfil a curse upon the ancient house. A. Conan Doyle's *The Terror of Blue John Gap* is a story of a monstrous animal, like a bear yet bigger than an elephant, that ravages the countryside. The theory for its being is that it is a survival, in a subterranean cave, of a long-extinct type, from prehistoric times, that comes out in its blindness to destroy. There are other examples of supernormal animals in modern fiction, yet these suffice to illustrate the *genre*.

Botany furnishes its ghostly plots in fiction as well as other branches of science, for we have plant vampires and witches and devils. Trees and flowers are highly psychic and run a gamut of emotions. Hawthorne shows us supernatural plants in several of his novels and stories, such as the mysterious plant growing from a secret grave, which has a strange poisonous power, or the flowers from Gaffer Dolliver's garden that shine like jewels and lend a glow to the living face near them, when worn on a woman's breast. In *Rappaccini's Daughter* the garden is full of flowers of subtle poison, so insidious that their venom has entered into the life of the young girl, rendering her a living menace to those around her. She is the victim of her father's dæmonic experiments in the effects of poison on the human body, and her kiss means death. Algernon Blackwood[1] tells of the uncanny power of motion and emotion possessed by the trees, where the forest exercises a magnetic force upon human beings sympathetic to them, going out after men and luring them to their fate. He describes the cedar as friendly to man and attempting but in vain to protect him from the creeping malignant power of the forest.

Fu-Manchu, Sax Rohmer's Chinese horror, performs

[1] In *The Man whom the Trees Loved.*

various experiments in botany to further his dreadful ends. He develops a species of poisonous fungi till they become giant in size and acquire certain powers through being kept in the darkness. When a light is turned on them, the fungi explode, turning loose, on the men he would murder, fumes that drive them mad. From the ceiling above are released ripe spores of the giant Empusa, for the air in the second cellar, being surcharged with oxygen, makes them germinate instantly. They fall like powdered snow upon the victims and the horrible fungi grow magically, spreading over the writhing bodies of the mad-men and wrapping them in ghostly shrouds. In *The Flower of Silence* he describes a strange orchid that has the uncanny habit of stinging or biting when it is broken or roughly handled, sending forth a poison that first makes a man deaf then kills him. Fu-Manchu introduces this flower into the sleeping-rooms of those he wishes to put out of the way, and sends them into eternal silence. *The Flowering of the Strange Orchid*, by H. G. Wells, is the story of a murderous plant, a vampire that kills men in the jungle, and in a greenhouse in England sends out its tentacles that grip the botanist, drinking his blood and seeking to slay him. This orchid has the power to project its vampiric attacks when it is a shriveled bulb or in the flower. This reminds us of Algernon Blackwood's story of the vampire soil, which after its psychic orgy burst into loathsome luxuriant bloom where before it had been barren.

It is a curious heightening of supernatural effect to give to beautiful flowers diabolical cunning and murderous motives, to endow them with human psychology and devilish designs. The magic associated with botany is usually black instead of white. One wonders if transmigration of soul does not enter subconsciously into these plots, and if a vampire orchid is not a trailing off of a human soul, the murderous blossom a revenge ghost expressing himself in that way. The plots in this type of fiction are wrought with much imagination and the scientific exactness combined with the supernatural gives a peculiar effect of reality.

There are varied forms of supernatural science that do not come under any of the heads discussed. The applications of research to weird fiction are as diverse as the phases of investigation and only a few may be mentioned to suggest the variety of themes employed. Inversion of natural laws furnishes plots,—as in Frank R. Stockton's *Tale of Negative Gravity* with its discovery of a substance that enables a man to save himself all fatigue by means of a something that inverts the law of gravity. With a little package in his pocket a man can climb mountains without effort, but the discoverer miscalculates the amount of energy required to move and finally rises instead of staying on the earth, till his wife has to fish him into the second-story window. Poe's *Loss of Breath* illustrates another infringement of a natural law, as do several stories where a human being loses his shadow.

In *The Diamond Lens*, Fitz-James O'Brien tells of a man who looking at a drop of water through a giant microscope sees in the drop a lovely woman with whom he falls madly in love, only to watch her fade away under the lens as his despairing eyes see the water evaporate. Supernatural acoustics enters[1] in the story of a man who discovers the sound-center in an opera house and reads the unspoken thoughts of those around him. He applies the laws of acoustics to mentality and spirituality, making astounding discoveries. Bram Stoker combines superstition with modern science in his books, as[2] where Oriental magic is used to fight the encroachments of an

[1] In *The Spider's Eye*, by Lucretia P. Hale.
[2] In *The Jewel of Seven Stars*.

evil force emanating from a mummy, as also to bring the
mummy to life, while a respirator is employed to keep
away the subtle odor.   He brings in blood transfusion
together with superstitious symbols, to combat the
ravages of vampires.[1]   Blood transfusion also enters into
supernaturalism in Stephen French Whitney's story,
where a woman who has been buried in a glacier for two
thousand years is recalled to life.

The Human Chord, by Algernon Blackwood, is a novel
based on the psychic values of sounds, which claims that
sounds are all powerful, are everything,—for forms, shapes,
bodies are but vibratory activities of sound made visible.
The research worker here believes that he who has the
power to call a thing by its proper name is master of that
thing, or of that person, and that to be able to call the
name of Deity would be to enable one to become as God.
He seeks to bring together a human chord, four persons
in harmony as to voice and soul, who can pronounce the
awful name and become divine with him.   He can change
the form or the nature of anything by calling its name, as a
woman is deformed by mispronunciation, and the walls
of a room expanded by his voice.   He can make of himself
a dwarf or a giant at will, by different methods of speaking his own name.   He says that sound could re-create or
destroy the universe.   He has captured sounds that strain
at their leashes in his secret rooms, gigantic, wonderful.
But in the effort to call upon the mighty Name he mis-
pronounces it, bringing a terrible convulsion of nature
which destroys him.   The beholders see an awful fire in
which Letters escape back to heaven in chariots of flame.

Psychology furnishes some interesting contributions
to recent fiction along the line of what might be called
momentary or instantaneous plots.   Ambrose Bierce's
The Occurrence at Owl Creek Bridge is a good example,—

[1] In *Dracula*.

where a man is being hanged and in the instant between the drop from the bridge and the breaking of the neck he lives through long and dramatic adventures, escaping his pursuers by falling into the river and swimming ashore, reaching home at last to greet his wife and children. Yet in a second his lifeless body swings from the bridge. *The Warning*, by Josephine Daskam Bacon, shows the case of a man who lives years in another country during a few moments of acute mental strain carried to the point of paranoia. Barry Pain has a story where in the time in which a man drives home from the theater he visits another planet and changes the current of his life, while Algernon Blackwood compresses a great experience into a few minutes of dreaming.

One noteworthy point in connection with the scientific supernaturalism is that these themes appear only in novels and short stories. They do not cross over into poetry as do most of the other forms of the ghostly art. Perhaps this is because the situations are intellectual rather than emotional, brain-problems or studies in mechanisms rather than in feelings or emotions. The province of science is removed from that of poetry because the methods and purposes are altogether different. The scientific methods are clear-cut, coldly intellectual. Science demands an exactness, a meticulous accuracy hostile to poetry which requires suggestion, vagueness, veiled mystery for its greatest effect. *The Flower of Silence*, for instance, would be a fitting title for a poem, but the poetic effect would be destroyed by the need for stating the genus and species of the orchid and analyzing its destruction of human tissue. Nature's mysterious forces and elements in general and vaguely considered, veiled in mists of imagination and with a sense of vastness and beauty, are extremely poetic. But the notebook and laboratory methods of pure science are antagonistic to poetry, though they fit admirably into the requirements of fiction, whose purpose is to give an impression of actuality.

Another reason why these scientific themes do not pass over into poetry may be that scientific methods as we know them are new, and poetry clings to the old and established conventions and emotions. There is amazing human interest in these experiments, a veritable wealth of romance, with dramatic possibilities tragic and comic, yet they are more suited to prose fiction than to poetry. We have adapted our brain-cells to their concepts in prose, yet we have not thus molded our poetic ideas. It gives us a shock to have new concepts introduced into poetry. An instance of this clash of realism with sentiment is shown in a recent poem where the setting is a physics laboratory. Yet in a few more decades we may find the poets eagerly converting the raw materials of science into the essence of poetry itself, and by a mystic alchemy more wonderful than any yet known, transmuting intellectual problems of science into magic verse. *Creation*, by Alfred Noyes, is an impressive discussion of evolution as related to God.

Perhaps another reason why these themes have not been utilized in poetry is because they are too fantastic, too bizarre. They lack the proportion and sense of artistic harmony that poetry requires. Strangeness and wonder are true elements of poetry, and magic is an element of the greatest art, but in solution as it were, not in the form observed in science. The miracles of the laboratory are too abrupt, too inconceivable save by intellectual analysis, and present too great a strain upon the powers of the imagination. They are fantastic, while true poetry is concerned with the fancy. Magic and wonder in verse must come from concepts that steal upon the imagination and make appeal through the emotions. Thus some forms of supernaturalism are admirably adapted to the province of poetry, such as the presence of spirits, visitations of angels or demons, ancient witchcraft, and so forth. The elements that have universal appeal through the sense of the supernatural move us in poetry, but the isolated instances, the peculiar problems that occur in scientific research if transferred to poetry would leave us cold. Yet they may come to be used in the next *vers libre*.

Nor do these situations come over into the drama save in rare instances. Theodore Dreiser, in a recent volume, *Plays of the Natural and the Supernatural*, makes use of certain motifs that are striking and modern, as[1] where a physician goes on the operating-table, the *dramatis personæ* including Demyaphon (Nitrous Acid), and Alcepheron (a Power of Physics), as well as several Shadows, mysterious personages of vagueness. These Shadows here, as in *The Blue Sphere*, are not altogether clear as to motivation, yet they seem to stand for Fate interference in human destiny. In the latter play Fate is also represented by a Fast Mail which is one of the active characters, menacing and destroying a child.

One reason why these motifs of science are not used in drama to any extent is that they are impossible of representation on the stage. Even the wizardry of modern producers would be unable to show a Power of Physics, or Nitrous Acid, save as they might be embodied, as were the symbolic characters in Maeterlinck's *Blue Bird*, which would mean that they would lose their effect. And what would a stage manager do with the rhythm of the universe, which enters into Dreiser's play? Many sounds can be managed off stage, but hardly that, one fancies. These themes are not even found in closet drama, where many other elements of supernaturalism which would be difficult or impossible of presentation on the stage trail off. William Sharp's *Vistas*, for instance, could not be shown on

[1] In *Laughing Gas*.

the stage, yet the little plays in that volume are of wonderful dramatic power. The drama can stand a good deal of supernaturalism of various kinds, from the visible ghosts and devils of the Elizabethans to the atmospheric supernaturalism of Maeterlinck, but it could scarcely support the presentations of chemicals and gases and supernatural botany and biology that fiction handles with ease. The miraculous machinery would balk at stage action. Fancy the Time Machine staged, for instance!

We notice in these scientific stories a widening of the sphere of supernatural fiction. It is extended to include more of the normal interests and activities of man than has formerly been the case. Here we notice a spirit similar to that of the leveling influence seen in the case of the ghosts, devils, witches, angels, and so forth, who have been made more human not only in appearance but in emotions and activities as well. Likewise these scientific elements have been elevated to the human. Supernatural as well as human attributes have been extended to material things, as animals are given supernormal powers in a sense different from and yet similar to those possessed by the enchanted animals in folk-lore. Science has its physical as well as psychic horrors which the scientific ghostly tales bring in.

Not only are animals gifted with supernatural powers but plants as well are humanized, diabolized. We have strange murderous trees, vampire orchids, flowers that slay men in secret ways with all the smiling loveliness of a treacherous woman. The dæmonics of modern botany form an interesting phase of ghostly fiction and give a new thrill to supernaturalism. Inanimate, concrete things are endowed with unearthly cunning and strength, as well as animals and plants. The new type of fiction gives to chemicals añd gases a hellish intelligence, a diabolic force of minds. It creates machinery and gives it an excess of force, a supernatural, more than human cunning, sometimes helpful, sometimes dæmonic. Machines have been spiritualized and some engines are philanthropic while some are like damned souls.

This scientific supernaturalism concerns itself with mortal life, not with immortality as do some of the other aspects of the *genre*. It is concrete in its effects, not spiritual. Its incursions into futurity are earthly, not of heaven or hell, and its problems are of time, not of eternity. The form shows how clear, cold intelligence plays with miracles and applies the supernatural to daily life. The enthusiasm, wild and exaggerated in some ways, that sprang up over the prospects of what modern science and investigation would almost immediately do for the world in the latter half of the nineteenth century, had no more interesting effect than in the stimulating of scientific fictive supernaturalism. And though mankind has learned that science will not immediately bring the millennium, science still exercises a strong power over fiction. This type shows a strange effect of realism in supernaturalism, because of the scientific methods, for supernaturalism imposed on material things produces an effect of verisimilitude not gained in the realm of pure spirit. Too intellectually cold for the purposes of poetry, too abstract and elusive for presentation in drama, and too removed by its association with the fantastic aspects of investigation and the curiosities of science to be very appropriate for tragedy, which has hitherto been the chief medium of expressing the dramatic supernatural, science finds its fitting expression in prose fiction. It is an illustration of the widening range of the supernatural in fiction and as such is significant.

CHAPTER VIII

Conclusion

IN the previous chapters I have endeavored to show the continuance and persistence of the supernatural in English fiction, as well as in other forms of literature, and to give some idea of the variety of its manifestations. There has been no period in our history from Beowulf to the present when the ghostly was not found in our literature. Of course, there have been periods when the interest in it waned, yet it has never been wholly absent. There is at the present a definite revival of interest in the supernatural appearing in the drama, in poetry and in fiction, evident to anyone who has carefully studied the recent publications and magazines. Within the last few years, especially in the last two years, an astonishing amount of ghostly material has appeared. Some of these stories are of the hoax variety, others are suggestive, allegorical or symbolic, while others frankly accept the forces beyond man's mortal life and human dominion. I hesitate to suggest a reason for this sudden rising tide of occultism at this particular time, but it seems clear to me that the war has had much to do with it. I have found a number of supernatural productions directly associated with the struggle. Among them might be mentioned Katherine Fullerton Gerould's extraordinary, elusive story of horror[1]; *The Second Coming*, by Frederick Arnold

[1] *The Eighty-Third.*

Kummer and Henry P. Janes, where Christ walks the
battlefields on Christmas Eve, pleading with the Kaiser
to stop the slaughter of men, but in vain, and the carnage
goes on till Easter, when the Christ stands beside the
dying Emperor, with the roar of the rioting people heard
in the streets outside, and softens his heart at last, so
that he says, "Lord, I have sinned! Give my people
peace!"; Kipling's ghost-story,[1] with its specters of children slain by the Germans; *The Gray Guest*, showing
Napoleon returning to lead the French forces to victory
in a crisis; *Jeanne, the Maid* where the spirit of Joan of
Arc descends upon a young French girl of to-day, enabling
her to do wonderful things for her countrymen; *War Letters
from a Living Dead Man*, a series of professed psychic
communications from the other world, by Elsa Barker;
Real Ghost Stories, a volume containing a number of stories
by different writers, describing some of the phantoms
seen by soldiers on the battlefield; and Arthur Machen's
The Bowmen, a collection of striking fictive instances
of crowd-supernaturalism associated with the war. The
last volume affords an interesting glimpse into the
way in which legends are built up, for it is a contemporary legend in connection with the Angels at
Mons. Carl Hauptmann has a striking play,[2] showing
the use of war-supernaturalism in the drama. When
the eyes of the world are turned toward the battlefields
and death is an ever-present reality, it is natural that
human thoughts occupy themselves with visions of a life
after death. *Kingdom Come*, by Vida Sutton, shows
the spirits of Russian peasants slain for refusing to fight,
specters unaware that they are dead. Various martial
heroes of the past are resurrected to give inspiration in
battle in recent stories.

[1] *Swept and Garnished.*
[2] *The Dead Are Singing*, in the May, 1916, *Texas Review.*

But whatever be the reason for this revival of the ghostly, the fact remains that this is distinctly the day for the phantom and his confrères. While romanticism is always with us, it appears in different manifestations. A few years ago the swashbuckling hero and his adventures seemed the most striking survival of the earlier days of romanticism, but now the weird and the ghostly have regained a popularity which they never surpassed even in the heyday of Gothic fiction. The slashing sword has been displaced by the psychographic pen. The crucial struggles now are occult, rather than adventurous, as before, and while realism in fiction is immensely popular—never more so than now—it is likely to have supernaturalism overlaid upon it, as in De Morgan's work, to give a single example. Recent poetry manifests the same tendency, and likewise the drama, particularly the closet drama and the playlet. While literary history shows clearly the continuity of the supernatural, with certain rise and fall of interest in it at different periods, it is apparent that now there is a more general fondness for the form than at any other period in English literature. The supernatural is in solution and exists everywhere. Recent poetry shows a strong predilection for the uncanny, sometimes in the manner of the old ballads, while in other instances the ghostly is treated with a spirit of critical detachment as in Rupert Brooke's sonnet,[1] or with skepticism as in his sardonic satire on faith.[2] In the recent volume of Brooke's collected poems, there are about a dozen dealing with the supernatural. Maeterlinck expressed the feeling that a spiritual epoch is perhaps upon us, as Poe said that we are in the midst of great psychal powers. As Francis Thompson says in his *Hound of Heaven*, "Nature, poor step-dame, cannot

---

[1] *Suggested by some of the Proceedings of the Society for Psychical Research.*
[2] In his *Heaven.*

slake our drought!'' The interest in certain lines of thought which lead to the writing of supernatural fiction, as Spiritualism or folk-lore, or science or psychical research, may have the reflex action of arousing interest in the subjects themselves. But at all events, there is no lack of uncanny literature at present.

One feature of the modern supernatural literature as distinguished from that of other periods, is in the matter of length. Of course, the ballad and the folk-tale expressed the ghostly in brief form, but the epic held the stage longer, while in Elizabethan times the drama was the preferred form as in the eighteenth century the Gothic novel. During the nineteenth century, particularly the latter half, the preference was decidedly for the short story, while more recently the one-act play has come into vogue. But in the last few years the supernatural novel seems to be returning to favor, though without displacing the shorter forms. Brevity has much to commend it as a vehicle for the uncanny. The effect of the ghostly may be attained with much more unity in a short story or playlet than in a novel or long drama, for in the more lengthy form much outside matter is necessarily included. The whole plot could scarcely be made up of the unearthly, for that would mean a weakening of power through exaggeration, though this is sometimes found to be the case, as in several of Bram Stoker's novels. Recently the number of novels dealing with supernatural themes has noticeably increased, which leads one to believe that the occult is transcending even the limitations of length and claiming all forms for its own. Now no literary type bars the supernatural, which appears in the novel as in the story, in the drama as in the playlet, and in narrative, dramatic, and lyric poetry. Even the epic of the more than mortal has not entirely vanished, as the work of Dr. William Cleaver Wilkinson attests, but

popular taste does not really run to epics nowadays.
The ghostly is more often seen in the shorter forms, where
brevity gives a chance for compression and intensity of
force difficult in longer vehicles. The rise of the one-act
play in popular favor is significant in this connection.
The short dramas of Synge, Yeats, Lady Gregory, William
Sharpe, Gordon Bottomley, and Theodore Dreiser show
the possibilities of the playlet for weird effect. Maeterlinck's plays for marionettes are especially powerful, but
the work of Lord Dunsany furnishes more peculiar ghostliness than that of any other present dramatist. His jade
idols, for instance, that wake to terrible life and revenge
themselves on presumptuous mortals, are a new touch in
dramatics. Algernon Blackwood is doing more significant
work in psychic fiction than anyone else, his prose showing
poetic beauty as well as eerie power.

Another significant fact to be noted in connection with
the later ghostly stories as compared with the Gothic is in
the greater number and variety of materials employed.
The early religious plays had introduced devils, angels, and
divinity to a considerable extent, while the Elizabethan
drama relied for its thrills chiefly on the witch and the
revenge-ghost. The Gothic romance was strong for the
ghost, with one or two Wandering Jews, occasional werewolves and lycanthropes, and sporadic satanity, but made
no use of angels or of divinity. The modern fiction,
however, gathers up all of these personages and puts them
into service freely. In addition to these old themes brought
up to date and varied astonishingly, the new fiction has
adapted other types. The scientific supernaturalism
is practically new—save for the Gothic employment of
alchemy and astrology—and now all the discoveries and
investigations of the laboratory are utilized and embued
with supernaturalism. Diabolic botany, psychological
chemistry, and supermortal biology appear in recent

fiction. The countless arts and sciences, acoustics, optics, dietetics, and what-not are levied on for plots, while astronomy shows us wonders the astrologer never dreamed of. The stars knew their place and kept it in early romance, but they are given to strange aberration and unaccountable conduct in late narration.

The futuristic fiction gives us return trips into time to come, while we may be transported into the far past, as with Mark Twain's Connecticut Yankee that visits King Arthur's Court. The extent to which a homespun realist like Mark Twain uses the supernatural is significant. No province or small corner of science has failed to furnish material for the new ghostly fiction, and even the Fourth and Fifth Dimensions are brought in as plot complications. Microscopes are bewitched, mirrors are enchanted, and science reverses its own laws at will to suit the weird demands.

Another modern material is the mechanistic. This is the age of machinery, and even engines are run by ghost-power. Examples of the mechanical spook are legion. There is the haunted automobile in Harriet Prescott Spofford's story, *The Mad Lady*, that reproduces through its speaking tube the long-dead voice, that runs away with its occupants, reliving previous tragic experiences. A phantom Ford is an idea combining romanticism with realism surely! In connection with this extraordinary car is a house that erects itself out of dreams and is substantial enough for living purposes. Other specimens are John Kendrick Bangs's enchanted typewriter that clicks off psychograms in the dark, between midnight and three o'clock in the morning; Frank R. Stockton's machine for negativing gravity; Poe's balloon in which Hans Pfaal makes his magic trip to the moon; Wells's new accelerator that condenses and intensifies vital energy, enabling a man to crowd the forces of a week into an hour of emergency, as likewise his time machine that permits the inventor to project himself into the future or the past at will, to spend a week-end in any era. The butterfly in Hawthorne's story shows the spiritualization of machinery as the poor artist of the beautiful conceived it, the delicate toy imbibing a magnetism, a spiritual essence that gives it life and beauty and power of voluntary motion. This etherealized machinery is manifest in modern fiction as well as the diabolic constructions that wreck and ruin.

Inanimate objects have a strange power in later fiction as Poe's ship that is said in certain seas to increase in size, as the trees told of by Algernon Blackwood that grow in the picture. There are various haunted portraits, as the picture of Dorian Grey that bears on its face the lines of sin the living face does not show, and whose hands are bloodstained when Dorian commits murder; and the painting told of in De Morgan's *A Likely Story*, that overhears a quarrel between an artist and his wife, the woman wrongly suspecting her husband and leaving him. The picture relates the story to a man who has the painting photographed and a copy sent to the wife. There is the haunted tapestry[1] that is curiously related to the living and to the long dead.

Another aspect of the later as distinguished from the earlier occult literature is the attention paid to ghostly children. Youngsters are coming to the front of the stage everywhere nowadays, particularly in America, so it is but natural that they should demand to be heard as well as seen, in supernatural fiction. In the Gothic ghosts I found no individualized children, and children in groups only twice. In one of James Hogg's short novels a vicious man is haunted on his death-bed by the specters of little ones dead because of him, but they

[1] In Poe's *Metzengerstein*.

are nameless and indistinguishable. In Maturin's *The Albigenses* a relentless persecutor, while passing through a lonely forest, sees the phantoms of those he has done to death, little children and babes at the breast, as well as men and women. But here again they are not given separable character, but are merely group figures, hence do not count.

There is a ghost-child mentioned in Hawthorne's *Blithedale Romance*, but it is not until more recent fiction that children's ghosts enter personated and individualized. The exquisitely shy little ones in Kipling's *They* are among the most wonderful of his child-creations, very human and lovable. In a war story,[1] he shows us the phantoms of several children whom the Germans have killed, natural youngsters with appealing childish attributes, especially the small boy with his pride in his first trousers. Arthur Machen[2] tells of a German soldier who has crucified a child against the church door and is driven to insanity by the baby spirit. Quiller-Couch[3] shows the specter of a little girl that returns at night to do housework for the living, visible only as two slender hands, who reminds us of the shepherd boy Richard Middleton tells of, who having died because of his drunken father's neglect, comes back to help him tend the sheep. Algernon Blackwood relates the story of a little child who has been wont to pray for the unquiet ghost of Petavel, a wicked man who haunts his house. After the child is dead, the mother sees the little boy leading Petavel by the hand, and says, "He's leading him into peace and safety. Perhaps that's why God took him."

Richard Middleton's story of a little ghost-boy[4] is poignantly pathetic. The little chap comes back to

---

[1] *Swept and Garnished.*
[2] In *The Monstrance*, another story of the war.
[3] In *A Pair of Hands.*   [4] *The Passing of Edward.*

play with his grieving sister, making his presence known by his gay feet dancing through the bracken, and his joyous imitations of an automobile's chug-chug. Mary MacMillan speaks of the spirits of little children that are "out earlier at night than the older ghosts, you know, because they have to go to bed earlier, being so young." Two very recent child ghosts are Wee Brown Elsbeth whom Frances Hodgson Burnett shows to us, the wraith of a little girl pitifully slain centuries ago by her father to save her from torture, who comes back to play with a living playmate; and the terrible revenge-ghost of the child slain by her stepfather, who comes back to cause his death, whom Ellen Glasgow describes.

The spirits of children that never were enter into the late stories, as in *The Children*, by Josephine Daskam Bacon, a story of confused paranoia and supernaturalism. A woman grieves over the children she never had till they assume personality and being for her. They become so real that they are finally seen by other children who wish to play with them. This reminds us of Thomas Bailey Aldrich's imagined child, Miss Mehitabel's son. Algernon Blackwood[1] shows us a multitude of baby spirits, with reaching arms, pattering steps, and lisping voices, spirits of the unborn that haunt childless women. The room which they enter seems sacred with the potentialities of motherhood, so that a man sleeping there sees his own dead mother return to him among the babes. These ghosts of little children that never were and never may be are like the spirits of the yet to be born children in Maeterlinck's dream-drama,[2] where, in the Land of the Future, the child-souls wait for the angel to summon them to life. In these stories associating children with the ghostly there is always a tender pathos, a sad beauty that is appealing.

[1] In *Clairvoyance*. [2] *The Blue Bird*.

The spectral insect or animal is another innovation in recent fiction, though there have been occasional cases before, as Vergil's *Culex*, the story of the ghost of a gnat killed thoughtlessly coming back to tell its murderer of its sufferings in the insect hades. Robert W. Chambers shows us several ghostly insects, a death's head moth that is a presager of disaster, and a butterfly that brings a murderer to justice, while Frederick Swanson in a story[1] makes a spectral insect a minister of fate. The most curdling example, however, of the entomological supernaturalism, is Richard Marsh's novel, *The Beetle*, a modernized version of the ancient superstitions of Egypt, whereby a priestess of Isis continues her mysterious, horrid life alternately as a human being and as a beetle. This lively scarab has mesmeric, magic power over mortals and by its sensational shape-shifting furnishes complicating terror to the plot.

The dog is frequently the subject of occult fiction, more so than any other animal, perhaps because the dog seems more nearly human than any save possibly the horse. Mrs. Elizabeth Stuart Phelps Ward shows us a dog very much at home in heaven, while she has a ghost-dog on earth coming back to march in a Decoration Day parade beside his master. Isabel Howe Fisk in a drama shows the Archangel Raphael accompanied by his dog, a cavortive canine, not apparently archangelic. Ambrose Bierce evokes one terrible revenge-ghost, a dog that kills the murderer of his master, while[2] Eden Phillpotts represents a pack of spectral dogs that pursue the Evil One over the earth till the Judgment Day, each being a lost soul. A young girl's little unbaptized baby is thought to be one of the number. Conan Doyle's Hound of the Baskervilles is a terrifying canine of legendary power. *Kerfol* by Edith Wharton shows the ghosts of five dogs,

[1] *The Ghost Moth.* [2] In *Another Little Heath Hound.*

each carefully individualized,—a Chinese sleeve-dog, a rough brindled bulldog, a long-haired white mongrel, a large white pointer with one brown ear, and a small black grayhound. These specters of animals that have been killed by a jealous husband—he had the cheerful habit of strangling every pet his wife cared for and laying it without a word on her pillow—appear once a year on the anniversary of the day on which the wife in desperation slew him. They preserve a most undoglike silence and follow the beholder with strange gaze. Kipling's dog Harvey is a supernatural beast, but what he represents I have never been able to determine. *At the Gate* is a recent story, showing a great concourse of dogs just outside the portals of heaven, unwilling to enter till their masters come to join them.

The diabolic horse in Poe's *Metzengerstein* is a curious composite of metempsychosis, haunted inanimate object, and straight ghost, but at all events sufficiently terrifying to the victim it pursued. Algernon Blackwood in *Wendigo* has created a supernatural animal that flies through the air and carries men away to insanity and death. Henry Rideout shows the ghost of a white tiger, while there are assorted elephant spooks, and Miss Burns in her studies in Shropshire folk-tales relates stories of human beings whose ghosts appear as animals suited to the personality of the deceased, as bears, bulls, hogs, and so forth. That adds a new terror to death!

Not only are new materials introduced in the later fiction of the uncanny but new types are stressed. In addition to the weird stories told with direct aim and art— ghosts for ghosts' sake—there are tales where the supernatural element is of secondary importance, being used to teach some truth or ridicule some fallacy. The symbolistic, humorous, and satiric methods abound in modern occult fiction and when well done have a double effect, that of primary supernatural impressiveness, and, in addition, of the subtler purposes behind the stories. Moralized legends, spiritual allegories such as Hawthorne wrote with consummate art, have continued to the present and form a contrast to the crude machinery of Gothic horrors. The delicacy of suggestion, the power of hinted ghostliness, though manifest in Shakespeare, are really modern achievements, for no one save him attained to them in earlier art. Mystic poetic fiction, spiritual symbolism appears in much of the modern unearthly writing. In certain cases it is interesting to note the change of old mythological stories into moral allegory. The plays and the stories of Lord Dunsany are peculiarly symbolic and have the force of antique mythology made instant and real. Yet they have a distinctive touch all their own. For instance, the story of the king who goes over the world seeking his lost yesterday, his dear past, who is told by the weird keeper of the bygone years that he cannot have it back, no not one golden second, has a delicate pathos of poetry. When the mournful king has gone back to his palace, a hoar harper comes who plays for him, and lo! to the strings of the harp have clung the golden seconds of his happiest hours, so that he lives them over again while the music lasts. *The Book of the Serpent* tells symbolic stories that are poems in prose, fantastic fables. The Creator is making experiments with dust-heaps, while the Serpent, the Turtle, and the Grasshopper look on, ask questions, and offer comments. The Serpent trails all through the dust-heap meant as stuff for artists, and the Maker drops a tear in that whereof He means to make mothers. He experiments with monkeys trying to learn how best to make man, and after man is complete, He makes woman. The stories of Oscar Wilde have, some of them, a beauty like that of some antique illuminated missal, with its jeweled words, its mystic figures. Wilde's ornate style, prose that trembles on the verge of poetry, full of passion and color and light, makes one think of his own words in *The Nightingale and the Rose*, where the poet's song was "builded of music by moonlight and stained with his own heart's blood."

The delicate suggestion of the unearthly, the element of suspense that gives the sense of the supernatural to that which may be mortal, is seen in such stories as *A Dream of Provence*, by Frederick Wedmore. The ancient belief that the soul may return to the body within a few days after death forms the basis for this dream-poem in prose. It shows the soul on tiptoe for the Unseen, with a love transcending the barriers of the grave, revealing idyllic sorrow in a father's love that denies death, and expresses the sense of expectancy in the hope of a miracle, with a beauty that is almost unbearable. Something of the same theme, of a father's waiting by his daughter's grave to hear the loved voice once more, is expressed in Andreyev's story.[1] But here there is horror and remorse instead of holy love. When the father cries out, the silence that issues from the grave is more terrible than ghostly sounds would be, more dreadful in its supermortal suggestion.

The purely humorous supernaturalism is essentially a new thing. The old religious dramas had used comic devils, and Peele's Ghost of Jack is supposed to be humorous, but not at all in the modern sense. There was nothing in early drama or fiction like the rollicking fun of Richard Middleton's Ghost Ship, or Frank R. Stockton's spectral humorists. The work of John Kendrick Bangs illustrates the free and easy manner of the moderns toward ghosts,

[1] *Silence.*

picturing them in unconventional situations and divesting
them of all their ancient dignity. He shows us the
wraith of the maiden who drowned herself in a fit of pique,
for which she is punished by having to haunt the ancestral
house as a shower-bath. His spectral cook of Bangletop
is an original revenge-ghost, with a villainous inversion
of h's, who haunts an estate because a medieval baron
discharged her without wages. His convivial spooks in
their ghost club, his astrals who play pranks on mortals,
and their confrères are examples of the modern flippancy
toward supernaturals.

The satirical use of supernaturalism is also new. Late
literature laughs at everything, with a daring familiarity
undreamed of before, save in sporadic cases. The devil
has been an ancient subject for laughter, but recent fiction
ridicules him still more, so that we have scant respect
for him, while the ghost, formerly a personage held in
great respect, now comes in for his share of ragging. No
being is too sacred to escape the light arrows of fun.
Heaven is satirically exploited, and angels, saints, and even
Deity have become subjects for jesting, conventionalized
with the mother-in-law, the tenderfoot, the Irishman, and
so forth. There is a considerable body of anecdotal
literature of the supernatural, showing to what extent
the levity of treatment has gone. Various aspects of
mortal life are satirized, as in Inez Haynes Gilmore's
Angel Island, which is a campaign document for woman's
suffrage. Satiric' supernaturalism is employed to drive
home many truths, to puncture conceits of all kinds,
and when well done is effective, for laughter is a clever
weapon.

The advance of the later supernatural fiction over the
earlier is nowhere seen more distinctly than in the increased effectiveness with which it manages the mechanics
of emotion, its skill in selecting and elaborating the details

by which terror and awe are produced. The present-
day artist of the uncanny knows how to strike the varied
tones of supernaturalism, the shrill notes of fear, the deep
diapason of awe, the crashing chords of horror. The
skillful writer chooses with utmost care the seemingly
trivial details that go to make up the atmosphere of the
unearthly. Shakespeare was a master of that, but none
other of his time. The knocking at the gate in *Macbeth*,
for instance, is a perfect example of the employment of a
natural incident to produce an effect of the supernatural,
as De Quincey has pointed out in his essay on the subject.

The Gothic novel relied largely for its impressiveness
on emphasizing ghostly scenes by representing aspects of
weather to harmonize with the emotions of the characters.
This was overworked in terror fiction, and while it still
possesses power it is a much less common method of
technique than it used to be. Poe's introductory paragraph in *The Fall of the House of Usher* is a notable example of skill in creating atmosphere of the supernatural by
various details including phenomena of weather, and
Hardy shows special power in harmonizing nature to the
moods and purposes of his characters. Yet many a
modern story produces a profound sense of awe, and
purges the soul by means of terror with no reference at all
to foreboding weather. However, the allusions now made
are more skillful and show more selective power than of
old.

Gothic fiction had much to say of melancholy birds
that circled portentously over ancient castles filled with
gloom and ghosts, but they were generic and not individual
specimens. The fowl was always spoken of as "a bird of
prey," "a night bird," "a bat," "an owl," or by some
such vague term. Natural history has become more
generally known since those times and writers of to-day
introduce their ominous birds with more definiteness and

appropriateness. The repulsive bat that clings to the window ledge in Bram Stoker's novel is a vampire, a symbol of the whole horrible situation, as the kite that soars menacingly overhead in another of his novels is individualized and becomes a definite thing of terror. Poe's raven is vastly more a bird of evil than any specimen in the Gothic aviary. Robert W. Chambers brings in a cormorant several times as a portent of ghostly disaster, particularly foreboding when it turns toward the land. "On the dark glistening cliffs, silhouetted against the glare of the sea, sat a cormorant, black, motionless, its horrible head raised toward heaven." There is in recent fiction no bird more dreadful in import than the belled buzzard that Irvin Cobb makes the leading figure in his story by that name. This is an excellent example of the use of the natural to produce terror and awe, for the murderer sees in the bird a minister of fate, and the faint tinkle of its bell as it soars over the marsh where the body lies buried paralyzes him with horror. At last he can bear no more, and hearing it, as he thinks, close at hand, he shrieks out his confession,—only to find this time that it is not the belled buzzard at all that he hears, but only an old cowbell that a little negro child has picked up in the barnyard!

Robert W. Chambers in his early stories contrives to give varying supernatural effects by descriptions of shadows as symbolic of life and character. He speaks of shadows of spirits or of persons fated to disaster as white; again his supernatural shadows may be gray—gray is a favored shade for ghostly effect whether for witches or for phantoms—and sometimes they are perfectly black, to indicate differing conditions of destiny. Quiller-Couch has a strange little allegory, *The Magic Shadow*, and other writers have used similar methods to produce uncanny effects.

The Gothic romance made much use of portents of the supernatural, which later fiction does as well, but differently and with greater skill. The modern stories for the most part abandon the conventional portents, the dear old clock forever striking twelve or one—there was no Gothic castle so impoverished as to lack such ghostly horologue!— the abbey bell that tolls at touch of spirit hands or wizard winds, the statuesque nose-bleed, the fire that burns blue at approach of a specter, and so forth. The later story is more selective in its aids to ghostly effect, and adapts the means desired to each particular case, so that it hits the mark. For instance, the sardonic laughter that sounds as the burglars are cracking the gate of heaven to get in, and imagining what they will find, is prophetic of the emptiness, the nothingness, that meets their astounded gaze when they are within. Ambrose Bierce in some of his stories describes the repulsiveness of the fleshly corpse, reanimated by the spirit, perhaps *not* the spirit belonging to it, with a loathly effect more aweful than any purely psychic phantom could produce, which reminds us somewhat of the corpse come to life in Thomas Lovell Beddoes's *Death's Jest Book*.

The horrors of invisibility in modern fiction avail to give a ghastly chill to the soul that visible apparitions rarely impart. Likewise the effect of mystery, of the incalculable element, in giving an impression of supernaturalism is a recognized method of technique in many stories, as the minister's black veil in Hawthorne's symbolic story. The unspeakable revolting suggestion in Edith Wharton's *The Eyes*, where a man is haunted by two hideous eyes that "have the physical effect of a bad smell, whose look left a smear like a snail," is built up with uncommon art. We do not realize how much is due to insanity and how much to the supernatural, when, after telling the story of his obsession, his fears that as a climax

he will become like those Eyes, the man suddenly sees
his reflection in the mirror and meets their dreadful
gaze. "He and the image confronted each other with a
glare of slowly gathering hate!" Mention might be made
of an incident in a recently published literary drama,
where a man seeks over the world for the unknown woman
with whom he has fallen in love, and on his calling aloud
in question as to who she is, "the grave, with nettle-
bearded lips replied, 'It is I, Death!'" These are only
suggestions of numberless instances that might be given
of a modern technique of supernaturalism that surpasses
anything in Gothic fiction.

The effectiveness of modern ghostly stories is aided by
the suggestiveness of the unearthly given by the use of
"sensitives," animals or persons that are peculiarly alert
to the occult impressions. We see in many stories that
children perceive the supernatural presences more quickly
than adults, as in Mrs. Oliphant's story of the ghost
returning to right a wrong, trying strenuously to make
herself known to the grown person and realized only by a
little child. In Belasco's play the little boy is the first
and for a long time the only one to sense the return of
Peter Grimm. In Maeterlinck's *The Blind*, the baby in
arms is aware of the unearthly presences better than the
men and women. Sometimes the sensitive is a blind
person, as the old grandfather in another of Maeterlinck's short plays, who is conscious of the approaching
Death before any of the others, or blind Anna in D'Annunzio's drama, *The Dead City*.

Animals are quick to perceive supernatural manifestations. Cats in fiction are shown as being at ease in the
presence of ghosts perhaps because of their uncanny
alliance with witches, while dogs and horses go wild with
fear. This is noticed in many stories, as in Bulwer-
Lytton's story of the haunted house where the dog dies of

terror in the face of the ghostly phenomena. The Psychic Doctor told of in Blackwood's uncanny stories, who goes to a house possessed by evil spirits, takes with him a cat and a dog which by their difference of action reveal to him the presence of the spirits long before they are visualized for him.

In general, there is more power of suggestion in the later ghostly stories than in the earlier. The art is more subtle, the technique more skillfully studied, more artfully accidental.

There is in modern fiction, notably the work of Poe, and that of many recent writers, Russian, French, and German as well as English, a type of supernaturalism that is closely associated with insanity. One may not tell just where the line is drawn, just how much of the element of the uncanny is the result of the broodings of an unbalanced brain, and how much is real ghostliness. Poe's studies of madness verge on the unearthly, as do Maupassant's, Hoffmann's, and others. Josephine Daskam Bacon illustrates this genre in a recent volume of stories, *The Strange Cases of Dr. Stanchion*, the plots centering round instances of paranoia occurring in the practice of a famous alienist, —yet they are *not paranoia alone!* One instance is of a young girl who is haunted by the ghost of a nurse who has died because given the wrong medicine by mistake. She is on the border-line of insanity when her lover cries aloud that he would take the curse on himself for her if he could, which, by some unknown psychic law, does effect a transference which frees her and obsesses him. Another is that of a man in the insane asylum, who recognizes in a mysterious housekeeper the spirit of his wife, who comes from the grave to keep him company and vanishes on the day of his death. These are curious analyses of the *idée fixe* in its effect on the human mind, of insanity as a cause or effect of the supernatural. Barry

Pain's *Celestial Grocery* is a recent example, a story of a man whose madness carries him to another planet, showing him inverted aspects of life, where emotions are the only real things, all else but shadows. Du Maurier's pathetic novel portraying the passion and anguish and joy of Peter Ibbetson that touches the thin line between sanity and madness, showing in his dream-metempsychosis a power to relive the past and even to live someone else's life, is a striking example. One interesting aspect of that story is the point where the spirit of Mary changes from the dream-lover of twenty-eight to the ghost of the woman fifty-two, since she has died and can no more come to her lover as she once did, but must come as her own phantom. There are extraordinary effects of insanity associated with the supernatural in the work of Ambrose Bierce, of Arthur Machen and others of the modern school. Italian literature shows some significant instances in Fogazzaro's *The Woman* and D'Annunzio's *Sogno d'un Mattino di Primavera*. As Lord Dunsany says of it, "Who can say of insanity,—whether it be divine or of the Pit?"

We have noticed in preceding chapters two aspects of modern supernaturalism as distinguished from the Gothic, —the giving of cumulative and more terrible power to ghostly beings, and on the other hand the leveling influence that makes them more human. The access of horror and unearthly force as shown in the characters described by certain writers is significant. In the work of Bierce, Machen, Blackwood, Stoker, and others supernaturalism is raised to the nth power and every possible thrill is employed. The carrion ghosts of Bierce, animated by malignant foreign spirits, surpass the charnel shudders produced by the Gothic. Algernon Blackwood's Psychic Invasions, where localities rather than mere apartments or houses alone are haunted, diabolized by undying evil influences with compound power, his Elementals that control the forces of wind and wave and fire to work their demon will, are unlike anything that the early terror novel conceived of. Horace Walpole and Mrs. Radcliffe knew no thrills like those of Bram Stoker's Count Dracula who is an immemorial evil, a vampire and werewolf as well as man, with power to change himself into a vampire bat or animal of prey at will. *The Unburied*, by Josephine Daskam Bacon, is more horrific than any mere revenge ghost, however much it shrieked "Vindicta!" The diabolism in Arthur Machen's work reeks obscurely of a Pit more horrible than epic or drama has portrayed. In general, many of the later ghostly characters are more complex, more intense in evil than the Gothic.

While it is true that certain writers show a tendency to create supernatural characters having an excess of evil power beyond the previous uncanny beings, on the other hand there is an equally strong and significant tendency to reduce the ghostly beings nearer to the human. Fiction here, as frequently, seems ahead of general belief, and refuses to believe in the altogether evil. Ghosts, angels, witches, devils, werewolves, and so forth are now made more human, more like to man, yet without losing any of their ancient power to thrill. Ghosts in late literature have more of the mortal characteristics than ever before, as has been pointed out in a previous chapter. They look more human, more normal, they are clad in everyday garments of varied colors, from red shirts and khaki riding-habits to ball-gowns,—though gray seems the favored shade for shades as well as witches,—and they have lost that look of pallor that distinguished early phantoms. Now they are more than merely vaporous, projections as they used to be, more than merely phantasmogenetic apparitions, — but are healthy, red-blooded spooks. They are not tongue-tied as their ancestors were, but are very chatty, giving forth views on everything they are interested in, from socialism to the present war. And their range of interests has widened immeasurably. It would seem that the literacy test has been applied to ghosts in recent fiction. Modern specters are so normal in appearance that often no one recognizes them as ghosts, —as in Edith Wharton's story *Afterwards*, where the peculiar thing about the apparition haunting a certain house is that it is not till long afterwards that one knows it was a ghost. The man in the gray suit whom the wife thinks a chance caller is the spirit of a man not yet dead, a terrible living revenge-ghost, who finally takes his victim mysteriously away with him. Modern ghosts have both motions and emotions like men, hence mortals are coming to regard them more sympathetically, to have more of a fellow-feeling for them.

Likewise the angels are now only a very little higher if any than men. Seraphs are democratic, and angels have developed a sense of humor that renders them more interesting than they used to be. The winged being that H. G. Wells's vicar goes gunning for is a charming youth with a naïve satire, as the angels in Mark Twain's story of heaven are realistically mortal and masculine in tastes. They care little for harps and crowns, grow fidgety under excess of rest, and engage in all sorts of activities, retaining their individual tastes. James Stephens's archangel, seraph, and cherub are chatty, cordial souls with an avidity for cold potatoes and Irish companionship.

The demons as well have felt the same leveling influence experienced by the ghosts and the angels. Only, in their case, the thing is reversed, and they are raised to the grade of humanity. We are coming to see, in modern fiction, at least, that the devil is not really black, only a pleasant mottled gray like ourselves. Satan, in Mark Twain's posthumous novel,[1] is an affable young fellow, claiming to be the nephew and namesake of the personage best known by that name. Bernard Shaw's devil is of a Chesterfieldian courtesy, willing to speed the parting as to welcome the coming guest. I have found no comic use of the werewolf or of the vampire, though there are several comic witch stories, yet all these personages are humanized in modern fiction. We feel in some recent supernatural stories a sense of a continuing current of life. These ghosts, devils, witches, angels, and so forth are too real to be cut short by an author's *Finis*.

Another aspect of the leveling influence is seen in the more than natural power of motion, feeling, and intelligence given to inanimate objects, machinery, plants, and animals, in late literature. The idea of endowing inanimate figures with life and personality is seen several times in Hawthorne's stories, as his snow image, Drowne's wooden image, the vivified scarecrow, Feathertop, that the witch makes. The clay figures that Satan in Mark Twain's novel models, endues with life, then destroys with the fine, casual carelessness of a god, remind one of an incident from mythology. The statue in Edith Wharton's *The Duchess at Prayer* that changes its expression, showing on its marble face through a century the loathing and horror that the living countenance wore, or Lord Dunsany's jade idol[2] that comes with stony steps across the desolate moor to exact vengeance on four men helpless in its presence, has a more intense thrill than Otranto's peripatetic statue. Lord Dunsany's *The Gods of the Mountains*, of which Frank Harris says, "It is the only play which has meant anything to me in twenty years," shows an inexorable fatality as in the Greek drama.

Science is revealing wonderful facts and fiction is quick to realize the possibilities for startling situations in every

[1] *The Mysterious Stranger.*   [2] In *A Night at an Inn.*

field. So diabolic botanical specimens, animals endowed with human or more than human craft—sometimes gifted with immortality as well—add a new interest to uncanny fiction. And the new machines that make all impossibilities come to pass inspire a significant class of supernatural stories. In general, a new force is given to all things, to raise them to the level of the human.

In the same way nature is given a new power and becomes man's equal,—sometimes far his superior—in thought and action. The maelstrom in Poe's story is more than merely a part of the setting,—it is a terrible force in action. Algernon Blackwood stresses this variously in his stories, as where Egypt is shown as a vital presence and power, or where the "goblin trees" are as awful as any of the other characters of evil, or in the wind and flame on the mountain that are elements of supernatural power, with a resistless lure for mortals, or in the vampire soil that steals a man's strength. This may be illustrated as well from the drama, as in Maeterlinck's where Death is the silent, invisible, yet dominant force, or in Synge's where the sea is a terrible foe, lying in wait for man, or in August Stramm's *The Daughter of the Moor*, where the moor is a compelling character of evil. Gothic fiction did associate the phenomena of nature with the moods of the action, yet in a less effective way. The aspects of nature in recent literature have been raised to the level of humanity, becoming mortal or else diabolic or divine.

In general, in modern fiction, man now makes his supernatural characters in his own image. Ghosts, angels, devils, witches, werewolves, are humanized, made like to man in appearance, passions, and powers. On the other hand, plants, inanimate objects, and animals, as well as the phenomena of nature, are raised to the human plane and given access of power. This leveling process democratizes the supernatural elements and tends to make them almost equal.

The present revival of interest in the supernatural and its appearance in literature are as marked in the drama as in fiction or poetry. Mr. E. C. Whitmore, in a recently published volume on *The Supernatural in Tragedy*, has ably treated the subject, especially in the Greek classic period and the Elizabethan age in England. His thesis is that the supernatural is most frequently associated with tragedy, and is found where tragedy is at its best. This may be true of earlier periods of the tragic drama, yet it would be going too far to make the assertion of the drama of the present time. The occult makes its appearance to a considerable extent now in melodrama and even in comedy, though with no decrease in the frequency and effectiveness of its use in tragedy. This only illustrates the widening of its sphere and its adaptability to varying forms of art.

A brief survey of some of the plays produced in the last few years, most of them being seen in New York, will illustrate the extent to which the ghostly motifs are used on the stage of to-day. Double personality is represented [1] by Edward Locke, in a play which is said by critics to be virtually a dramatization of Dr. Morton Prince's study, [2] where psychological apparatus used in laboratory experiments to expel the evil intruder from the girl, a chronoscope, a dynograph, revolving mirrors, make the setting seem truly psychical. But the most dramatic instance of the kind, of course, is the dramatization of Dr. Jekyll's alter ego.

The plays of Charles Rann Kennedy [3] and Jerome K. Jerome [4] are akin to the old mystery plays in that they

[1] In *The Case of Becky.* [2] *The Disassociation of a Personality.*
[3] *The Servant in the House.* [4] *The Passing of the Third Floor Back.*

personate divinity and show the miracle of Christly influence on sinful hearts. Augustus Thomas[1] and Edward Milton Royle[2] introduce hypnotism as the basis of complication and dénouement. Supernatural healing, miraculous intervention of divine power, occur in plays by William Vaughan Moody,[3] Björnson,[4] and George M. Cohan.[5] Another[6] turns on converse with spirits, as does Belasco's *Return of Peter Grimm*, while a war play by Vida Sutton[7] shows four ghosts on the stage at once, astonishing phantoms who do not realize that they are dead. Others[8] have for their themes miracles of faith and rescue from danger, though the first-named play satirizes such belief and the latter is a piece of Catholic propaganda.

Magic, by G. K. Chesterton, introduces supernatural forces whereby strange things are made to happen, such as the changing of the electric light from green to blue. *Peter Ibbetson*, the dramatization of Du Maurier's novel, shows dream-supernaturalism, and various other psychic effects in a delicate and distinctive manner. And *The Willow Tree*, by Benrimo and Harrison Rhodes, is built upon an ancient Japanese legend, relating a hamadryad myth with other supermortal phantasies, such as representing a woman's soul as contained in a mirror.

We have fairy plays by J. M. Barrie,[9] W. B. Yeats,[10] and Maeterlinck,[11] and the mermaid has even been staged,[12] Bernard Shaw shows us the devil in his own home town, while Hauptmann gives us Hannele's visions of heaven. The Frankenstein theme is used to provoke laughter

[1] In *The Witching Hour*.   [2] In *The Unwritten Law*.
[3] *The Faith Healer*.   [4] *Beyond Their Strength*.
[5] *The Miracle Man.*   [6] *The Spiritualist.*   [7] *Kingdom Come.*
[8] As *The Eternal Mystery*, by George Jean Nathan, and *The Rosary*.
[9] *Peter Pan.*   [10] *The Land of Heart's Desire.*
[11] *The Blue Bird.*   [12] *The Mermaid.*

mixed with thrills.[1]   Owen and Robert Davis[2] symbolize man's better angel, while *The Eternal Magdalene*, a dream-drama, shows another piece of symbolic supernaturalism. Lord Dunsany's plays have already been mentioned.

Yet the drama, tnough showing a definite revival of the supernatural, and illustrating various forms of it, is more restricted than fiction. Many aspects of the occult appear and the psychic drama is popular, but the necessities of presentation on the stage inevitably bar many forms of the ghostly art that take their place naturally in fiction. The closet drama does not come under this limitation, for in effect it is almost as free as fiction to introduce mystical, symbolic, and invisible presences. The closet drama is usually in poetic form and poetry is closer akin to certain forms of the supernatural than is prose, which makes their use more natural.

The literary playlet, so popular just now, uses the ghostly in many ways. One shows the Archangel Raphael with his dog, working miracles, while another includes in its *dramatis personæ* a faun and a moon goddess who insists on giving the faun a soul, at which he wildly protests. As through suffering and human pain he accepts the gift, a symbolic white butterfly poises itself on his uplifted hand, then flits toward Heaven. In another, Padraic yields himself to the fairies' power as the price of bread for the girl he loves. Theodore Dreiser's short plays bring in creatures impossible of representation on the stage, "persistences" of fish, animals, and birds, symbolic Shadows, a Blue Sphere, a Power of Physics, Nitrous Acid, a Fast Mail (though trains have been used on the stage), and so forth.

Instances from recent German drama might be given,

[1] In *The Last Laugh*, by Paul Dickey and Charles W. Goddard.
[2] In *Any House*.

as the work of August Stramm, who like Rupert Brooke and the ill-starred poets of the Irish revolution has fallen as a sacrifice to the war.   An article in the *Literary Digest* says of Stramm that "he felt behind all the beauty of the world its elemental passions and believed these to be the projections of human passions in the waves of wind and light and water, in flames of earth."   He includes among his characters[1] a Spider, Nightingales, Moonlight, Wind, and Blossoms.   Carl Hauptmann[2] likewise shows the elemental forces of nature and of super-nature.   On the battlefield of death the dead arise to join in one dreadful chant of hate against their enemies.

Leonid Andreyev's striking play[3] might be mentioned as an example from the Russian.   King-Hunger, Death, and Old time Bell-Ringer, are the principal actors, while the human beings are all deformed and distorted, "one continuous malicious monstrosity bearing only a remote likeness to man."   The starving men are slain, but over the field of the dead the motionless figure of Death is seen silhouetted.   But the dead arise, and a dull, distant, manifold murmur, as if underground, is heard, "We come! Woe unto the victorious!"

But as I have said, these are literary dramas, impossible of presentation on the stage, so that they are judged by literary rather than dramatic standards.   For the most part fiction is infinitely freer in its range and choice of subjects from the supernatural than is the drama.   The suggestive, symbolic, mystic effects which could not in any way be presented on the stage, but which are more truly of the province of poetry, are used in prose that has a jeweled beauty and a melody as of poetry.   Elements such as invisibility, for instance, and various occult agencies may be stressed and analyzed in fiction as

[1] In *Sancta Susanna*.   [2] In *The Dead Are Singing*.
[3] *King-Hunger*.

would be impossible on the stage. The close relation between insanity and the weird can be much more effectively shown in the novel or short story than in the drama, as the forces of mystery, the incalculable agencies can be thus better emphasized. Ghosts need to be seen on the stage to have the best effect, even if they are meant as "selective apparitions" like Banquo, and if thus seen they are too corporeal for the most impressive influence, while in fiction they can be suggested with delicate reserve. Supernatural presences that could not be imaged on the boards may be represented in the novel or story, as Blackwood's Elementals or Psychic Invasions. How could one stage such action, for instance, as his citizens turning into witch-cats or his Giant Devil looming mightily in the heavens? Likewise in fiction the full presentation of scientific supernaturalism can be achieved, which would be impossible on the stage.

In conclusion, it might be said that fiction offers the most popular present vehicle for expression of the undoubtedly reviving supernaturalism in English literature. And fiction is likewise the best form, that which affords the more varied chances for effectiveness. The rising tide of the unearthly in art shows itself in all literary forms, as dramatic, narrative, and lyric poetry, with a few epics —in the playlet as in the standard drama, in the short story as in the novel. It manifests itself in countless ways in current literature and inviting lines of investigation suggest themselves with reference to various aspects of its study. The supernatural as especially related to religion offers an interesting field for research. The miracles from the Bible are often used, as in Lew Wallace's *Ben Hur*, and Christ is introduced in other times and places, as the war novel,[1] or in Marie Corelli's satire on Episcopacy,[2] where the cardinal finds the Christ child outside the cathedral.

[1] *The Second Coming.*　　　　[2] *The Master Christian.*

The more than mortal elements, as answers to prayer, the experience of conversion, spiritual miracles, and so forth, are present to a considerable extent in modern fiction. Two very recent novels of importance base their plots on the miraculous in religion, *The Brook Kerith*, by George Moore, and *The Leatherwood God*, by William Dean Howells. I have touched on this aspect of the subject in a previous article.[1]

One might profitably trace out the appearances of the ghostly in modern poetry, or one might study its manifestations in the late drama, including melodrama and comedy as well as tragedy. This present treatment of the supernatural in modern English fiction makes no pretensions to being complete. It is meant to be suggestive rather than exhaustive, and I shall be gratified if it may help to arouse further interest in a significant and vital phase of our literature and lead others to pursue the investigations.

[1] "Religion in Recent American Novels," in the January, 1914, *Review and Expositor*.

INDEX

A

Accusing Spirit, The, 21
Address to the De'il, An, 131
Æsop, *Fables,* 231
Affair of Dishonor, An, 91
Afterwards, 102, 202
Afterwards, 302
Ahasuerus, 176
Ahrinziman, 88, 183, 213
Aids to Gothic Effect, 36 *et seq.*
Ainsworth, W. H., 181
Albigenses, The, 9, 11, 94, 168, 288
Aldrich, Thomas Bailey, 63
—— *Miss Mehitabel's Son,* 68, 85, 287
—— *Père Antoine's Date Palm,* 63
—— *Queen of Sheba, The,* 122
Amazonian Tortoise Myths, 232
Amboyna, 41
Amiel, Friedrich, 144
Among the Immortals, 217
Amos Judd, 40, 257
Amphitryton, 122
Amycus and Celestine, 63
Anansi Stories, 232
Ancient Legends and Superstitions of Ireland, 229
Ancient Records or the Abbey of St. Oswyth, 9, 21
Ancient Sorceries, 65, 105, 124, 153, 194
Andersen, Hans Christian, 155, 176, 233
—— *The Little Mermaid,* 155, 176, 233
Andreyev, Leonidas, 69
—— *King-Hunger,* 308
—— *Red Laugh, The,* 69
—— *Silence,* 293
Angel Island, 294
Angel Message, An, 207
Ankerwich Castle, 34
Another Little Heath Hound, 290

Anti-Jacobin, The, 51
Any House, 307
Apuleius, Lucius, *Metamorphoses,* 145
Applier, Arthur, *Vendetta of the Jungles, A,* 168
Arabian Nights' Tales, 252
Architecture, Gothic, 8 *et seq.*
Ariel, or the Invisible Monitor, 24
Arnim, Achim von, *Die Beiden Waldemar,* 122
Arnold, Edwin Lester, *Strange Adventures of Phra, the Phœnician, The,* 188
Arnold, Matthew:
—— *Forsaken Merman, The,* 155, 233
—— *Neckan, The,* 155
Arrest, An, 85
Arthur and Gorlogon, 30
Arthur Mervyn, 35
Artist of the Beautiful, The, 287
Astral Bridegroom, An, 207
At the End of the Passage, 120
At the Gate, 201, 291
Auerbach, Berthold, 176
Austen, Jane, 47, 49
—— *Northanger Abbey,* 47, 51
Austin, Alfred, *Peter Rugg, the Missing Man,* 189
Austin, M. H., *Readjustment,* 107
Avengers, The, 56
Ayesha, 183, 193

B

Bacon, Josephine Daskam, 94
—— *Children, The,* 289
—— *Heritage, The,* 94
—— *Miracle, The,* 254
—— *Strange Cases of Dr. Stanchion, The,* 254, 299
—— *Unburied, The,* 66, 301
—— *Warning, The,* 276
Bahr-geist, The, 115, 225

Balzac, Honoré de, 182
—— Elixir of Life, The, 60
—— Magic Skin, The, 60
—— Melmoth Reconcilie, 59
—— Unknown Masterpiece, The, 60
Bangs, John Kendrick, 112, 293
—— Enchanted Typewriter, The,
207, 286
——— House-boat on the Styx, The,
112, 216
—— Pursuit of the House-boat, The,
112, 187, 216
—— Rebellious Heroine, The, 197
—— Speck on the Lens, The, 255
—— Thurlow's Christmas Story, 121
—— Water-Ghost and Others, The,
112
Banshee, The, 99
Bardic Stories of Ireland, 243
Baring-Gould, S., 181
—— Eve, 246
Barker, Elsa, 206, 207
—— Letters from a Living Dead Man,
207
—— War Letters from a Living
Dead Man, 206, 292
Barker, Granville, 123, 198
—— Souls on Fifth, 123, 198, 215
Barrett, Eaton Stannard, 8, 49
—— Heroine, The, 49, 50
Barrie, J. M., 240
—— Little White Bird, The, 240
—— Peter Pan, 240, 306
Baynim, John, 246
Baynim, Michael, 246
Beckford, William, 17
—— Vathek, 8, 17, 22, 25, 29, 33, 37,
70
Beddoes, Thomas Lovell, 53, 297
—— Death's Jest Book, 53, 115, 297
Beetle, The, 290
Belasco, David, Return of Peter
Grimm, The, 201, 298
Beleaguered City, The, 211
Bellamy, Edward, 189
—— Looking Backward, 189, 262
Belled Buzzard, The, 296
Benet, William Rose, Man with the
Pigeons, The, 218
Ben Hur, 309
Bennett, Arnold, Ghost, The, 117
Beowulf, 281
Berenice, 62
Besant, Walter, Ivory Gate, The,
122
Betrothed, The, 225
Beyond Their Strength, 306

Bierce, Ambrose, 53, 61, 109, 116,
290, 300
—— Arrest, An, 85
—— Damned Thing, The, 61, 92
—— Death of Halpin Frazer, The,
110, 192
—— Eyes of the Panther, The, 170,
271
—— Middle Toe of the Right Foot,
The, 61, 92
—— Mysterious Disappearances, 259
—— Occurrence at Owl Creek Bridge,
The, 275
—— Two Military Executions, 116
—— Vine on the House, A, 90
Biology, Supernatural, 270
Biology, Supernatural in Gothicism,
34
Birthmark, The, 185, 270
Bisclaveret, 30, 168
Bisland, Elizabeth, The Case of John
Smith, 215
Björnson, Björnstjerne, 306
—— Beyond Their Strength, 306
Black Magic, 146
Black Monk, The, 69
Black Patch, The, 255
Blackmore, R. D., Lorna Doone, 226
Blackwood, Algernon, 68, 76, 79,
85, 96, 105, 166, 171, 235, 273,
285, 287, 300, 304, 309
—— Ancient Sorceries, 65, 124, 153,
194
—— Camp of the Dog, The, 170
—— Clairvoyance, 289
—— Empty House, The, 98, 117
—— Glamour of the Snow, The,
231
—— Haunted Island, A, 114
—— Heath Fire, The, 231
—— Human Chord, The, 275
—— Jules Le Vallon, 194
—— Keeping His Promise, 98
——Man from the Gods, The, 121
——Man Whom the Trees Loved,
The, 230, 272
——Nemesis of the Fire, A, 98
——Old Clothes, 124, 194
——Psychic Invasion, A, 106
——Regeneration of Lord Ernie,
The, 230
———Return, The, 123, 198
—— Sand, 230
—— Sea Fit, The, 230
—— Secret Worship, 105, 117, 137
—— Temptation of the Clay, The,
231

Blackwood, Algernon (*Continued*)
—— *Terror of the Twins, The*, 122, 192
—— *Transfer, The*, 164
—— *Wave, The*, 194
—— *With Intent to Steal*, 62, 117
Bleek, W. H. I., *Reynard, the Fox, in South Africa*, 232
Blind, The, 64, 298
Blithedale Romance, The, 188, 199
Blue-Bird, The, 64, 278, 280, 306
Blue Roses, 268
Blue Sphere, The, 208, 278
Blythe, James, *Mine Host and the Witch*, 148
Bon Bon, 95, 141
Bones, Sanders, and Another, 156
Bonhote, Mrs., 20
—— *Bungay Castle*, 20, 45
Book of the Serpent, 292
Book of Wonder, The, 245
Borderland, The, 124
Botany, Supernatural, 272 *et seq.*
Bottle Imp, The, 70
Bottomley, Gordon, 65, 153, 285
—— *Crier by Night, The*, 65, 238
—— *Riding to Lithend*, 152
Bowmen and Others, The, 204, 258, 282
Brand, 65
Brandes, Georg, 122
—— *Romantic Reduplication and Personality*, 122
Brentano, *Die Mehreren Wehmüller*, 122
Bride of Lammermoor, The, 38
Brieux, Eugene, 252
Brissot's Ghost, 89
Brontë, Emily, 86
—— *Wuthering Heights*, 86, 226
Brook Kerith, The, 310
Brooke, Rupert, 308
—— *Failure*, 222
—— *Heaven*, 221, 283
—— *On Certain Proceedings of the Psychical Research Society*, 281, 283
Brown, Alice, 101, 211
—— *Here and There*, 101, 107
—— *Tryst, The*, 126, 211
Brown, Charles Brockden, 35
—— *Arthur Mervyn*, 35
—— *Edgar Huntley*, 39
—— *Wieland*, 35, 39
Brownie of Bodbeck, The, 26, 38
Browning, Elizabeth Barrett, 148
—— *Drama of Exile, A*, 133

—— *Lay of the Brown Rosary, The*, 148
Browning, Robert, 69
—— *Sludge, the Medium*, 69
Brushwood Boy, The, 195
Bubble Well Road, 138
Buchanan, Robert, 177
—— *Wandering Jew, a Christmas Carol, The*, 177, 180
—— *Haunters and the Haunted, The*, 60, 78, 188, 299
—— *Strange Story, A*, 90, 182
Bungay Castle, 20, 45
Bunyan, John, 213
Burger, 56
—— *Lenore*, 56
Burnett, Frances Hodgson, *White People, The*, 203, 298
Burns, Robert, 232
—— *Address to the De'il, An*, 131
—— *Tam O'Shanter*, 156
Burns, Miss, *Shropshire Folk-tales*, 291
Butler, Ellis Parker, *Dey Ain't No Ghosts*, 128
Butler, Katherine,
—— *In No Strange Land*, 96, 212
Butler, Samuel, 262
—— *Erewhon*, 262
By the Waters of Paradise, 83
Byron, Lord:
—— *Cain*, 136
—— *Giaour, The*, 160
—— *Heaven and Earth*, 221
—— *Vision of Judgment, A*, 134

C

Cable, George W., 226
Calderon, 27, 133
—— *El Embozado*, 119
—— *El Magico Prodigioso*, 100, 143
Camp of the Dog, The, 170
Campbell-Praed, Mrs., 207
—— *Nyria*, 207
Captain Stormfield's Visit to Heaven, Extracts from, 201, 217
Car of Phœbus, The, 207
Carmen Sylva, 176, 233
Case of Becky, The, 305
Case of John Smith, The, 215
Castle of Caithness, The, 20
Castle of Otranto, The, 4, 8, 16, 25, 31, 36, 40, 52, 101
Castle of Wolfenbach, The, 48
Castle Specter, The, 53
Celestial Grocery, The, 265, 300

Celestial Railroad, The, 213, 265, 300
Celtic Revival, The, 227
Celtic Twilight, The, 239
Chambers, Robert W., 87, 290, 296
—— *The Messenger,* 88
Chamisso, 59, 176
—— *Erscheinung,* 122
Chansons de Gestes, 7
Chaucer, Geoffrey, 87, 140, 217
—— *Friar's Tale, The,* 140
Chemistry, Supernatural, 267
Cher, Marie, 197
—— *Immortal Gymnasts, The,* 197
Chesterton, G. K., 306
—— *Magic,* 306
Children, The, 289
Children of the Mist, The, 226
Christabel, 148, 238
Clairvoyance, 289
Clara Militch, 68, 162
Clark, Rev. T., *Wandering Jew, or the Travels of Bareach, the Prolonged, The,* 178
Clarke, Laurence, 94
—— *Grey Guest, The,* 94, 282
Clermont, 48
Cloak, The, 68
Closed Cabinet, The, 107
Cobb, Irvin, *Belled Buzzard, The,* 296
Cobb, Palmer, *Influence of E. T. A. Hoffmann on Edgar Allan Poe, The,* 58
Cocotte, 61
Coffin Merchant, The, 254
Cohan, George M., 306
—— *Miracle Man, The,* 306
Coleridge, Samuel Taylor, 65, 118
—— *Christabel,* 148, 238
—— *Wanderings of Cain, The,* 118
Collins, Wilkie, 78
—— *Dream Woman, The,* 78
—— *Ghost Touch, The,* 103
—— *Haunted Hotel, The,* 89, 100
—— *Queen of Hearts, The,* 107, 113
Collins, William, *Ode on the Popular Superstitions of the Highlands,* 74
Collison-Morley, Lacy, 202
—— *Greek and Roman Ghost Stories,* 202
Comer, Cornelia A. P., *Little Grey Ghost, The,* 118
Comus, 7, 148
Confessions of a Justified Sinner, 29
Confessions of an English Opium-Eater, 268

Connecticut Yankee at King Arthur's Court, A, 189, 262, 286
Converse, F., 93
—— *Co-operative Ghosts,* 93, 98
Conway, Hugh, 103
—— *Our Last Walk,* 103
Conway, M. D., 180
Cooper, J. Fenimore, 226
Co-operative Ghosts, 93, 98
Corbin, John, 76
Corelli, Marie:
—— *Master Christian, The,* 309
—— *Romance of Two Worlds, A,* 213
—— *Sorrows of Satan, The,* 136, 144
Count Roderick's Castle, or *Gothic Times,* 20
Countess Cathleen, 65, 143
Courting of Dinah Shadd, The, 152
Coward, The, 61
Craddock, Charles Egbert, 83, 104, 226
—— *His Unquiet Ghost,* 83
Crawford, F. Marion, 37, 68, 94, 109, 116, 117
—— *Among the Immortals,* 217
—— *By the Waters of Paradise,* 83
—— *Dead Smile, The,* 70, 109
—— *Doll's Ghost, A,* 98
—— *For the Blood Is the Life,* 62, 78, 162
—— *Khaled,* 62, 70, 147
—— *Man Overboard,* 97
—— *Mr. Isaacs,* 37, 71
—— *Screaming Skull, The,* 60, 89, 92
—— *Upper Berth, The,* 100
—— *Witch of Prague, The,* 149, 195, 266
Crawford, Hope, *Ida Lomond and Her Hour of Vision,* 207
Creation, 277
Crier by Night, The, 65, 238
Crock of Gold, The, 241, 246
Croly, George, 179
—— *Salathiel,* or *Tarry Thou Till I Come,* 179
Crystal Egg, The, 263
Cuchulain of Muirthemne, 243
Culex, 290
Curran, Mrs. John H., *Patience Worth,* 197, 207
Curse of the Cashmere Shawl, The, 153
Curse of the Fires and the Shadows, The, 154
Curse of the Wandering Jew, The, 177
Curtin, Jeremiah, 244

Curtis, George William, 121, 258
—— *Prue and I*, 121, 258

D

Dacre, Mrs., 10, 77
—— *Zofloya*, 10, 17, 28, 33, 35, 37, 38, 53, 154, 251
Damned Thing, The, 61, 92
Danby, Frank, *Twilight*, 268
Daniel and the Devil, 141
D'Annunzio, Gabriel, 66
—— *Daughter of Jorio, The*, 67, 149
—— *La Città Morta*, 66, 298
—— *Sogno d'un Mattino di Prima-vera*, 67, 300
—— *Sogno d'un Tramonto d'Au-tunno*, 67, 152
Dante, 27, 130, 133, 144, 209, 215
Dark Nameless One, The, 155
Darwin, Charles, 73, 251
Darwin, Erasmus, 14
Daughter of Jorio, The, 67, 149
Daughter of the Moor, The, 304
Davis, Owen, and Robert, *Any House*, 307
Davis, Richard Harding, *Vera, the Medium*, 200
Day of My Death, The, 199
Days of the Comet, The, 264
Dead Are Singing, The, 282
Dead City, The, 298
Dead Ship of Harpswell, The, 187
Dead Smile, The, 70, 109
Deakin, Lumley, 146
—— *Red Debts*, 146
Death of Halpin Frazer, The, 110, 192
Death's Jest Book, 53, 115, 297
Defoe, Daniel, 205
—— *Apparition of Mrs. Veal*, 205
—— *History of Duncan Campbell, The*, 225
Demi-gods, 242
Demi-gods, The, 219, 221
Dæmonic Spirits, 158 *et seq.*
Dæmonology, Gothic, 33
De Morgan, William Frend, **92**, 283
—— *Affair of Dishonor, An*, 91
—— *Likely Story, A*, 287
De Quincey, Thomas
—— *Avengers, The*, 56
—— *Confessions of an English Opium-Eater*, 268
—— *Dream Fugue*, 15
—— *Klosterheim*, 56

—— *On the Knocking at the Gate in Macbeth*, 295
Descent into the Maelstrom, The, 231, 253
Devil, The, 138
Devil and His Allies, The, 130 *et seq.*
Devil, Gothic, The, 27 *et seq.*
Devil and Tom Walker, The, 140
Devil in the Belfry, The, 141
Dey Ain't No Ghosts, 128
Diamond Lens, The, 274
Dickey, Paul, 307
—— *Last Laugh, The*, 307
Dickens, Charles:
—— *Haunted House, The*, 171
—— *Signal Man, The*, 114
Die Beiden Waldemar, 122
Die Braut von Corinth, 162
Die Mehreren Wehmüller, 122
Disassociation of a Personality, The, 305
Divine Adventure, The, 248
Dr. Bullivant, 185
Dr. Faustus, 15, 143
Dr. Heidigger's Experiment, 184, 252
Dr. Jekyll and Mr. Hyde, 120, 268, 305
Dog Harvey, The, 291
Doings of Raffles Haw, The, 267
Dolliver Romance, The, 183, 184
Doll's Ghost, A, 98
Door in the Wall, The, 258
Doppelgänger, 57, 119
Doppelgänger, The, 122
Dorset, St. John, 159
—— *Vampire, The*, 159
Double Personality, 305
Doyle, A. Conan, 79
—— *Doings of Raffles Haw, The*, 267
—— *Hound of the Baskervilles, The*, 290
—— *Los Amigos Fiasco, The*, 187, 270
—— *Lot No. 49*, 62
—— *Secret of Goresthorpe Grange, The*, 79
—— *Silver Mirror, The*, 259
—— *Terror of Blue John Gap, The*, 272
Dracula, 78, 163, 188, 301
Dream, The, 68
Dream Fugue, 15
Dream Gown of the Japanese Ambas-sador, The, 79
Dream of Armageddon, A, 196, 262
Dream of Provence, A, 293
Dream Woman, The, 78

Dreams, 13, 77
Dreiser, Theodore:
—— Blue Sphere, The, 208, 278
—— In the Dark, 208
—— Laughing Gas, 278
—— Plays of the Natural and the Supernatural, 208
—— Spring Recital, A, 208
Dromgoole, Will Allen, 226
Dryden, John, 41
—— Amboyna, 41
Duchess at Prayer, The, 121, 303
Duchess of Malfi, The, 8, 166
Dumas, Alexandre, Père, 159
—— Le Vampire, 159
Du Maurier, George:
—— Martian, The, 196, 207, 264
—— Peter Ibbetson, 186, 196, 206, 300
—— Trilby, 267
Dunbar, Aldis, 244
Dunbar, Olivia Howard, 85
—— Shell of Sense, The, 85, 212
Dunsany, Lord, 52, 63, 235, 242, 244, 247, 249, 285, 292, 300
—— Book of Wonder, The, 245
—— Glittering Gate, The, 221, 222
—— Gods of Pegana, The, 245
—— Gods of the Mountain, The, 244, 303
—— Night at an Inn, A, 244, 303
—— Time and the Gods, 245
—— Usury, 198
—— When the Gods Slept, 63, 74

E

Edgar Huntley, 39
Edwards, Amelia, 86
—— Four-fifteen Express, The, 86
Eel-King, The, 233
Eighty-third, The, 61, 281
El Embozado, 119
Elementals, 300
Eleonora, 103
Eliot, George, 167, 257
—— Lifted Veil, The, 157
Elixière des Teufels, 57
Elixir of Life, The, 35, 182 et seq.
Elixir of Life, The, 60
Elixir of Youth, The, 186
Elizabethan Drama, The, 139
El Magico Prodigioso, 100, 143
Elsie Venner, 170
Elves, 247
Emperor and Galilean, 42, 66
Empty House, The, 98, 117

Enchanted Typewriter, The, 207, 286
Erckmann-Chatrian, 62
—— Invisible Eye, The, 62
—— Owl's Ear, The, 62
—— Waters of Death, The, 62
Erewhon, 262
Erscheinung, 122
Eternal Magdalen, The, 27
Eternal Mystery, The, 306
Ethelwina, or the House of Fitz-Auburne, 25
Eubule-Evans, A. 177
—— Curse of the Wandering Jew, The, 177
Eve, 246
Evil Eye, The, 152
Exchange, The, 153, 156, 197
Extract from Captain Stormfield's Visit to Heaven, An, 217
Eyes, The, 297
Eyes of the Panther, The, 170, 271

F

Fable for Critics, A, 57
Fables, 231
Facts in the Case of M. Waldemar, 266
Faerie Queene, The, 7
Failure, 22
Fair God, The, 246
Fairies of Pesth, The, 240
Fairy Faith in Celtic Countries, 237
Fairy, The, 239 et seq.
Faith Healer, The, 306
Fall of the House of Usher, The, 295
Faraway Melody, A, 97
Faust, 143, 175
Feathertop, 152, 156
Fenn, George M., Man with the Shadow, The, 122
Fiction of the Irish Celts, 243
Field, Eugene, 141
—— Daniel and the Devil, 141
—— Eel-King, The, 233
—— Holy Cross, The, 181
—— Moon Lady, The, 233
—— Mother in Paradise, The, 213
—— Pagan Seal-wife, The, 233
—— Werewolf, The, 169, 172
Finch, Lucine, Butterfly, The, 307
First Men in the Moon, The, 264
Fisherman and His Soul, The, 134, 153, 236
Fisk, Isabel Howe, 290
Flaireurs, 64
Flower of Silence, The, 273

Flowering of the Strange Orchid, The,
  62, 164, 273
Flying Dutchman, The, 187
Fogazzaro, Antonio, 66
—— *Saint, The,* 66
—— *Sinner, The,* 66
—— *Woman, The,* 66, 194, 300
Folk-lore, 73
Ford, James L., 266
Forest Lovers, 149
Forsaken Merman, The, 155, 233
For the Blood Is the Life, 62, 78, 162
Fouqué, Henri Auguste, 57, 59
—— *Undine,* 57
Four-fifteen Express, The, 86
Fourth Dimension, The, 256
Fox, John, Jr., 226
France, Anatole, 63
—— *Amycus and Celestine,* 63
—— *Isle of the Penguins, The,* 63
—— *Juggler of Notre Dame, The,* 63
—— *Mass of Shadows, The,* 63
—— *Putois,* 63
—— *Revolt of the Angels, The,* 220
—— *Scholasticus,* 63
Frankenstein, 14, 17, 34
Franklin, Andrew, 176
—— *Wandering Jew, The,* 176
Freeman, Mary Wilkins, 78
—— *Faraway Melody,* 97
—— *Hall Bedroom, The,* 79, 260
—— *Shadows on the Wall, The,* 78,
  99, 104, 226
Freud, 79
Friar's Tale, The, 140
Fu Manchu Stories,
Furnished Room, The, 60, 101
Future, Magic Views of the, 256

G

Garland, Hamlin, 69, 76, 200
——*Shadow World, The,* 200
—— *Tyranny of the Dark, The,* 200
Garments of Ghosts, 92 *et seq.*
Gaston de Blondeville, 19
Gates Ajar, The, 210
Gates Between, The, 210
Gates Beyond, The, 210
Gautier, Théophile, 62
—— *La Morte Amoreuse,* 62, 163
—— *Mummy's Foot, The,* 62
—— *Romance of the Mummy, The,*
  62
*General William Booth Enters into
  Heaven,* 217
German Romanticism, 67

Gerould, Gordon H., 202
—— *Grateful Dead, The,* 202
Gerould, Katherine Fullerton, 61,
  71, 104
—— *Eighty-Third, The,* 61, 281
—— *Louquier's Third Act,* 61
—— *On the Stairs,* 83, 114, 122
Ghost, The, 60
Ghost at Point of Rock, The, 83
Ghost-children, 287 *et seq.*
Ghost Moth, The, 290
Ghost of Miser Brimpson, The, 83
Ghost of the White Tiger, 291
Ghost Ship, The, 111, 293
Ghost of Futurity, 114
Ghost of Jack, The, 110
Ghost Touch, The, 101, 103
Ghostly Doubles, 119
Ghostly Odor, 100
Ghostly Perfume, 101
Ghostly Psychology, 106
Ghostly Sounds, 97 *et seq.*
Ghosts, Gothic, 18 *et seq.*
Ghosts, Modern, 81 *et seq.*
Ghouls, 158
Giaour, The, 160
Gigantism, 36
Gilmore, Inez Haynes, 294
—— *Angel Island,* 294
Glamour of the Snow, The, 231
Glanville, Joseph, 191
Glasgow, Ellen, *Shadowy Third, The,*
  203
Glass of Supreme Moments, The, 157
Glittering Gate, The, 221, 222
Glover, Richard, *Ballad of Hosier's
  Ghost,* 89
Gnoles, 247
Gnomes, 347
Goblin Market, 148
Goddard, Charles W., 307
—— *Last Laugh, The,* 307
Gods, 242
Gods and Fighting Men, 244
Gods of Pegana, 245
Gods of the Mountains, The, 244, 303
Godwin, William, 35, 182
—— *St. Leon,* 35, 36
Goethe, 133, 162
—— *Die Braut von Corinth,* 162
—— *Faust,* 143, 175
Gogol, 68
—— *Cloak, The,* 68
Gothic Romance, *et seq.*
Granville, Charles, 179
—— *Plaint of the Wandering Jew,
  The,* 179

318 Index

Great God Pan, The, 247
Great Stone of Sardis, The, 262
Greek and Roman Ghost Stories, 202
Gregory the Great, Dialogues, 202
Gregory, Lady, 229, 234, 237, 240, 285
—— Cuchulain of Muirthemne, 243
—— Gods and Fighting Men, 243
Grey Guest, The, 94, 282
Grosse, Marquis, 49
—— Horrid Mysteries, 49
Guy Mannering, 150
Gypsy Christ, The, 181

H

Hag, The, 148
Haggard, Rider, 183, 193
—— Ayesha, 183, 193
—— She, 183
Hale, Lucretia P., Spider's Eye, The, 62, 274
Hall Bedroom, The, 79, 260
Hall of Eblis, The, 8
Hamlet, 18, 118, 144
Hand, The, 61
Hannele, 218
Hans Pfaal, 286
Happy Prince, The, 238
Hardy, Thomas:
—— Return of the Native, The, 150
—— Tess of the D'Urbervilles, 143
—— Under the Greenwood Tree, 150
—— Withered Arm, The, 225
Harper, Olive, Sociable Ghost, The, 111
Harris, Joel Chandler, 74, 226
—— Uncle Remus Tales, 232, 235
Hart, Charles F., Amazonian Tortoise Myths, 232
Hartley, Randolph, Black Patch, The, 255
Haunted Hotel, The, 89, 100
Haunted House, The, 171
Haunted Island, A, 114
Haunted Subalterns, The, 138
Haunters and the Haunted, The, 60, 78, 188, 299
Hauptmann, Carl, 282
—— Dead Are Singing, The, 282
Hauptmann, Gerhardt:
—— Hannele, 218
—— Sunken Bell, The, 158
Hawkesworth, John, 70, 190
—— Transmigration of a Soul, 190
Hawthorne, Julian, 121

—— Lovers in Heaven, 121, 144, 213
Hawthorne, Nathaniel:
—— Artist of the Beautiful, The, 287
—— Birthmark, The, 185, 270
—— Blithedale Romance, The, 188, 199
—— Celestial Railroad, The, 213
—— Dr. Heidigger's Experiment, 184, 252
—— Dolliver Romance, The, 183, 184
—— Feathertop, 152, 156
—— House of Seven Gables, The, 158
—— Howe's Masquerade, 122
—— Intelligence Office, The, 265
—— Main Street, 152
—— Marble Faun, The, 57
—— Prophetic Pictures, 121
—— Rappacini's Daughter, 252, 272
—— Scarlet Letter, The, 152
—— Select Party, A, 178
—— Septimius Felton, 143, 150, 183, 252
—— Virtuoso's Collection, A, 78
—— Young Goodman Brown, 151
Hearn, Lafcadio, 1, 77
—— Interpretations of Literature, 1, 77
Heath Fire, The, 231
Heaven, 221, 283
Heaven and Earth, 221
Heijermans, 176
Hellas, 176
Henry, O., Furnished Room, The, 60, 101
Here and There, 101, 107
Heretic, The, 207
Heritage, The, 94
Herodotus, 166
Heroes, 242
Heroine, The, 49, 50
Herrick, Robert, Hag, The, 148
Hewlett, Maurice, Forest Lovers, 149
Heywood, Eliza, Lasselia, 42
His Unquiet Ghost, 83
History of Duncan Campbell, The, 255
History of Jack Smith, or the Castle of St. Donats, 20
Hoax Ghosts, 82
Hodder, Reginald, Vampire, The, 68, 163
Hoffmann, David, 181
Hoffmann, E. T. A., 51, 59, 69, 182, 190, 199
—— Doppelgänger, 58

Hoffman, E. T. A. (*Continued*)
—— *Elixière des Teufels*, 58
—— *Kater Murr*, 58
—— *Magnetizeur*, 58
Hogg, James:
—— *Brownie of Bodbeck*, 26, 38
—— *Confessions of a Justified Sinner*, 29
—— *Hunt of Eildon, The*, 26, 27, 30, 32
—— *Witch of Fife, The*, 148
—— *Wool-gatherer, The*, 23, 29, 30, 32
Holmes, Oliver Wendell, *Elsie Venner*, 170
Holy Cross, The, 181
Horrid Mysteries, 49
Horsley-Curties, T. J., 9
—— *Ancient Records or the Abbey of St. Oswyth*, 9, 12, 21, 32, 42, 43
—— *Ethelwina, or the House of Fitz-Auburne*, 25, 38
Hound of the Baskervilles, The, 290
Hound of Heaven, The, 283
House of Judgment, The, 214
House of Souls, The, 271
House-boat on the Styx, The, 112, 216
House of Seven Gables, The, 158
Howells, William Dean, 76
—— *Leatherwood God, The*, 310
—— *Undiscovered Country, The*, 200, 267
Howe's Masquerade, 122
Human, Chord, The, 275
Human Personality, 202
Humorous Ghosts, 110
Hunt, Leigh, 105
Hunt of Eildon, The, 26, 27, 30, 32
Huxley, Thomas Henry, 73, 252
Hyde, Dr., *Paudeen O'Kelley and the Weasel*, 237

I

Ibsen, Henrik, 35, 42
—— *Brand*, 65
—— *Emperor and Galilean*, 42, 66
—— *Lady from the Sea, The*, 66
—— *Master Builder*, 35, 66
—— *Pretenders, The*, 65
—— *Rosmersholm*, 66
—— *Vikings of Helgeland, The*, 65
Ida Lomond and Her Hour of Vision, 207
Immortal Gymnasts, The, 197
In Castle Perilous, 118
In Mr. Eberdeen's House, 124

In No Strange Land, 96, 212
In the Dark, 208
In the House of Suddoo, 146
Inferno, 144
Insanity and the Supernatural, 69, 299
Insanity in Gothic Fiction, 35 *et seq.*
Intelligence Office, The, 265
Interior, 64
Interpretations of Literature, 1, 77
Intricate Personality of Specters, 119
Invisible Man, The, 95, 269
Invisible Eye, The, 62
Irving, Washington, 110, 226·
—— *Devil and Tom Walker, The*, 140
—— *Legend of Sleepy Hollow, The*, 89
—— *Rip Van Winkle*, 246
—— *Specter Bridegroom, The*, 83, 110
—— *Tales of the Alhambra*, 226
Island of Dr. Moreau, The, 271
Isle of the Penguins, The, 63
Italian, The, 48
Ivan, the Fool, 68, 138, 144
Ivory Gate, The, 122
In the Track of the Wandering Jew, 178

J

Jacobs, W. W., *Monkey's Paw, The*, 98, 253
James, Henry:
—— *Jolly Corner, The*, 122
—— *Turn of the Screw, The*, 86, 91, 109
Janvier, Thomas A., *Legends of the City of Mexico*, 226
Jealousy of Ghosts, 117
Jeanne, The Maid, 282
Jerome, Jerome K., *Passing of the Third Floor Back, The*, 305
Jewel of Seven Stars, The, 191, 274
Jigar-Khor, The, 165
John Inglesant, 87, 98
Johnson, Arthur, *In Mr. Eberdeen's House*, 124
Johnston, Mary, *Witch, The*, 150
Jolly Corner, The, 122
Joyzelle, 64
Judgment of God, The, 234
Juggler of Notre Dame, The, 63
Jules Le Vallon, 194
Julius Cæsar, 18, 84

Jungle Tales, 232

K

Kaffir Tales, 232
Kater Murr, 58
Keats, John, 148
—— *La Belle, Dame sans Merci*, 148
—— *Lamia*, 162
Keeping His Promise, 98
Kelpie, The, 155
Kennedy, Charles Rann, *Servant in the House, The*, 66, 305
Kennedy, Patrick, 243
—— *Bardic Stories of Ireland*, 243
—— *Fiction of the Irish Celts*, 243
Kentucky's Ghost, 199
Kerfol, 290
Khaled, 62, 70, 147
Kinetoscope of Time, The, 256
King, Basil, 203
—— *Old Lady Pingree*, 203
King Lear, 13
Kingdom Come, 282, 306
Kingemann, 176
King Hunger, 207, 308
Kingsley, Charles, *Water Babies*, 240
Kipling, Rudyard, 53, 71, 99, 104, 180
—— *At the End of the Passage*, 120
—— *Brushwood Boy, The*, 195
—— *Bubble Well Road*, 138
—— *Courting of Dinah Shadd, The*, 152
—— *Dog Harvey, The*, 291
—— *Haunted Subalterns, The*, 138
—— *In the House of Suddoo*, 146
—— *Jungle Tales*, 232
—— *Last of the Stories, The*, 197, 215
—— *Mark of the Beast, The*, 100, 167
—— *Phantom Rickshaw, The*, 88, 94
—— *Swept and Garnished*, 94, 282, 288
—— *They*, 84, 93, 288
Kittredge, George Lyman, 30, 224
—— *Arthur and Gorlogon*, 30
Kleist, 59
Klosterheim, 56
Knock! Knock! Knock! 68
Kummer, Frederick Arnold, *Second Coming, The*, 281
Kundry, 181

L

Le Belle Dame sans Merci, 148

La Città Morta, 66, 299
Lady from the Sea, The, 66
La Horla, 61, 95
Lair of the White Worm, The, 188
Lais, 7
Lamia, 162
La Morte Amoreuse, 62, 163
Land of Darkness, The, 212
Land of Heart's Desire, The, 65, 240, 306
Lang, Andrew, 118, 188, 242
—— *In Castle Perilous*, 118
—— *St. Germain, the Deathless*, 188
Lasselia, 42
Last Ghost in Harmony, The, 104, 201
Last Laugh, The, 307
Last of the Stories, The, 197, 215
Later Influences, 54 *et seq.*
Latham, Francis, *Midnight Bell*, 49
Laughing Gas, 278
Lay of the Brown Rosary, The, 148
Leatherwood God, The, 310
Leaves from the Autobiography of a Soul in Paradise, 207
Lee, Robert James:
—— *Astral Bridegroom, An*, 207
—— *Car of Phœbus, The*, 207
—— *Heretic, The*, 207
—— *Leaves from the Autobiography of a Soul in Paradise*, 207
—— *Life Elysian, The*, 207
—— *Through the Mists*, 208
—— *Vagrom Spirit, The*, 207
Legend of Sleepy Hollow, The, 89
Legend of Sharp, A, 134
Leprechauns, 239
Letters from a Living Dead Man, 207
Le Vampire, 159
Lewis, Arthur, 242
—— *London Fairy Tales*, 242
Lewis, Mary L., *Stranger than Fiction*, 207
Lewis, Matthew Gregory ("Monk"), 14, 16, 77
—— *Castle Specter, The*, 53
—— *Monk, The*, 12, 16, 22, 24, 26, 27, 30, 33, 34, 35, 37, 177
Liebgeber Schappe, 122
Life after Death, 209 *et seq.*
Lifted Veil, The, 257
Ligeia, 123, 191
Likely Story, A, 287
Lindsay, Nicholas Vachell, *General William Booth Enters into Heaven*, 217
Little Crow of Paradise, The, 234

Little Gray Ghost, The, 118
Little Mermaid, The, 155, 176, 233
Little Pilgrim in the Unseen, The, 212
Little White Bird, The, 240
Lloyd, N. M., Last Ghost in Harmony, The, 104, 201
Locke, Edward, Case of Becky, The, 305
Lodge, Sir Oliver, 74
—— Raymond, or Life and Death, 75
London Fairy Tales, 242
London, Jack:
—— Scarlet Plague, The, 262
—— Star Rover, The, 264
Long Chamber, The, 118
Looking Backward, 189, 262
Los Amigos Fiasco, The, 187, 270
Loss of Breath, The, 74
Lot No. 49, 62
Louquier's Third Act, 61
Love Philter, The, 267
Lovers in Heaven, 121, 144, 213
Lowell, James Russell, Fable for Critics, A, 57
Lucas, Charles, History of Jack Smith, or the Castle of St. Donats, The, 20
Lycanthrope, The, 39
Lytton, Edward George, Earle Lytton Bulwer-Lytton, 1st baron, 60

M

Macaulay, Thomas Babington, 110
Macbeth, 18, 98, 153, 295
Machen, Arthur, 52, 70, 79, 117, 247, 250, 300, 301
—— Bowmen and Others, The, 204, 258, 282
—— Hill of Dreams, The, 79
—— House of Souls, The, 271
—— Monstrance, The, 288
—— Red Hand, The, 247
—— Seeing the Great God Pan, 139
—— Three Impostors, The, 247, 269
Mad, 61
Mad Lady, The, 286
Madness, 61
Maeterlinck, Maurice, 6, 42, 64, 299
—— Blind, The, 64, 298
—— Blue-bird, The, 64, 278, 289, 306
—— Interior, 64
—— Intruder, The, 64, 304
—— Joyzelle, 64
Magic, 306
Magic Shadow, The, 296

Magic Skin, The, 60
Magnetiseur, 58
Maighdeanmhara, The, 155
Main Street, 152
Man and Superman, 217
Man in Black, The, 137
Man from the Gods, The, 121
Man Overboard, 97
Man with a Shadow, The, 122
Man Whom the Trees Loved, The, 230, 272
Man with the Pigeons, The, 218
Man Who had been in Fairyland, The, 241
MS. found in a Bottle, The, 253
Marble Faun, The, 57
Marie de France, 30, 118
—— Bisclaveret, 30, 168
Markheim, 120
Mark of the Beast, The, 100, 167
Marlowe, Christopher, 27, 153
—— Doctor Faustus, 15, 143
Marsh, Richard, Beetle, The, 290
Martian, The, 196, 207, 264
Mass of Shadows, The, 63
Master Builder, The, 35, 66
Master Christian, The, 309
Mather, Cotton, 130
Matthews, Brander:
—— Dream Gown of the Japanese Ambassador, The, 79
—— Kinetoscope of Time, The, 256
—— Primer of Imaginary Geography, A, 181, 216
—— Rival Ghosts, 112
Maturin, Charles Robert, 9, 17, 38, 59, 182
—— Albigenses, The, 9, 11, 94, 168, 288
—— Melmoth, the Wanderer, 8, 10, 12, 24, 26, 36, 41, 44, 138
Maupassant, Guy de, 60, 69, 299
—— Cocotte, 61
—— Coward, The, 61
—— Ghost, The, 60
—— Hand, The, 61
—— La Horla, 61, 95
—— Mad, 61
—— Madness, 61
—— Tress, The, 61
—— Wolf, The, 172
McDonald, George, Portent, The, 266
McLeod, Fiona:
—— Dark Nameless One, The, 155
—— Divine Adventure, The, 248
—— Judgment of God, The, 234

McLeod, Fiona (*Continued*)
—— *Sin Eater, The,* 138
Mechanistic Supernaturalism, 286 *et seq.*
Meg Merrilies, 150
Meinhold, 56
Melmoth Reconcilie, 59
Melmoth, the Wanderer, 8, 10, 12, 24, 26, 36, 41, 44, 138
Meredith, George, 71, 127
—— *Shaving of Shagpat, The,* 71
Merlin, 145
Mermaid, The, 234
Mermaid, The, 306
Merman and the Seraph, The, 234
Meroe, 145
Mesmeric Revelations, 266
Messenger, The, 88
Metamorphoses, 145
Metempsychosis, 180 *et seq.*
Metzengerstein, 287, 291
Middle Toe of the Right Foot, The, 61, 92
Middleton, Jessie Adelaide, 92
—— *Ghost with Half a Face, The,* 92
Middleton, Richard, 111, 288
—— *Coffin Merchant, The,* 254
—— *Ghost Ship, The,* 111, 293
—— *Passing of Edward, The,* 99, 288
Midnight Bell, 49
Midsummer Night's Dream, A, 64
Milne-Horne, Mary Pamela, *Anansi Stories,* 232
Milton, John, 27, 133, 239
—— *Comus,* 7, 148
—— *Paradise Lost,* 144, 209, 211, 215
Mine Host and the Witch, 148
Miracle, The, 254
Miracle Man, The, 306
Miss Mehitabel's Son, 63, 68, 85, 287
Mistaken Ghost, The, 62
Mitchell, J. A., *Amos Judd,* 40, 257
Molnar, Fernac, *Devil, The,* 138
Monastery, The, 225
Monk, The, 12, 16, 22, 24, 26, 27, 30, 33, 35, 37, 177
Monkey's Paw, The, 98
Monstrance, The, 288
Moody, William Vaughn, *Faith Healer, The,* 306
Moon Lady, The, 233
Moon Madness, 139, 231
Moore, George, *Brook Kerith, The,* 310
Morella, 123, 190
Morris, William, 236, 250

—— *Water of the Wondrous Isle, The,* 236
—— *Well at the World's End, The,* 236
—— *Wood beyond the World, The,* 236
Mosen, Julius, 176
Mother in Paradise, The, 213
Motives for Ghost Appearance, 113
Mr. Isaacs, 37, 71
Mrs. Veal, 205
Mummy's Foot, The, 62
Mummy's Tale, The, 110
My Aunt Margaret's Mirror, 225
Myers, *Human Personality,* 202
Mysteries of Udolpho, The, 9, 48
Mysterious Mother, The, 53
Mysterious Stranger, The, 142
Mysterious Warnings, 49
Mystery and Mystification in Gothicism, 43
Mystery of Joseph Laquedem, The, 181, 195
Myths and Legends of Our Land, 187

N

Nathan, George Jean, *Eternal Mystery, The,* 306
Neckan, The, 155, 233
Nemesis of Fire, A, 98
Never Bet the Devil Your Head, 140
New Accelerator, The, 286
New Arabian Nights, The, 70
Night at an Inn, A, 244, 303
Night Call, The, 83
Nightingale and the Rose, The, 235, 293
Nightmare Abbey, 51
Norris, Frank, *Vandover and the Brute,* 167
Northanger Abbey, 47, 51
Notch on the Axe, The, 89, 188
Noyes, Alfred, *Creation,* 277
Nyria, 207

O

O'Brien, Fitz-James, 61
—— *Diamond Lens, The,* 274
—— *What Was It? A Mystery,* 61, 96
Occult Magazine, The, 163
Occurrence at Owl Creek Bridge, The, 275
Ode on the Popular Superstitions of the Highlands, 74

O'Donnell, Elliot, 88, 110
—— Mummy's Tale, The, 110
—— Werewolves, 170
Old Clothes, 124, 194
Old English Baron, The, 16, 19, 40
Old Fires and Profitable Ghosts, 154
Old Lady Mary, 211
Old Men of the Twilight, The, 234
Old Wives' Tale, 110, 145
Oliphant, Mrs. Margaret:
—— Beleaguered City, The, 211
—— Land of Darkness, The, 212
—— Little Pilgrim in the Unseen,
The, 212
—— Old Lady Mary, 211, 298
—— Open Door, The, 211
—— Portrait, The, 211
On Certain Proceedings of the
Psychical Research Society, 221
On the Knocking at the Gate in
Macbeth, 295
On the Stairs, 61, 114, 122
Open Door, The, 211
Origin of Individual Gothic Tales,
13 et seq.
O'Shaughnessy, Arthur, 168
Our Last Walk, 103
Oval Portrait, The, 58
Ovid, 166
Owl's Ear, The, 62

P

Pagan Seal-wife, The, 233
Page, Thomas Nelson, 226
Pain, Barry, 53, 79, 157
—— Blue Roses, 268
—— Celestial Grocery, The, 265, 300
—— Exchange, The, 153, 156, 197
—— Glass of Supreme Moments,
The, 157
—— Love Philter, The, 267
—— Moon Madness, 139, 231
—— Undying Thing, The, 271
—— Wrong Elixir, The, 186
—— Zero, 257
Paine, Albert Bigelow, Elixir of
Youth, The, 186
Pair of Hands, A, 103, 288
Panghorne, Georgia Wood, Substi-
tute, The, 88
Paradise Lost, 144, 209, 211, 215
Parsifal, 181
Parsons, Francis, Borderland, The,
124
Parsons, Mrs. M., Mysterious Warn-
ings, 49

Passing of Edward, The, 99, 288
Passing of the Third Floor Back,
The, 66, 303
Passionate Crime, The, 242
Patience Worth, 197, 207
Paudeen O'Kelley and the Weasel,
237
Peacock, Thomas Love, Nightmare
Abbey, 51
Pearce, J. H., Little Crow of Para-
dise, The, 234
Peele, George, 145
—— Old Wives' Tale, 110, 145, 202,
293
Père Antoine's Date Palm, 63
Peter Ibbetson, 186, 196, 206, 300
Peter Pan, 240, 306
Peter Rugg, the Missing Man, 189
Phantom Rickshaw, The, 88, 94
Phantoms, 68
Phelps, William Lyon, 41
—— Beginnings of the English Ro-
mantic Movement, 41
Phillpotts, Eden, 83
—— Another Little Heath Hound,
290
—— Children of the Mist, 226
—— Ghost of Miser Brimpson, The,
83
—— Witch, The, 151, 226
Picture of Dorian Grey, The, 32,
60, 121, 134
Pit and the Pendulum, The, 253
Plaint of the Wandering Jew, The,
179
Planche, J. R., 160
—— Vampire, or the Bride of the
Isles, 160
Plattner Case, The, 260
Plays of the Natural and the Super-
natural, 208
Pliny, 72
Poe, Edgar Allan, 58, 69, 252, 299
—— Berenice, 62
—— Bon Bon, 41, 95
—— Descent into the Maelstrom,
The, 231, 253
—— Devil in the Belfry, The, 141
—— Eleonora, 103
—— Facts in the Case of M. Walde-
mar, The, 266
—— Fall of the House of Usher,
The, 295
—— Hans Pfaal, 286
—— Ligeia, 123, 191
—— Loss of Breath, 74
—— MS. Found in a Bottle, 253

Poe, Edgar Allen (*Continued*)
—— *Mesmeric Revelations*, 266
—— *Metzengerstein*, 287, 291
—— *Morella*, 123, 190
—— *Never Bet the Devil Your Head*, 140
—— *Oval Portrait, The*, 58
—— *Pit and the Pendulum, The*, 253
—— *Raven, The*, 56
—— *Tale of the Ragged Mountains, A*, 58, 190
—— *William Wilson*, 58, 120
Polidior, *Vampyre, The*, 160
Pomponius Mela, 166
Portent, The, 266
Portents in Gothic Romance, 39
Portrait, The, 211
Powell, J. W., 232
Pretender, The, 65
Primer of Imaginary Geography, The, 181, 216
Primitive Culture, 227
Prince, Morton, 305
—— *Disassociation of a Personality, The*, 305
Prince of India, The, 179
Proby, W. C., *Spirit of the Castle, The*, 40
Prophetic Pictures, 121
Prue and I, 121, 258
Psychic Invasion, A, 106
Psychical Research, 73, 199 *et seq.*
Pursuit of the House-boat, The, 112, 187, 216
Pushkin, Alexander, *Queen of Spades, The*, 69
Putois, 63
Pyle, Howard, *Evil Eye, The*, 152

Q

Queen Mab, 176
Queen of Hearts, The, 107, 113
Queen of Sheba, The, 122
Queen of Spades, The, 69
Quiller-Couch, A. T., 154
—— *Magic Shadow, The*, 296
—— *Mystery of Joseph Laquedem, The*, 181, 195
—— *Old Fires and Profitable Ghosts*, 154
—— *Pair of Hands, A*, 103, 288
—— *Roll-call of the Reef, The*, 107
Quinet, Edgar, 176

R

Radcliffe, Anne, 9, 16, 23, 43, 44, 45, 46, 71, 82
—— *Gaston de Blondeville*, 19
—— *Italian, The*, 48
—— *Mysteries of Udolpho, The*, 9, 48
—— *Romance of the Castle, The*, 44
—— *Sicilian Romance, A*, 45, 50, 301
Raleigh, Sir Walter, *English Novel, The*, 46
Rappacini's Daughter, 252, 272
Raven, The, 56
Raymond, or Life and Death, 75
Readjustment, 107
Real Ghost Stories, 282
Rebellious Heroine, The, 197
Recent Carnival of Crime in Connecticut, The, 122
Red Debts, 146
Red Hand, The, 247
Red Ranrahan, 186, 243
Reeve, Clara, 16
—— *Old English Baron, The*, 16, 19, 40
Regeneration of Lord Ernie, The, 230
Reineche Fuchs, 213
Religion in Recent American Novels, 310
Remarkable Case of Davidson's Eyes, The, 256
Return, The, 123, 198
Return of Peter Grimm, The, 201, 298
Return of the Native, The, 150
Revolt, of the Angels, The, 220
Reynard the Fox, 231
Reynard the Fox, in South Africa, 232
Rhodes, Benrimo and Harrison, *Willow Tree, The*, 306
Richter, Jean Paul, *Leibgeber Schappe*, 122
Rideout, Henry, *Ghost of the White Tiger, The*, 291
Riders to the Sea, 10, 304
Riding to Lithend, 152
Rip Van Winkle, 246
Rival Ghosts, 112
Roche, Regina Maria, 10, 43, 45, 50
—— *Clermont*, 45, 49
Roger of Wendover's Chronicles, 175
Rohmer, Sax, 146
—— *Flower of Silence, The*, 273
—— *Fu-Manchu Stories*, 253, 268, 270, 272

Roll-call of the Reef, The, 107
Romance of the Castle, The, 40
Romance of the Mummy, The, 62
Romance of Two Worlds, A, 213
Romantic Movement, 55
Romantic Reduplication and Psychology, 122
Rosary, The, 306
Rosmersholm, 66
Rossetti, Christina, Goblin Market, 148
Rossetti, Dante Gabriel, Sister Helen, 67, 153
Royle, Edward Milton, Unwritten Law, The, 306
Russian Literature, 67

S

St. Germain, the Deathless, 188
St. Irvyne, the Rosicrucian, 17, 35, 36
St. Leon, 35, 36
St. Oswyth, 12
Saintsbury, George, Tales of Mystery, 48
Saint, The, 66
Salathiel, or Tarry Thou Till I Come, 179
Sancta Susanna, 307
Satire on Gothicism, 47 et seq.
Satirical Supernaturalism, 294
Scarlet Letter, The, 152
Scarlet Plague, The, 262
Scenery, Gothic, 10
Schiller, Robbers, The, 16
Schlegel, 176
Scholasticus, 63
Science, Gothic, 33
Science, Supernatural, 251 et seq.
Scott, Sir Walter, 38, 56, 115, 225, 246
—— Betrothed, The, 225
—— Bride of Lammermoor, The, 38
—— Guy Mannering, 150
—— Monastery, The, 225
—— My Aunt Margaret's Mirror, 225
—— Talisman, The, 134, 146, 147, 225
—— Two Drovers, The, 151, 225
—— Woodstock, 225
Screaming Skull, The, 60, 89, 92
Sea Fit, The, 230
Sea Lady, The, 234
Second Coming, The, 281
Second Wife, The, 122
Secret of Goresthorpe Grange, The, 79

Secret Worship, 105, 117, 137
Seeing the Great God Pan, 139
Select Party, A, 178
Selfish Giant, The, 246
Sensitives, 298
Septimius Felton, 143, 150, 183, 252
Servant in the House, The, 66, 305
Shadow World, The, 200
Shadows on the Wall, The, 78, 99, 104, 226
Shadowy Third, The, 203
Shakespeare, 13, 18, 56, 84, 115, 119
—— Hamlet, 18, 118, 144
—— Julius Cæsar, 18, 84
—— King Lear, 13
—— Macbeth, 17, 98, 152, 153, 295
—— Midsummer Night's Dream, 64
—— Tempest, The, 64
Sharp, William, 65, 285
—— Gypsy Christ, The, 181
—— Vistas, 65, 278
Shaving of Shagpat, The, 71
Shaw, George Bernard, Man and Superman, 217, 306
She, 183
Sheldon, Edward:
—— Mermaid, The, 234
Shell of Sense, The, 85, 212
Shelley, Mary, 14
—— Frankenstein, 14, 17, 34
Shelley, Percy Bysshe, 17, 35, 176, 180, 182
—— Fragment of an Unfinished Drama, 48
—— Hellas, 176
—— Queen Mab, 176
—— St. Irvyne, the Rosicrucian, 17, 35, 36
—— Witch of Atlas, The, 148
—— Wandering Jew, The, 176
—— Zastrozzi, 10, 12
Shorthouse, J. H.:
—— Countess Eve, 138
—— John Inglesant, 66, 87, 98
Shropshire Folk Tales, 291
Sicilian Romance, A, 45, 50, 301
Sidhe, The, 242
Signal Man, The, 114
Silence, 293
Silvani, Anita, 88, 207
—— Ahrinziman, 88, 183, 213
Silver Mirror, The, 259
Sin Eater, The, 138
Sinner, The, 66
Sister Helen, 67, 153
Skinner, C. M., 187

Skinner, C. M. (*Continued*)
—— *Myths and Legends of Our Land*, 187
Smale, Fred C., *Afterwards*, 102, 202
Smith, Benjamin, *Merman and the Seraph, The*, 234
Sociable Ghost, The, 111
Sogno d'un Mattino di Primavera, 67, 300
Sogno d'un Tramonto d'Autunno, 67, 152
Solomon, Simeon, *Vision of Love Revealed in Sleep*, 79
Song of Love Triumphant, The, 68
Songs from a Vagrom Spirit, 207
Song of the Wandering Jew, The, 176
Sorcerer, The, 145
Sorrows of Satan, The, 136, 144
Soul of the Moor, The, 207
Soul on Fire, A, 193
Souls on Fifth, 123, 198, 215
Southey, Robert, *Thalaba*, 161
Spearmen, F. H., *Ghost at Point of Rock, The*, 83
Speck on the Lens, The, 255
Specter Bridegroom, The, 83, 110
Spectral Mortgage, The, 63
Spencer, Herbert, 251
Spenser, Edmund, 239
—— *Faerie Queene, The*, 7
Speranza (Lady Wilde), 229, 240
—— *Ancient Legends and Superstitions of Ireland*, 229
Spider's Eye, The, 62, 274
Spirit of Turrettville, The, 23
Spiritualism, 73, 199 *et seq.*
Spofford, Harriet Prescott, 286
—— *Mad Lady, The*, 286
Spring Recital, A, 208
Star, The, 264
Star Rover, The, 264
Stead, W. T., 74
Stephens, James, 219
—— *Crock of Gold, The*, 241, 246
—— *Demi-gods, The*, 219, 221
Stevenson, Robert Louis, 70
—— *Bottle Imp, The*, 70
—— *Dr. Jekyll and Mr. Hyde*, 120, 268, 305
—— *Markheim*, 120
—— *New Arabian Nights, The*, 70
—— *Thrawn Janet*, 137
Stockton, Frank R., 293
—— *Great Stone of Sardis, The*, 262
—— *Spectral Mortgage, The*, 63
—— *Tale of Negative Gravity, A*, 274, 286

—— *Transferred Ghost, The*, 63, 87, 111, 122
Stoker, Bram, 78, 92, 117, 180
—— *Dracula*, 78, 163, 188, 301
—— *Jewel of Seven Stars, The*, 191, 274
—— *Lair of the White Worm, The*, 188
Stories of Red Ranrahan, 186, 243
Story of Days to Come, A, 262
Story of the Late Mr. Elvesham, The, 122, 185
Stramm, August, 209, 251, 308
—— *Daughter of the Moor, The*, 304
—— *Sancta Susanna*, 307
Strange Adventures of Phra, the Phœnician, The, 188
Strange Cases of Dr. Stanchion, The, 254, 299
Strange Story, A, 90, 182
Stuart, Ruth McEnery, 226
Styx River Anthology, The, 216
Subjective Ghosts, 83
Substitute, The, 88
Sue, Eugene, 176, 178
—— *Wandering Jew, The*, 176, 180
Suggested by Some of the Proceedings of the Psychical Research Society, 283
Sunken Bell, The, 158
Supernatural in Folk-tales, 233 *et seq.*
Supernatural in Tragedy, The, 305
Supernatural Life, 174 *et seq.*
Supernatural Science, 251 *et seq.*
Sutton, Vida, *Kingdom Come*, 282, 306
Swept and Garnished, 94, 282, 288
Synge, John, 10, 229, 240
—— *Riders to the Sea*, 10, 304
Swanson, Frederick, *Ghost Moth, The*, 290
Swift, Dean, 35

T

Tale of Negative Gravity, A, 274, 286
Tale of the Ragged Mountains, A, 58, 190
Tales of the Alhambra, 226
Tales of Mystery, 48
Talisman, The, 134, 146, 147, 225
Tam O'Shanter, 156
Tchekhov:
—— *Black Monk, The*, 69
—— *Sleepyhead*, 69
—— *Ward No. 6*, 69

Temperament, Gothic, 46
Tempest, The, 64
Temptation of the Clay, The, 231
Terror of Blue John Gap, The, 272
Terror of the Twins, The, 122, 192
Tess of the D'Urbervilles, 143
Thackeray, W. M., 55, 89
—— Fairy Pantomime, A, 240
—— Notch on the Axe, A, 89, 188
Thalaba, 161
Theal, Kaffir Tales, 232
Theodora, 103
They, 84, 93, 288
They That Mourn, 85, 108
They That Walk in Darkness, 136
Thomas, Augustus, 306
—— Witching Hour, The, 306
Thompson, Francis, Hound of
Heaven, The, 283
Thorndike, Ashley Horace, 42
—— Tragedy, 42
Thrawn, Janet, 137
Three Impostors, The, 247, 269
Through the Mists, 207
Thurlow's Christmas Story, 121
Thurston, E. Temple, Passionate
Crime, The, 242
Ticket-of-leave Angel, The, 221
Tieck, Ludwig, 56, 59
Time and the Gods, 245
Time Machine, The, 189, 260
Tolstoi, Ivan, 68
—— Ivan, the Fool, 68, 138, 144
Tompkins, Juliet Wilbur, They
That Mourn, 85, 108
Tragedy, 42
Transfer, The, 164
Transferred Ghost, The, 63, 87, 111,
122
Transmigration of a Soul, The, 190
Tress, The, 61
Trilby, 267
Triumph of Night, The, 121
Tryst, The, 126, 211
Turgeniev, Ivan, 68, 69, 163
—— Clara Militch, 68, 162
—— Dream, The, 68
—— Knock! Knock! Knock! 68
—— Phantoms, 68
—— Song of Love Triumphant, The,
68
Turn of the Screw, The, 86, 91, 109
Twain, Mark, 142
—— Connecticut Yankee at King
Arthur's Court, A, 189, 262, 286
—— Extracts from Captain Storm-
field's Visit to Heaven, 201, 217

—— Mysterious Stranger, The, 142,
303
—— Recent Carnival of Crime in
Connecticut, The, 122
Twilight, 268
Two Drovers, The, 151, 225
Two Military Executions, 116
Two Voices, 97
Tylor, Primitive Culture, 227
Tyranny of the Dark, The, 200

U

Unburied, The, 66, 301
Uncle Remus Tales, 232, 235
Under the Greenwood Tree, 150
Undine, 57
Undiscovered Country, The, 200, 267
Unknown Masterpiece, The, 60
Undying Thing, The, 271
Unwritten Law, The, 306
Upper Berth, The, 100
Usury, 198

V

Vampire, The, 159
Vampire, The, 68, 163
Vampire Bride, The, 159
Vampire, or the Bride of the Isles,
The, 159
Vampires, 158 et seq.
Vampyre, The, 160
Vandover and the Brute, 167
Van Dyke, Henry, Night Call, The,
83
Van Lerberghe, Charles, Flaireurs,
64
Vathek, 8, 17, 22, 25, 29, 33, 37, 70
Vendetta of the Jungle, A, 168
Vera, the Medium, 200
Vergil, Culex, 290
Views of Other Planets, 263
Vikings of Helgeland, The, 65
Vine on the House, The, 90
Virtuoso's Collection, The, 78
Vision of Judgment, A, 214
Vision of Judgment, A, 134
Vision of Love Revealed in Sleep, A,
79
Vistas, 65, 278
Vorse, Mary Heaton, Second Wife,
The, 122, 192

W

Wallace, Edgar, Bones, Sanders,
and Another, 156

Wallace, Lew, 179
—— Fair God, The, 256
—— Prince of India, 179
Wandering¡Jew, The, 8, 175 et seq.
Wandering Jew, The, 176
Wandering Jew, The, 176
Wandering Jew, The, 176, 180
Wandering Jew, A Christmas Carol, The, 177
Wandering Jew, or the Travels of Bareach, the Prolonged, The, 178
Wanderings of Cain, The, 118
Walpole, Horace, 6, 8, 11, 14, 71, 92, 188, 309
—— Castle of Otranto, The, 6, 8, 16, 17, 25, 31, 32, 36, 40, 41, 52, 101
—— Mysterious Mother, The, 53
War Letters from a Living Dead Man, 207, 292
War of the Wenuses, The, 263
War of the Worlds, The, 263
Ward, Elizabeth Stuart Phelps, 199, 290
—— Day of My Death, The, 199
—— Gates Ajar, The, 210
—— Gates Between, The, 210
—— Gates Beyond, The, 210
—— Kentucky's Ghost, 199
Ward No. 6, 69
Warning, The, 276
Water Babies, The, 240
Water Ghost and Others, The, 112
Water of the Wondrous Isle, The, 236
Waters of Death, The, 62
Wave, The, 194
Webster, John, Duchess of Malfi, The, 8, 166
Wedmore, Frederick, Dream of Provence, A, 293
Well at the World's End, The, 236
Wells, Carolyn, Styx River Anthology, The, 216
Wells, H. G.:
—— Crystal Egg, The, 263
—— Days of the Comet, The, 264
—— Door in the Wall, The, 258
—— Dream of Armageddon, A, 196, 262
—— First Men in the Moon, The, 264
—— Flowering of the Strange Orchid, 62, 164, 273
—— In the Days of the Comet, 264
—— Invisible Man, The, 95, 269
—— Island of Dr. Moreau, The, 271

—— Man Who Had Been in Fairyland, The, 241
—— New Accelerator, The, 286
—— Plattner Case, The, 260
—— Remarkable Case of Davidson's Eyes, The, 256
—— Sea Lady, The, 234
—— Star, The, 264
—— Story of Days to Come, A, 262
—— Story of the Late Mr. Elvesham, The, 122, 185
—— Time Machine, The, 189, 260
—— Vision of Judgment, A, 214
—— War of the Worlds, The, 263
—— When the Sleeper Wakes, 262
—— Wonderful Visit, The, 218, 221, 302
Wentz, W. Y. E., 239
—— Fairy Faith in Celtic Countries, 239
Werewolf, The, 166 et seq.
Werewolf, The, 169, 172
Werewolves, 170
Weston, Jessie Adelaide, 146
—— Black Magic, 146
—— Mummy's Foot, The, 62
Wetmore, Elizabeth Bisland, Doppelgänger, The, 122
Weyman, Stanley J., Man in Black, The, 137
Wharton, Edith, 53, 121
—— Afterwards, 302
—— Duchess at Prayer, The, 121, 303
—— Eyes, The, 297
—— Kerfol, 290
—— Triumph of Night, The, 121
What Was It? A Mystery, 61, 96
When the Gods Slept, 63, 74
When the Sleeper Wakes, 262
Whicher, George Frisbee, Life and Romances of Mrs. Eliza Heywood, 42
White Lady of Avenel, 225
White People, The, 203, 298
White Sleep of Auber Hurn, The, 121
Whitman, Stephen French, Woman from Yonder, The, 126, 187
Whitmore, E. C., 305
—— Supernatural in Tragedy, The, 305
Wieland, 35, 39
Wilde, Oscar, 32, 240, 249
—— Fisherman and His Soul, The, 134, 153, 236
—— Happy Prince, The, 238

Wilde, Oscar (*Continued*)
—— *House of Judgment, The*, 214
—— *Legend of Sharp, A*, 134
—— *Nightingale and the Rose, The*, 235, 293
—— *Picture of Dorian Grey, The*, 32, 60, 121, 134
——*Selfish Giant, The*, 246
Wilkinson, William Cleaver, 284
William of Newbury, 159
William Wilson, 58, 120
Williams, Blanche Colton, 83
Williams, Frances Fenwick:
—— *Soul on Fire, A*, 193
—— *Theodora*, 193
Willow Tree, The, 306
Wisdom of the King, The, 154
Witch, The, 149
Witch, The, 151
Witch, The, 145 *et seq.*
Witch of Atlas, The, 148
Witch of Edmondton, The, 150
Witch of Endor, The, 145
Witch of Fife, The, 148
Witch of Prague, The, 149, 195, 266
Witch Hazel, 157
Witches, Gothic, 26 *et seq.*
Witching Hour, The, 306
With Intent to Steal, 62, 117
Withered Arm, The, 225
Wizard, The, 145 *et seq.*
Wolf, The, 172
Woman, The, 66, 194, 300
Woman from Yonder, The, 126, 187
Wonderful Visit, The, 218, 221, 302

Wood beyond the World, The, 236
Woodstock, 225
Wool-gatherer, The, 23, 29, 30
Word with a Mummy, A, 62
Wordsworth, William, *Song of the Wandering Jew, The*, 176
Wrong Elixir, The, 186
Wuthering Heights, 86, 226

Y

Yeats, W. B., 226, 237, 240, 248, 285
—— *Celtic Twilight, The*, 239
—— *Countess Cathleen*, 65, 143
—— *Curse of the Fires and the Shadows, The*, 154
—— *Land of Heart's Desire, The*, 65, 340, 306
—— *Old Men of the Twilight, The*, 234
——*Stories of Red Ranrahan*, 186, 243
—— *Wisdom of the King, The*, 154
Young Goodman Brown, 151

Z

Zangwill, Israel, *They That Walk in Darkness*, 136
Zastrozzi, 17
Zero, 257
Zofloya, 10, 17, 28, 33, 37, 38, 53, 154, 251
Zola, Émile, 252